The Ten Keys
to
Total Freedom

A Conversation with
Gary M. Douglas
and
Dr. Dain C. Heer

ACCESS
CONSCIOUSNESS®
PUBLISHING

The Ten Keys to Total Freedom
A Conversation with Gary M. Douglas and Dr. Dain C. Heer

Copyright © 2015 by Gary M. Douglas and Dr. Dain Heer

ISBN 978-1-939261-00-7
Hardcover ISBN 978-1-63493-021-5

Published by
Access Consciousness Publishing, LLC
www.accessconsciousnesspublishing.com

Printed in the United States of America

Contents

Introduction

Originally The Ten Keys were called The Ten Commandments. It was intended as a joke—it was not a serious thing—but people got up in arms about it, so we changed the name to The Ten Demandments and all kinds of other things. None of those names ever really worked.

Now they're The Ten Keys to Total Freedom, which is a pretty good name for them.

We still like the joke—and the name The Ten Commandments—because they are commandments. They're commandments or demands you have to make of yourself if you really want to create total awareness and freedom. All we care about is having total awareness. None of the rest of it matters.

So, here are The Ten Keys to Total Freedom, which can open the doors to total freedom and total awareness. The Ten Keys will help you expand your capacity for consciousness so you have greater awareness about you, your life, this reality and beyond. With greater awareness, you can begin generating the life you always knew was possible and haven't yet created.

This book is based on a series of telecalls or conversations that we had over a period of ten weeks with a number of Access Consciousness® facilitators and other people from all over the world. We liked the conversational format because it allowed people to ask questions about things that weren't clear to them—and everyone listening in on the conversation got a lot out of the questions other people asked.

We also did lots of clearings, and people told us this changed everything in terms of their understanding of the keys and their ability to apply them to their life.

We hope these talks will help you apply The Ten Keys to your life as well.

Many thanks to Marilyn Bradford and Donnielle Carter
for reading the manuscript of this book
and showing us what was missing.

Would an Infinite Being Truly Choose This?

Gary: Hello everyone. Welcome to our first conversation about The Ten Keys to Total Freedom.

Tonight we're going to talk about the first key: Would an infinite being truly choose this? We invite you to ask this question many times a day in response to the situations that come up in your life. It will remind you that you always have a choice—because you are an infinite being.

Let's start out by talking about what an infinite being is.

Dain: Most people have no idea what an infinite being is. They don't have the concept, even when we talk about it, because, where do you see it showing up in this reality? You don't see it anywhere. The best you can do is to create a fantasy of what an infinite being would be. But that's not what an infinite being is—so under those conditions, when you don't know what an infinite being actually is, you don't have the choice to be one.

Gary: The way I personally understood infinite being was by meditating to see how far outside my body I could go in all directions. Initially, I thought being an infinite being meant I was outside of my body, but that led to the idea that an infinite being didn't have a body.

A lot of people think that an infinite being wouldn't need a body—but that isn't it. You have to get that you, as an infinite being, chose to have a body. You chose to be embodied. You have chosen to be embodied since the beginning of time. You chose to have the kind of body you have and you chose everything that's going on in your life.

An infinite being is one who chooses. You keep thinking an infinite being wouldn't choose this embodiment because you assume that an infinite being would not have a body. That's not correct. You're an infinite being and you chose to have a body. Why did you choose to have a body?

Dain: Well, first of all, there are all kinds of cool things you can do with a body that you can't do without one. Right now, take your right hand, put it on your left arm and touch it lightly. If you didn't have a body, you wouldn't be able to do that. If you didn't have a body, you wouldn't be able to climb into a bathtub and feel hot, wonderful water on your skin, and you wouldn't be able to feel the sun on your face. You wouldn't be able to have sex.

Gary: You wouldn't be able to touch your breasts or your crotch or any of the other things that are fun to do. What would you have to do instead? You'd have to stand outside and look at everything. Most people think infinite being is standing outside and looking at things. No, that's not it. Infinite being is being aware of everything and being infinite choice.

Dain: It's being aware of everything, being infinite choice, and embracing total embodiment as the joy—the greatness—of embodiment that's possible.

Gary: How many definitions of what an infinite being is do you have that are not what it is? Everything that is times a godzillion, will you destroy and uncreate it all? Right and wrong, good and bad, POD and POC, all 9, shorts, boys and beyonds.*

Dain: What fantasies do you have about what an infinite being is that you've made so real that even in the face of total awareness, you cannot and will not change, choose or cure them? Everything that is times a godzillion, will you destroy and uncreate it all? Right and wrong, good and bad, POD and POC, all 9, shorts, boys and beyonds.

Gary: Dain and I have been looking at this area, and we realized that the reason reincarnation occurs, the reason you have to come back and do it again and again, is because you have the point of view that you never get it right. You buy into the idea that there is a right and wrong way to be an infinite being. Then you decide that you always get it wrong. You didn't get it right based on what? Based on some idea that you bought into.

This is the reason we do reincarnation. If you don't want to reincarnate, you have to get that there is a greatness in embodiment, which is the greatness of being totally aware of this reality.

Unfortunately, that's the way people live and think. That's what goes on in their mind. "I'm right. I'm wrong. I'm right. I'm wrong; therefore I'm right so therefore I'm wrong. But then I'm right. But I'm wrong that I'm right." People drive themselves crazy with these insane points of view. Could you just give it all up?

---

* There is an explanation of the clearing process at the end of the book.

How many right and wrong ways of being an infinite being have you made yourself wrong about, while trying to be right about, while refusing to be right about so you can be wrong about, so that you know that you're wrong about right about, and right about wrong about, so that you are right where you're wrong, because you're wrong about right and everything? Everything that is times a godzillion, will you destroy and uncreate it all? Right and wrong, good and bad, POD and POC, all 9, shorts, boys and beyonds.

The main thing you've got to get about being an infinite being is that you would not choose judgment. Anywhere you're choosing judgment, you're not choosing from infinite being. When you are truly being conscious, you see that everything is in consciousness and oneness. Everything is included (including judgment) and nothing is judged (not even judgment). That's the sign of infinite being.

It's not about trying to eliminate judgment. It's simply about being aware when anyone, including you, is doing judgment.

Question: I ask myself, "Would an infinite being truly choose this?" and I get "No." Well, in my logical-thinking, opinionated, judgmental universe, this seems to set up a paradox. How does one deal with the answer to this question and embrace or even love the now on a day-to-day basis?

Gary: You have some reason or justification for why you're choosing what you're choosing at every moment of every day. Try asking:

- Would an infinite being truly choose this?
- So, if an infinite being wouldn't choose this, then why the hell am I?
- Do I really need to choose this?
- Do I want to choose this?
- What's the purpose of choosing this?

Dain: The question, "What's the purpose of choosing this?" will take you out of blindly choosing something that may not be from an infinite point of view and move you into an infinite point of view, into the awareness of, "Wait a minute, there's actually something I'm trying to achieve by choosing this."

Once you realize that you can ask, "Is this choice actually achieving that purpose?" you will often find out that it's not.

Question: If a person doesn't know, perceive or feel that they are an infinite being, what would be your way to guide that person to have a knowing experience and to perceive that as a truth for them?

Gary: The best way to know that you are an infinite being is to close your eyes and feel the outside edges of you. You're going to find that everywhere you look, there you are, because an infinite being has no limitation. As infinite beings, we have the ability to perceive, know, be and receive everything.

You keep trying to define what you can perceive, know, be and receive in relationship to this reality and your body, but that isn't it.

Question: If an infinite being can be any energy at will and at choice and wants to experience every aspect of their being, what wouldn't they choose? For example, doesn't experiencing sadness give you a much deeper awareness of the amazing aspect of being? Even cutting off awareness is a choice. It has some interesting results.

Gary: No, you're coming to a conclusion here. The first part of the question, "If an infinite being can be any energy at will and at choice and wants to experience every aspect of their being, what wouldn't they choose?" is correct. But the question is "Would an infinite being choose this?" And if an infinite being wouldn't choose it, why are you? That's the way you've got to look at it. Would you really like to experience sadness? Would an infinite being choose sadness? The birds are infinite beings. Do they choose sadness?

Dain: Do they ever wake up and have a bad feather day? I'm not going to sing today because I am pissed off at the worms.

Gary: You've got to look at this from the point of view of, "Okay, what is it I'm willing to have here? What is it I'm not willing to have here?" It's about choices. An infinite being chooses.

Dain: It requires having a larger perspective than this reality. Does sadness give you a greater awareness of infinite being? Not necessarily. You mentioned the idea of wanting to experience all aspects of self. What's the difference between experiencing that and having the awareness that it's not a choice you would like to make or that you have to make, thank you very much?

Gary: We have a weird point of view on this planet that we have to experience something to know it. No, you don't. You can know things without ever experiencing them.

Dain: Would an infinite being have to experience something to know it and be aware of it?

Gary: You said, "Even cutting off awareness is a choice. It has some interesting results." It is interesting that we have the point of view that something occurs as a result of the choice to cut off our awareness. Why would an infinite being choose to cut off their awareness so they could appreciate what it's like when they're not cutting off their awareness? Would an infinite being have to cut off awareness in order to appreciate having awareness? I don't think so!

Question: What is doubt? Can it be cleared? Is it linked to a kind of validation of awareness or fact? I've entrenched myself in choices that were made because they were the right thing to do, and now I find myself thinking that there's a part of my life where I'd like to make different choices. How can I break through the chains of obligations, societal pressures and mindsets without totally alienating and hurting others? What about situations where we're in relationships, jobs or situations that have come about from many years of choices?

Gary: First of all, doubt is what you use to eliminate awareness and everything you know. Why would you choose that?

Ask, "Would an infinite being truly choose to doubt himself or herself?" No. "Then why the hell am I? What if I were willing to know everything I know?"

That's the way it should work. Would an infinite being choose the "right" thing to do or would an infinite being choose what would create greater awareness?

You also have to ask, "Are obligations, societal pressures and mindsets something an infinite being would choose? Or are they something a finite being would choose?"

And why are you assuming that as an infinite being choosing to break the chains of obligations, societal pressures and mindsets, you would alienate and hurt others? Maybe you won't. You don't know, because I can guarantee you that you haven't actually chosen that.

Would an infinite being choose to make their choice permanent for all eternity? That's what you're talking about when you speak about relationships, jobs or situations that have come about from many years of choices. You're talking about the idea that there's some kind of finite purpose in all of that.

Dain: If you were to ask yourself the question from the place of, "Wow, would an infinite being have chosen the relationship I chose?" you can look at it and say, "Okay, there are aspects of this relationship that an infinite being would have chosen as an acknowledgement of infinite being. They were a contribution to being. I probably wouldn't have chosen the rest if I had been functioning from infinite being, but what if now I truly could have all of that?"

You look at it and ask, "What would it be like if I had chosen all those things from infinite being? What choices would I have available now?" Choosing as an infinite being, for the most part, isn't done in this reality, but it's something that builds. When you make your first choice as an infinite being, it's "Ooh, I don't know if I can do this." After about 100 choices, it's "Wait a minute, this is something I can actually do. This is something I can actually choose. This is something that's actually available to me. It's not something that's foreign to me." That's why we're having this conversation, so it becomes something that's a reality for you. You don't feel like we're speaking Greek when we talk about functioning from no judgment or functioning from infinite being. If you're not judging what you've chosen, you take judgment out of the computation, and it's not part of the equation.

Gary: That's actually the reason for having this key—to take judgment out of all computations.

Dain: Hmm...does that include my stepmother? How does that work? Would an infinite being choose to have my stepmother? That's my question right now. I don't know.

Gary: The question is "Were you functioning as an infinite being when you chose to let your father have your stepmother?"

Dain: Oh, do you mean I could have totally stopped it?

Gary: Yeah, you could have.

Dain: I could have been "Flash! No way! Not happening!"

Gary: Yeah.

Dain: Aw, man. That's interesting.

Gary: But you weren't allowed to have that kind of control or power in your life, and because you weren't allowed to have it, you thought you didn't have it. It's a big mistake to think that because you're not allowed to have something, that you can't have it. No, no, you can have it all, if you're willing to have it.

Question: I think of an infinite being as formless and expanded. There is no need of food, work or anything this world can offer. So for me, when I ask this question in different situations, the answer is always no. If I were an infinite being, I would not need to make that choice. I'm following the feeling of what it would be like to be an infinite being. There would be no more doing, and of course, the body would not be necessary any more. I am a massage therapist and I find it increasingly difficult to motivate my body to do this physical work. I often feel a dislike of moving the body and doing bodywork or training.

Gary: Once again, it's a fantasy that an infinite being doesn't have any of the things that you have chosen. You're judging that every choice you have made is a wrongness in some way.

> Everything you've done to make all your choices a wrongness, will you destroy and uncreate it all? Right and wrong, good and bad, POD and POC, all 9, shorts, boys and beyonds.

You've got to understand that there is no such thing as *need*. *Need* is a created construct of this reality. There are many constructs in this reality that are not real. We create them in order to justify the choices we make or to prove they were right. A finite being uses "need" to justify what they're not willing to choose. If you have the point of view that there's any need in your life, you're creating a reality that doesn't actually exist.

When somebody dies, we think we "need" to be unhappy. This is another construct. What if it's someone who has been in pain for a year or two? It's hard to be sorry for a person who finally dies after a year of pain. The relief for them and their body is extraordinary. Shouldn't you be happy they are no longer in pain?

What about the need to work? Would an infinite being need to work? You chose an embodiment in this reality. If you didn't live in a reality in which work was part of the reality, would you need to work? No. But you chose this reality. You chose this reality, and working is part of what this reality is about. So, why wouldn't you be great at working? Why wouldn't you love it instead of hating it? An infinite being doesn't choose to hate things!

As an infinite being, you are willing to receive everything. Would you need to eat? Not necessarily. You've got to be willing to recognize the choice. Do you need to eat? No. Do you need to work? No. Do you need anything this world offers? No, but you've chosen to be here for some reason. You chose to come, you're here, so why don't you learn to live as an infinite being in the choices you've made instead of thinking you have no choice?

Working is creating and generating. The reason you work is to create and generate something in life. You keep trying to find a reason not to create and generate something greater than what you currently have. That's why you think an infinite being wouldn't do any of these things. Why do you assume there would be no more doing? An infinite being is creative and generative. An infinite being could and would be able to do anything.

> What fantasy about work have you made so real that even in the face of total awareness you cannot or will not change, choose or cure it? Everything that is times a godzillion, will you destroy and uncreate it all? Right and wrong, good and bad, POD and POC, all 9, shorts, boys and beyonds.

You're misunderstanding the meaning of an infinite being. An infinite being is one who can choose to do anything, to experience anything, to have anything, to create anything and to generate anything.

Dain: An infinite being loves to do things. An infinite being gets off on doing all kinds of cool stuff. There is no judgment. It's "Ooh, what else can I do? Ooh, what else can I do? Ooh, what else can I do?"

Gary: For example, an infinite being could kill. Is that a choice you want to make? You've got to be willing to look at it and recognize "Okay, I can kill." Years ago, a man was coming after me, and I woke up with his hands in my pants. I said, "Take your hands off me now, or I'm going to kill you."

He said, "I won't!"

I said, "Okay," and I started strangling him. I strangled him until he passed out. At that moment, I said, "Okay, I've got another ten seconds until he's dead. Do I want to clean up the mess?" No. I didn't want to deal with the mess. Did I think I could stay out of jail? Sure, yes, why not? I can stay out of anything. I'm an infinite being. But did I want to deal with all the other things this would create? No.

This is where, when you make a choice, you have to be willing to have the awareness of how that choice is going to affect you and everybody around you. Would I kill just for the fun of it? No, why would I kill? Cause I could, but so can you.

Question: Can you expand on killing energy and the judgment system we have in this reality for someone killing someone?

Gary: Killing energy is about realizing "This person is being totally unconscious, totally anti-conscious. He is being a complete shit. Would I like to kill him? Yes. Would an infinite being kill this person? Yes. Can I get away with it with ease? Wait, too much work, never mind."

You have to have a willingness to have killing energy and recognize that if you do kill, you will have to deal with things in this reality that you may not want to deal with. As an infinite being, you'll know that having killing energy and being willing to kill doesn't require you to kill if you don't want to deal with the consequences of having killed.

In this reality, there's a fantasy that death is wrong and keeping people alive is right. They will take people who have killed at one time or another and put them in jail forever. They won't kill them. That's supposed to be punishment. Interesting reality. Does it change people to be in jail? Yes. For the better or the worse? Usually for the worse. Why? Because they learn better ways of being criminal when they're in jail. You put all the criminals in the same school. They're all going to learn the same things. Put them all in there so they can learn how to do everything they do bad, better. Then we wonder why our justice system doesn't work. Would an infinite being truly change based on being in jail? No. What's going to change an infinite being? Only their point of view will change them.

When you use the question, "Would an infinite being choose this?" you begin to look at the fact that you could choose anything. You've got infinite choice. I ask, "If I choose this, what results am I going to have? How are things going to be?"

Do I choose to get angry sometimes? Yeah. Do I hold onto it? Usually not. Why? Because it doesn't do any good. My getting angry can only justify, in the other person's world, the rightness of the fact that they've chosen not to do what I asked them to do.

That works, doesn't it? Not at all! Watch other people. Say you're in an airport. There is a problem with the plane, and the flight has been cancelled. People are walking up and screaming at the lady behind the desk as though she's responsible. She's not responsible; she didn't do anything. She's just the poor soul who has to deal with re-routing you.

Are the people who scream at her acting like infinite beings or complete spoiled brats? Complete spoiled brats. I'm nice to the lady, and I get all kinds of help. She looks at the people who are screaming at her and she says to herself, "I'm sorry, sir, I won't help you."

I get up there and I say, "Hey, what can I do to make your life easier? I can see you're having a bad day."

She says, "What?"

I'm acting like an infinite being who knows that she isn't responsible for the problem and that the only way I'm going to get what I want is if I'm willing to help her through whatever the problem is. It works every time.

Dain: It requires a different level of awareness than most people are willing to function from. It's an awareness of what will create a greater result for everyone. Initially you may want to get upset, but would an infinite being truly choose that? No. You create a result that is totally different from anybody else—and your life gets easier.

Gary: That's the reason for this key. It makes your life easier. Would an infinite being truly be upset with their child? Yes, damn it, I would be … for ten seconds, and then I'm over it. Because I realize that my getting upset isn't going to change anything.

Dain: You have ten seconds to live the rest of your life. Here are your two choices. Take your right hand and punch yourself in the eye—or choose something else. Which did you choose? Why did you punch yourself in the eye? You're not going to like the result.

Gary: You're already willing to know what the result is going to be. Punching myself in the eye is going to hurt. I don't think I'll do that.

You've got to recognize "Wait a minute, the fact that I'm even asking this question is the beginning of awakening all the places in which infinite being actually exists for me." That's the reason you ask the question. That's the reason it's there. That's the reason it's considered one of The Ten Keys.

Question: What part does having a purpose play in what an infinite being chooses? Would an infinite being choose to be uncomfortable on their way to consciousness?

Gary: Purpose is what you think you have to have in order to have a reason to choose. That's not the way it works. You don't have to have a reason to choose; you just get to choose.

An infinite being wouldn't choose to be uncomfortable on their way to awareness, but you keep choosing to be uncomfortable. So, what are you really choosing? Are you choosing to be aware—or are you choosing to diminish your awareness so you can suffer? In this reality, suffering is next to godliness, which is another construct of this reality. You think the only way you're going to get your god-dom is if you suffer and make the choice difficult and hurtful. You make infinite being hard. It's like thinking that life should be a penis. The only time its valuable is when it's hard.

Question: I'm wondering why an infinite being would choose to have created two fabulous men in her life and what question she would ask of herself about the following situation she has created: One man is a fantastic father, the other is a fantastic lover. Both of them are good looking, smart, funny, healthy, kind, creative, successful, totally humanoid* guys. She has asked her husband about their relationship, but all he asks her is "What do you want?" She knows she cannot ask him to change but can only be the invitation for him to change, which has not happened so far, and she's curious about what to do.

Gary: Well, number one, an infinite being wouldn't define herself as a *she*. Number two, why wouldn't you have twenty-five fabulous men in your life instead of just two? Are you making what you have chosen wrong? As an infinite being, you wouldn't choose to have two fabulous men for what reason?

You've chosen to judge that you are somehow wrong for having multiples of anything in your life. You already have two or three kids. You have

---

* See glossary for definition.

multiples already. Why wouldn't you have multiples of everything? If you've got three kids, shouldn't you have three fathers? You're trying to judge infinite being by the standards of this reality.

Everything that is times a godzillion, will you destroy and uncreate it all? Right and wrong, good and bad, POD and POC, all 9, shorts, boys and beyonds.

As far as your husband asking you what you want, he's a man. What is he supposed to do? He chose to come in as a man, which means, "What do you want of me?" That's all he can say, "What do you want of me?" Nothing else is possible. Why is that so? In this reality, a man is a particular way. That's primarily the way a man is. He wants to know what he has to do to please you, the woman.

Everything that is times a godzillion, will you destroy and uncreate it all? Right and wrong, good and bad, POD and POC, all 9, shorts, boys and beyonds.

You can ask him for what you want. If he chooses not to do it, then he makes a choice. If you ask him to change, does he have to change? No. Is it his choice to change? Yeah. Most of you have the point of view that you can't ask for what you want anywhere in life. Would an infinite being not ask for what they want? Would an infinite being expect somebody else to deliver what they want? Or would they be able to deliver it for themselves? You keep thinking you can't ask, because if you did, you'd lose something. Why don't you just ask, "What do I really want to create here?"

Everything that is times a godzillion, will you destroy and uncreate it all? Right and wrong, good and bad, POD and POC, all 9, shorts, boys and beyonds.

Question: Are there people in this reality who function as infinite beings all the time?

Gary: Me. Dain. As an infinite being, you're always in question. You're never in answer. When you come to a conclusion or you try to come to an answer, you have to come to judgment. You have to function from a totally different reality.

Here's an example. At one point, everybody was telling me, "You've got to stop giving your daughter so much. You're spoiling her." I asked, "Would an infinite being get spoiled?" No. An infinite being can't be spoiled.

Dain: Gary asks questions every time he thinks about giving her something. Will this increase the possibilities in her life and in the world? And if the answer is yes, that's all an infinite being is interested in.

Asking a question is the way you get the possibility for creating something greater than this reality. Whenever you go to choose something, ask, "Will this create greater possibilities?" Use this question whether you're buying a car, taking a lover, starting a relationship, having a job or whatever it is. It's:

- Will this create greater possibilities?
- Will this be rewarding?

Gary: Don't make it about this reality. It's about what you can choose that would create and generate a different reality for you. This reality can't ever be better for you. You can try. Love you lots, but you're insane.

Dain: As long as you're choosing from this reality or through this reality, you can't create it as better. Choose from another place, where you ask the question, "Would an infinite being truly choose this?" Just ask that one question.

If you ask that question, let the energy be there and then choose. It will open the door for that to become a choice that you have available. Please don't judge you for not having access to what an infinite being would choose in this ten seconds. Start asking the question and give yourself a chance to learn how to do it.

Gary: What would it be like if you were to choose what was going to expand your life? The best way I can describe this in terms of this reality is: You've got a choice. You can go to McDonalds and have a Big Mac, fries and a Coke, or you can go to the restaurant next door where they serve pâté, caviar, champagne, blintzes and all kinds of other wonderful things to eat. You can have a taste treat or you can have the ordinary food of this reality. You simply have to choose where you want to go.

And it's not an either/or situation. Will I go to McDonalds? If I'm in Australia and I want to have french fries, yeah, I'll go to McDonald's. But that's all I'm going to eat from McDonalds anywhere in the world—except I do like their iced tea. I won't go to the most expensive place in the world where they have mango iced tea because I don't like mango iced tea. Would an infinite being choose not to drink mango iced tea? Only if they choose not to. I choose what works for me. You've got to be willing to recognize what works for you and choose that. It's not that McDonalds is wrong. It's that you've got ordinary fare and a limited menu or you've got an unlimited menu with unlimited possibilities and delicious things to eat. Where do you want to live? That's what you've got to look for.

Question: It seems like I'm resisting this reality rather than including it. Can you say a little bit about that?

Gary: Well, that's pretty much where everybody functions from. You try to make a better version of this reality or you resist this reality rather than asking, "Okay, what in this reality is working for me? What isn't working for me? Which choice do I have here to make everything work for me?"

You can also ask, "How can I use this to my advantage?" For example, I wanted to bring my Costa Rican horses out to ride in the Fiesta of the Spanish Horse. I spent ten grand to bring the horses out to ride in this event for two and a half minutes so I could create and establish communication lines with people who might be interested in them. I found a bunch of people; some of them were interested, some of them didn't respond and some of them did. I now have two people who are interested in these horses. It has created a different possibility. It cost me $10,000 to get two communication lines. Was it worth it? Do I have a judgment of it? No, I have no judgment on it, and I don't put a worth or a value on it. In this reality, we try to put a value on what we're choosing as though that's going to make the difference in what we choose. What it's really about is what's going to make everything work for you.

I once went shopping with Dain when he wanted a new printer. He looked at all of the printers in the store and he said, "I don't know which one to choose."

Dain: At first I was going to get the $500 printer because my point of view was I wanted the most expensive one. Then Gary asked me, "Which one would you choose if you could have anything? If money weren't the issue, what would you choose?" I said, "I'd choose the one that would work the best and give me what I desired." It didn't matter whether it cost a lot more or a lot less.

Just around the corner from the $500 printer, I found a printer for $150 that did everything I was looking for. I said, "Wow! If money weren't the issue, I would choose this one!" I bought it and I took it home, and I was really glad I chose it because the $500 printer would have been too big to fit anywhere in my office. I'm glad I didn't make money the issue because I would have had to return the expensive printer, anyway, and get the $150 one.

Gary: Choose from the place of "What is going to work best for me? What's going to give me what I would really like to have?" When you do this, you end up buying the thing that works best for you. Money isn't the issue.

This is the reason you ask, "Would an infinite being truly choose this?" That question includes everybody else who's involved with you. It's not as if you, as an infinite being, are separate from everything else. You have to be involved in everything. When Dain bought the $150 printer, it worked because the whole universe was included in his decision. That's why it fit in his office.

I know people who buy the most expensive bottle of wine when they go to a store rather than the one that will taste best. Would an infinite being always choose the most expensive thing?

Years ago, I went to a wine tasting with a friend. We started out the evening with a $25 bottle of wine and then he ordered a second bottle he thought was $25. It turned out that it was $125. He was horrified at first then he decided to have his own personal wine tasting. He let everybody have a little sip of his wine. It was very interesting. There was only a minimal difference between the $25 bottle and the $125 bottle. The $125 bottle was about ten percent better.

Would an infinite being choose what tastes better? Would an infinite being choose what is a good price and tastes good? Or would an infinite being always go for the top of the line? We assume in this reality that the top of the line is what you get if you're an infinite being because as an infinite being, you could have anything you want.

Dain: But that's looking from this reality's point of view. An infinite being would choose that which would work out the best and have the greatest result. It's the Kingdom of We.* When you choose as an infinite being, you include everything and everyone in the choices you make.

Gary: The whole idea of this key is to get you out of judgment and into awareness. You're not trying to get to the "best" choice or the "right" choice.

Let's say you're going out to buy a black dress. How do you determine which black dress you're going to choose? Do you choose the one that looks best on you, the one that feels best on you, the one that costs the least? Or are you going to choose the one that will work for more events than the one you're buying it for? That's when it turns out great. The dress becomes something that's building on every aspect of your life.

Question: I often get annoyed with my son because he's so ungrateful. I drove him to an event a couple of days ago and he showed no gratitude. I thought, "You little shit!" I almost stopped the car and said, "Okay, get out." Then I went to "This is how I brought him up. He has no gratitude." I get annoyed over and over again because he takes me for granted. How do I stop being annoyed?

Gary: Whenever I get annoyed, I always know I'm not doing infinite being. I know I'm doing judgment.

---

* See glossary for definition.

So, are you annoyed with your son—or are you annoyed with you? Ask, "Who am I annoyed with? Am I annoyed with him—or am I annoyed with me?" Maybe you're annoyed with you for being annoyed about this.

Half of the time when I'm annoyed, it's because I'm trying to take a point of view that my parents put on me about how I had to raise children.

I stop being annoyed by realizing I'm trying to create something I don't even believe in. I'm trying to create my life from somebody else's reality. I ask, "Would an infinite being create from this place I'm creating from? Is annoyance going to create what I would really like to create here?" Yes or no? It's simple.

Children will always give you their worst and give everybody else their best. When your son stayed here with us, he was grateful for everything. And he will be grateful with other people; he will just never be grateful with you. You're the mom, and the mom doesn't require anything. The mom is like a piece of furniture that you get to sit on and walk on. Moms are rugs, sorry.

Somewhere I believe that if I tell him, "You're being an ungrateful shit," he will change. I suppose that's what I believe when I go there. The other day when I dropped him off, I ended up ranting at him for a few minutes about being ungrateful, in the hope that he would get it. I feel so unappreciated.

Gary: Why waste your breath? I get annoyed and then I realize that it doesn't matter how many ways I say it, how I say it or how much I talk about it. It ain't going to change.

Would an infinite being feel unappreciated? Or would an infinite being be willing to say, "Okay, my son is an ungrateful little git," and then move on? You've got to look at what is in front of you. At one point, my youngest son was always late. I would fume and rant and rave every time it happened.

One day my daughter, Grace, looked at me and asked, "Why are you bothering, Dad?"

I said, "What do you mean?"

She asked, "Do you actually think he's going to change?"

I said, "Oh, good point, never mind," and I stopped carrying on about it.

The next time my son said he wanted to meet me, I asked, "What time do you want to get together?" He gave me a time and I said fine. I was out shopping with Dain when it was time for us to meet, and I said to Dain, "We've got an extra 45 minutes. He's never on time."

When we arrived 45 minutes later, he was there, waiting, irritated as hell. He was tapping his foot on the ground exactly the way I did with him when he was late.

I thought, "This is funny!"

You have to recognize what the other person is going to do. Would an infinite being always be late? Would an infinite being always be ungrateful? No. But, people are always not functioning as infinite beings; they're functioning as finite beings. Are you going to change a finite being into an infinite being? That would be a no.

Ninety percent of what you give nobody appreciates. It's okay. An infinite being would stop giving for what reason?

Question: If you know what works for you and what doesn't, could that be a limitation?

Gary: Well, would an infinite being always choose the same thing? Would you always choose to eat at McDonalds—or would you go to other places as well? You have multiple choices about everything in life, but you act like the only choices you have are a good choice or a bad choice. An infinite being would have infinite choice. How much of your life are you functioning from no choice?

Question: If we're making the same mistake again and again, is that because we're creating a fantasy?

Gary: Yes, fantasies are the way we continue to make mistakes. Every time we create a fantasy about anything, we totally cut off our awareness of the future, and we only allow a result that's going to match the fantasy.

How many fantasies around The Ten Keys have you made so real that even in the face of total awareness you absolutely will not change, choose or alter them? Everything that is times a godzillion, will you destroy and uncreate it all? Right and wrong, good and bad, POD and POC, all 9, shorts, boys and beyonds.

I've tried so many things, and I have the fantasy that Access Consciousness is not going to work, either.

That's not a fantasy; it's an absolute reality.

That it's not going to work?

Yeah. It's not going to work. Access Consciousness doesn't work—but *you* do. What is it you're not willing to have work? Access Consciousness—or you?

As an infinite being, would you be able to work things out and make things work for you? You will be able to make anything work for you that you are willing to make work for you.

All the fantasies that keep you locked out of making you work for you, will you destroy and uncreate them all? Right and wrong, good and bad, POD and POC, all 9, shorts, boys and beyonds.

What fantasy have you made so real about The Ten Keys to Total Freedom that even in the face of total awareness you cannot change, choose or alter it? Everything that is times a godzillion, will you destroy and uncreate it all? Right and wrong, good and bad, POD and POC, all 9, shorts, boys and beyonds.

Question: It was a real hit for me when you were talking about how when you choose something, you need to look at how things are going to roll out or see the consequences of what's going to come from it. I do that brilliantly for other people, especially in my practice, but I don't go there for myself.

Gary: That's the reason you have to ask the question, "Would an infinite being truly choose this?"

Dain: The question opens the door so you can go there. Right now, in your own life, you can't see where the doors for getting there are located. Once you ask the question, you'll see doors of possibility that are available. They have always been there. As an infinite being, you could see these doors for other people, but you would never see them for yourself because you never see you as an infinite being.

That's good. I'll play with that.

Gary: Please do. You don't get the value of you. You keep looking at you as less-than. An infinite being would never be less than anybody else, would they? They would always just be different.

Dain: In your practice when you work with people, are you willing to see them as greater than they're willing to see themselves? Do you know that's true about them?

Yes, all the time.

Dain: That is part of the reason people come to you, because you're willing to see something greater in them than they're willing to see.

Gary: It's what makes you good.

Dain: It's what makes you great at what you do. Is it possible you'd be willing to take five to fifteen minutes every day to do a session on you as though you were coming to you for a session, and just be there with you? Do it as though you were coming to you for a session and look at you the way you see your clients.

I can do that.

Gary: We buy a whole lot of crap from our families, our peer group and the people around us. It's always about the way we're better or we're worse. What if you were neither better nor worse, but only different? That's what you, as an infinite being are; you are different. Not better, not worse, not more, not less, just different. That's why infinite being is so important. It makes it okay to be different, and it also gives you a place where you begin to realize you don't have to judge yourself.

Dain: You begin to see how being that difference can have your life show up differently. The difference that you are will create your life as different from other people's lives. Different from the pain and suffering, the trauma and drama that everybody else finds so valuable. Asking this question is one great way of opening up a door to getting there.

Gary: What fantasies about not being the infinite being you are have you made so real that even in the face of total awareness, you absolutely will not change, choose or alter them? Everything that is times a godzillion, will you destroy and uncreate it all? Right and wrong, good and bad, POD and POC, all 9, shorts, boys and beyonds.

Question: I work with large groups of people in my classes. I expand out before I do my classes, but more often than not, after the class, I feel like I've been run over by a truck. I feel like anything but infinite being. How do I get over that?

Gary: Do you have any fantasies about being run over by a truck? Or how much energy it takes to do a class?

How many fantasies about feeling like being run over by a truck have you made so real that even in the face of total awareness you cannot or will not change, choose or alter them? Everything that is times a godzillion, will you destroy and uncreate it all? Right and wrong, good and bad, POD and POC, all 9, shorts, boys and beyonds.

I did a version of this process on myself. I was tired all the time. I would tell Dain, "I'm so tired!"

Dain would ask, "What are you tired of?" I would give him a long list of things I was tired of, but nothing changed.

I asked, "Okay, what am I missing here?" Then one day, I asked, "Oh! Would an infinite being choose to be tired? No! So, why the hell am I?"

I asked, "What fantasy do I have here that's making me tired?" I realized I had come to the conclusion that if I worked as hard as I did, then I had to be tired. I started to run a fantasy process about being tired, and all of a sudden, my tiredness went away.

Yesterday after having done four days of very intense classes, I felt like I had been run over by a Mack truck. So I asked, "Okay, how many fantasies do I have creating this as a reality?" All of a sudden, I started to feel better. Then I asked, "Would an infinite being truly choose to be run over by a truck? Would an infinite being choose to feel tired? Would an infinite being have to feel bad?" Fantasies are what you create in order to make the decisions and choices you've made real.

You've got to look at these two things. Recognize that they can go together. You can change them because you're an infinite being. You can change frigging anything if you want to.

Question: I was in the class you just mentioned and since then, I've been extremely irritated by how slow everybody is—in the car, at the supermarket and everywhere I go. I'm more irritated than I've ever been. People are slower than I've ever noticed.

Gary: I know, your basic point of view is: An infinite being would move this slowly for what frigging reason? Get out of my way!

That's exactly what I sound like!

Gary: As you become more aware, you begin to realize how slowly the world operates. It can be irritating to a degree that's unbelievable. The good news is there comes a point where your awareness surpasses your allowance.* Right now your awareness has exceeded your allowance.

Yes, I need more allowance.

Gary: You need more allowance and more interesting point of view. Recently Dain and I were flying home from a class in Australia, and I was so frigging irritated I hated everybody. I said, "I just want to kill everybody on this plane."

Dain asked, "Wow, what's really going on?"

I said, "I don't know, but I have no allowance for anybody here. They're all assholes." Usually on our long flights, we get really nice stewardesses. This time we had one who was a frumpy, ugly bitch who was so frigging condescending and obnoxious that I wanted to jump up out of my chair and throttle her. Everything she said was irritating.

Dain asked, "So, has your allowance been exceeded by your awareness?"

I said, "Yes! Okay, I've got to expand my allowance." You will go through phases when you'll have to expand your allowance because your awareness has exceeded the level of allowance you're willing to be.

_____

* See glossary for definition.

Getting your Bars* run helps. That helps a lot—but it's not enough. You have to expand your allowance level, and then it gets okay.

I have allowance to a degree that's almost unbelievable most of the time, and when I get to one of those places where my allowance is gone, it's "Zow! What do I do now?" If getting my Bars run doesn't help, I know my awareness has exceeded my level of allowance and I have to do more interesting point of view.

One of the reasons we're having this conversation is that I noticed people didn't understand how to apply The Ten Keys to their life. So I'm trying to give you examples of how I use them in my life.

The more you apply this key, the sooner you will start to function as the infinite being you are instead of having to ask the question. But you have to start out asking the question, "Would an infinite being truly choose this?"

Let's say you are a student and you have to go to school. Why do you have to go to school? Because you want an education. Why do you want an education? Because you know that it's going to help you in some way. How do you know that? You just know. You're going to school and you hate the tests. Would an infinite being truly choose to hate tests? No. Then, what the hell am I doing here, hating tests? You have to look at it and ask, "Okay, how do I change this? What can I do differently? What can I be differently that will change this?"

When you ask these questions, especially "Would an infinite being choose this?" you begin to see that you're functioning as a finite being.

You ask, "How can I change this?" The whole purpose of having this conversation is to encourage you to recognize when you're functioning as a finite being—so you can choose to function from a different place. You can choose something different.

The Ten Keys are not hard and fast rules that you have to follow. You get to play with them so you can get to the place where you are a playmate of consciousness. You want playmates, don't you? The only way you're going to create playmates of consciousness is if you become the one who's willing to play with consciousness. It doesn't come from trying to get it right or wrong.

Dain: Please don't choose from right or wrong. Don't choose from judgment. Choose from "What else can I play with here to make my life everything I'd like it to be?"

---

* See glossary for definition.

Start running the fantasy process and asking, "How many fantasies do I have holding this in place?" It's your fantasy that doesn't allow you to actually see a future and to change something easily.

~~~

Everything Is Just an Interesting Point of View

Gary: Hello everyone. Tonight we're going to discuss the second key: Everything is just an interesting point of view.

First of all, let's talk about *point of view* and *awareness*. A point of view is a position from which something is observed; it's a particular way of looking at something. A point of view is different from awareness.

Awareness is seeing what you can see—and not having a point of view about it. Otherwise, you may be trying to create something that may not exist.

Dain: The definition of point of view is contained in the phrase *point of view*; it's the point from which you view something, which means you can only occupy one place in the universe at any one time. You can't be in multiple places.

When you take a point of view, you eliminate space and compress it down to one point, which is where you create a limitation, because you cannot be aware of any other choice, possibility or contribution. You're not functioning from question.

Gary: In Robert A. Heinlein's book, *Stranger in a Strange Land,* there were people called Fair Witnesses, who had been trained to report exactly what they saw and heard without making any extrapolations or assumptions. Fair Witnesses were prohibited from drawing conclusions about what they observed.

Someone would ask a Fair Witness, "What color is this house?"

The Fair Witness, from the place he was standing, could see two sides of the house, so he would say, "On this side, it's this color, and on this side, it's this color. I cannot assume a point of view about what color the other sides are."

Unlike the Fair Witnesses, most of us make assumptions in our lives. We look at two sides of something and we assume the other sides are congruent with what we've already seen. That's a point of view we impel ourselves to take, as though by assuming that this matches this, it is awareness. It's not awareness!

When you take a point of view, you cannot have all-encompassing awareness. All you can have is a point of view.

In this reality, you can align and agree with a point of view, which is the positive polarity—or you can resist and react to a point of view, which is a negative polarity.

Either one—aligning and agreeing or resisting and reacting—gets you caught in the stream of everybody else's trauma, drama, upset and intrigue, and you get washed away. You're not perceiving and receiving what is.

Let's say you meet a homeless man on the street, and he asks you for money. If you do alignment and agreement, you might say, "Oh, this poor, unfortunate man! It's awful that he's on the street. Maybe I should give him some money."

If you do resistance and reaction, you might say, "Look at this guy! He's a bum! Get a job, buddy!"

When you are in interesting point of view, you neither align and agree with a point of view nor do you resist and react to it. You would see the homeless guy and say, "Well, that's an interesting choice." You don't get swept away with the trauma and drama. You are the Rock of Gibraltar that keeps everything in order around you.

When you do interesting point of view, the stream of life comes at you and goes around you—and you're still you. (And the homeless guy usually won't ask you for money.) When you aren't in interesting point of view, you get caught in the stream of this reality and get washed away. You lose you utterly.

A while ago, it hit the news that a Congressman from New York named Weiner posted a picture of his wanger on his Twitter account. Everybody got all riled up about it and they eventually forced him to resign. My point of view was "Well, interesting point of view. What does that have to do with the job? Does the fact that he has to show his wanger mean he's incapable of doing his job? If that were the case, we would have no politicians. They all have to show their wangers, one way or another." So it's just an interesting point of view.

Someone said to me, "I try to do interesting point of view but I don't really get how to do it, because I only do interesting point of view with the things I've already decided are interesting points of view."

It's not about what you've *decided* ought to be an interesting point of view, it's about every single solitary thought, feeling and emotion you have! Everything is just an interesting point of view—because none of those points of view are even yours to start with.

You've got to do interesting point of view with every single solitary point of view, not judge which ones are right, which ones are wrong, which ones are good, which ones are bad, which ones you like and which ones you don't like.

You're willing to do interesting point of view on the thing you've decided you don't like, but you're not willing to do interesting point of view on the things you decided you do like and therefore you cannot actually ever achieve interesting point of view.

What fantasy and beingness* are you using to squelch and suppress the quantum entanglements* that would allow you to be interesting point of view? Everything that is times a godzillion, will you destroy and uncreate it all? Right and wrong, good and bad, POD and POC, all 9, shorts, boys and beyonds.

Dain: Would an infinite being actually have any points of view? When you begin to function from interesting point of view I have this point of view, you can get to the place where you don't have any solidity about anything that comes up. In other words, rather than getting emotional about something, it's "Well, that was interesting." Rather than getting fearful about something, it's "That was interesting." Rather than getting angry about something, it's "Oh, that's interesting." You end up *being* interesting point of view. You can *be* it when you start to choose interesting point of view.

Interesting point of view is what little kids have. It's the way they function—and it's exactly how we've been taught *not* to be. Interesting point of view is the antithesis of everything you've learned from the time you were tiny. You naturally are interesting point of view. You have to teach yourself not to be it.

All the fantasies and beingnesses you have specifically not to be interesting point of view, will you destroy and uncreate it all? Right and wrong, good and bad, POD and POC, all 9, shorts, boys and beyonds.

---

* See glossary for definition.

We're inviting you to do something that will create a totally different possibility for you. But you have to *do* it. That's why we're having these conversations about The Ten Keys—so you can apply them and do them and become them and live as them instead of feeling like they're something outside of you that you only do sometimes or don't do well or don't understand.

Every one of these Ten Keys is about a different way of being in the world. They're different from anything you're taught on this planet.

Gary: They are the keys to absolute freedom. For those of you who are facilitators of others, ninety percent of what you have to deal with when you work with people is The Ten Keys.

Ninety percent of everything in your life has to do with one of The Ten Keys.

Dain: Ninety-nine plus percent of the limitations people create come from not functioning from interesting point of view. Ninety-nine point nine, nine, nine, nine percent of what is creating difficulty in your life is where you haven't been able or willing to function from interesting point of view.

Gary: How can you be a good facilitator if you're not doing interesting point of view? You can't! You have to do interesting point of view in order to be a great facilitator—because if you take a point of view, you'll stick the person you're trying to facilitate with something that is not true for them or for you.

What fantasy and beingness are you using to squelch and suppress the quantum entanglements that would allow you to be interesting point of view? Everything that is times a godzillion, will you destroy and uncreate it all? Right and wrong, good and bad, POD and POC, all 9, shorts, boys and beyonds.

Gary: I guess the reason this key has worked so well for me is that I am not interested in fantasy; I am interested in total awareness. If you're not functioning from "I want total awareness, no matter what that entails," you cannot do these things. It may be that you can't live The Ten Keys because you're still functioning from some fantasy or some beingness as though that's going to get you where you want to go or give you what you want to have.

Dain: This is interesting, because I was interested in fantasies. At the same time, I was also interested in total awareness, and awareness has eventually destroyed most of the fantasies I had. And life is getting better.

I look back and see all the places where I was interested in fantasies, especially with regard to women and relationships. That was the area where it happened for me. Whenever I didn't know what else to do, which was often, I would draw upon interesting point of view.

I made the choice to sit there, be with the energy that came up, no matter what it was, and do interesting point of view I have that point of view. When I did that, whatever was in the fantasy and/or the beingness and whatever seemed valuable about it dissipated. The more I did interesting point of view, the more I felt like I could be in the presence of anything and not be swallowed up by it.

If you're not doing interesting point of view, if you're not being interesting point of view, then every point of view that comes along that you might have charge on, owns you. It causes you to go into resistance and reaction.

If it's of value to you to be able to be in the presence of any point of view that anybody has, even points of view that everyone on the entire planet seems to share, and not lose you, this is the way to get there.

Gary: Right now, think about something that has been bugging you, something that you can't get free of. I know you've got something. It could be stupid, slow people. It could be something to do with money.

- Look at that point of view right now and do: Interesting point of view I have this point of view.
- Look at it again and do: Interesting point of view I have this point of view.
- Look at it one more time and do: Interesting point of view I have this point of view.
- Is it still there or has it changed?

Question: I'm trying to get more clients for my business. I have joined a few groups and I have done some other things to meet people and make new contacts, but I have a lot of frustration in my universe. I can't even do interesting point of view with this. I don't even know how to put words to it.

Gary: Get the emotion of the frustration. Now do: Interesting point of view I have that point of view with it. Do it again. Get the feeling of the frustration, then do: Interesting point of view I have that point of view. And one more time: Interesting point of view I have that frustration.

Now how does it feel? Does the frustration feel the same or is it different?

It's different. It's getting better, and I've just become aware that I don't want to have it.

Gary: Okay, good. I'm grateful you brought this up. In order to feel frustrated, you have to take a point of view that you are frustrated. Once you take the point of view that you can be frustrated, you can be.

This example of feeling frustrated should help people understand that you can use this tool with anything you're making significant or valuable. When you have frustration in your world or when you feel helpless or overwhelmed by the lack of money or by having too much money, just do: Interesting point of view I have this point of view.

I realize that I've gone to frustration because that makes me feel like I'm doing something about the situation I'm in. If I just sit back and relax, I feel like this problem isn't going to change.

Gary: But is it a problem?

This is the situation I'm getting massively frustrated with right now. I'm doing people's Bars, but I don't see any real change happening. I'm sure more change is occurring than I realize, but I find it...

Gary: If you are doing people's Bars from interesting point of view, they can change. But if you're doing Bars from the point of view that you want them to change, that is not interesting point of view. You have to allow people to receive whatever they receive, however they receive it. You shouldn't desire somebody to change.

The only thing you need to desire is that you can allow things to open up for people and go the way they want them to go. The purpose of Bars is to allow people to have whatever change they get. If they change, they do, and if they don't, that's their choice.

Frustration only occurs when you come from a fixed point of view. That's the reason we're trying to get you to interesting point of view. If you're doing sessions on somebody, and you're not in interesting point of view about it, they can't change. You are preventing them from changing. You have stuck them with a "not interesting point of view" as though that's the way to get them to change.

Dain: It's as though you think there's something wrong with them rather than realizing that there is something right about everything they are at this moment. There's something right about all of it but not from the sense of "right" or "wrong." It's just a choice they've made. If you approach your work with them from interesting point of view, it's amazing what can happen.

If somebody wants you to change, Gary, what do you do?

Gary: Me? I change.

Dain: Hah! When anybody wants a humanoid to change, what do we do? We say, "F--- you! I will not change. I won't. Just because you want me to, I won't change."

Gary: We say, "You can't make me do that."

Dain: When you want someone to change, you actually impel energy into their world that says, "You should be changing. You should be different. You should have the better life that I know is possible for you, stupid."

And they say, "No, I'm not going to change at all because you're trying to do this to me."

You have to recognize "I seem to have a vested point of view in these people changing. Interesting point of view I have the point of view that they should change."

Gary: And what if your interesting point of view was "Okay, it's their choice. If they want to be sick and die, no problem. If they want to do whatever they're doing, it's up to them."

Someone recently said to me, "My friend is dying, but I don't want him to die."

I asked, "Is he suffering a lot?"

She said, "Yes. I hate the fact that he's suffering, and I don't want him to die."

I said, "Those two fixed points of view you've taken stick him with trying to stay around for you. He has to suffer more because you're not willing for him to suffer. What if that's what he's going to do to get out of here? You've got to be in interesting point of view."

When I work with people, I can see that something isn't working for them, and they can also see that it's not working for them, but I can't seem to get them to…

Gary: Well, first of all, you're assuming that they actually want to change it.

Dain: And you're also coming to a conclusion that whatever they are doing is not working for them. You don't know what's going on for them.

Gary: Not changing is working for them in some way.

Dain: It's the same with your frustration. In some way, your frustration is working for you. Otherwise you wouldn't be choosing it.

That frustration is so not working for me.

Dain: Yeah, but once you started using this tool, you realized, "Wow, I wanted it to be there. I wanted to be frustrated. I'm actually creating it."

Gary: Maybe you're creating people who don't really want to change in order to maintain your frustration.

You're saying that I'm attracting people who don't want to change?

Gary: People look at you and they see you have money handled. They say, "Oh, I want to have what she has," which means they want to have your money. You think they want to change the condition they're in, but that's not it. They want what you already have, which is money.

There are a lot of people who have the point of view that if they don't make money, you'll eventually give them some of yours. I have this happen all the time. I always find it an interesting point of view that people think I'm going to give them money.

Dain: And because he has it as an interesting point of view, he's not affected by it. In other words, he just says, "Okay, that's interesting." He doesn't have to give them money unless he wants to, and he doesn't have to feel bad if he doesn't give them money—because the idea that he's supposed to do that is just an interesting point of view.

Here's another example. I had an affair with a woman. Some time later, she called me and said she had a terrible problem she had to have handled. (She had cancer.) I said, "Okay, I'll give you ten sessions to see if we can handle it." In each session, instead of handling the issue, she talked about how we belonged together. She said we should be together—and would be together for the rest of our lives. She was not interested in handling the cancer at all. She was interested in the sympathy, trauma and drama that from her point of view would make us closer. A lot of people think they can get closer to others by having a major problem that cannot be solved.

So you have to ask, "Am I trying to solve a problem that this person doesn't want to solve? What's really going on here?" This is the whole idea of interesting point of view. When you use this tool, you can see what's actually going on. If you don't have an interesting point of view, you will choose a point of view that eliminates the awareness you could have of what's actually going on. When you do that, you can only see from that one point; you can't see what's actually occurring.

Gary: When people call me and say, "I need some help," I ask, "What's going on?"

They say, "I don't know."

I ask, "You wanted help? What do you want help for?"

They say, "Well, I'm not sure. I think I have a question."

I ask, "Okay, what's your question?"

They say, "I'm not sure. Can't you tell me what my question is?"

People want me to tell them what's wrong with them so they can handle what I tell them is wrong rather than looking at what is true for them and seeing what's going to work for them. That's the reason I start every call with a question, "Okay, what's up? What can I do for you?" I don't anticipate that I will help anybody when I start a session. My point of view is never that they want to change. My point of view is never that they actually desire what they say they desire. As a result, I can be in interesting point of view, and it works.

So, something attracts people and they come along for a Bars session. They don't necessarily want change, they just want...

Gary: They want to have what you've got. From their point of view, if they can get what you have, then their life will be good.

How do I change this?

Dain: You could do: Interesting point of view I have this point of view five times every time it comes up.

Gary: And you could do: Interesting point of view that this person is coming to me for anything other than just to look at me.

Dain: If you can have that, then something else can occur besides what you've decided or concluded is going to occur. You would have a different choice available.

Gary: I've seen time and again that when Dain got involved with women, they would have to have private sessions with him and he would do ten, twelve, fifteen or twenty private sessions, twenty hours worth of work. They actually just wanted to know that there was a connection there with Dain. That's all they were looking for.

You may be incredibly psychic and pick up their point of view. You keep thinking that you have to do something with the point of view you receive. No, you only have to be interesting point of view. If you do that, then no point of view can stick you—theirs, yours or anybody else's.

Question: I'm attempting to live The Ten Keys, but I just don't seem to be getting it. There's something that's stopping me, I'm not sure what it is except maybe I haven't chosen them yet.

Gary: If you do each key, one at a time, for six months, you will be free. Each key builds on the others and makes it possible for you to live as The Ten Keys. Start where you are and do interesting point of view the way we have described. Eventually it will all start to work. It all starts to come together.

Or take the key you're most resistant to and do that one first.

Question: It seems like the points of view that really stick us are the ones we don't even know we have. How do we get to the points of view we don't know we have? Is it:

Interesting point of view I have this point of view that I don't know I have?

Gary: Well, that could be the case.

Here is what interesting point of view is not: If you look at something, for example cars, and you say, "Oh, I'm thinking about Fords. Interesting point of view I'm thinking about Fords. That must mean I like Fords. I guess it's not bad that I have that point of view about Fords." That's not being interesting point of view.

You've got to look at your point of view and say, "I like BMWs. Interesting point of view I like BMWs."

Do I spend my life thinking about BMWs? No. Do I occasionally think about a BMW? Usually not, because if I do, I say, "Interesting point of view I have that point of view," and all of a sudden I realize I'm getting the point of view of a person who's driving a BMW and is so frigging happy to be driving their car that they're saying, "I love my BMW!" And I, being the psychic Sponge Bob of the universe, pick it up.

I use interesting point of view with every single thought, feeling and emotion that I have, whether it's mine or somebody else's.

Question: When you first started doing interesting point of view, did it drive you crazy because of everything that came up?

Gary: The first thing that happened is that I began to realize that none of the points of view I had were mine.

Dain: Even the point of view about going crazy. That's kind of funny, because you think about it and then you say, "Interesting point of view I have this point of view that I'm going crazy."

Gary: Interesting point of view that I think I'm going crazy. Would an infinite being choose to go crazy? No. Could they? Yeah.

Let's run a process:

What fantasy and beingness are you using to squelch and suppress the quantum entanglements that would allow you to be interesting point of view? Everything that is times a godzillion, will you destroy and uncreate it all? Right and wrong, good and bad, POD and POC, all 9, shorts, boys and beyonds.

Dain: We talked about fantasy in our first conversation. We have all kinds of fantasies about the way things are, the way things should be, ought to be or have to be. Or the way they are that they're not. We have fantasies like "This is what's going on here" and "That's not what's going on at all."

Gary: A great example of not being interesting point of view is when we say, "This is what's going on." It's a conclusion. When you come to a conclusion, a judgment, a decision or a computation, you cannot see what's actually occurring

What you should be saying is, "Well, interesting point of view that I have that point of view. What if something other than what I think is going on is actually going on?" When you function from interesting point of view, you can actually see what is going on. Why is that? Because you are not imposing your idea, judgment, conclusion, fantasy or whatever it is, on what is happening. You are able to see what is, apart from any reactions or ideas you may have about it.

What fantasy and beingness are you using to suppress and squelch the quantum entanglements that would give you interesting point of view as a reality? Everything that is times a godzillion, will you destroy and uncreate it all? Right and wrong, good and bad, POD and POC, all 9, shorts, boys and beyonds.

Gary: Beingness is always a point of view. It's something you do to prove you are being. You're trying to prove that you are something. Let's say you decide to be extremely feminine.

What if you didn't have to prove you were feminine? What if you were just being you—and that was the ultimate in femininity? The thing that's most attractive about you to other people is you being you.

Instead of being who we are, we put out an image of what we think we need to be in order to prove that we are whatever we think we're supposed to be. We try to prove we are being something rather than actually being what we are. That's what beingness is.

Being, on the other hand, is just being. You can't do interesting point of view unless you're being.

Dain: That's very interesting. If you're doing fantasy at all, you're not being interesting point of view.

Gary: Exactly.

Dain: If you're doing beingness at all, you're not being interesting point of view.

Gary: Yep.

What fantasy and beingness are you using to suppress and squelch the quantum entanglements that would give you interesting point of view as a reality? Everything that is times a godzillion, will you destroy and uncreate it all? Right and wrong, good and bad, POD and POC, all 9, shorts, boys and beyonds.

Dain: Quantum entanglements are, in essence, your connection with the creative, generative elements of the universe.

Gary: They are what allow you to receive communication from other people. If you didn't have quantum entanglements, you would not have psychic awareness, intuition or the capacity to hear somebody else's thoughts.

Quantum entanglements are basically the string theory of the universe. They are the way that everything is interrelated and interconnected. You can ask for something from these conscious elements of the universe and have it show up simply by asking for it. We have a far greater capacity to do that when we function from The Ten Keys, and especially when we function from interesting point of view.

Dain: You squelch and suppress the quantum entanglements with your fantasies and your beingnesses.

What fantasy and beingness are you using to squelch and suppress the quantum entanglements that would allow you to be interesting point of view? Everything that is times a godzillion, will you destroy and uncreate it all? Right and wrong, good and bad, POD and POC, all 9, shorts, boys and beyonds.

Gary: Somebody recently said, "I'm trying to do interesting point of view, but I only do it about the things I've already decided are interesting points of view."

I said, "You're willing to do interesting point of view on the things you've decided you don't like, but you're not willing to do it on the things you've decided you do like. As a result you can never actually achieve interesting point of view."

It's not about what you've decided ought to be an interesting point of view; it's that every single solitary thought, feeling and emotion you have is just an interesting point of view.

You've got to do interesting point of view with every point of view you have—not judge which points of view are right, which ones are wrong, which ones are good, which ones are bad, which ones you like and which ones you don't like.

What fantasy and beingness are you using to suppress and squelch the quantum entanglements that would allow you to be interesting point of view? Everything that is times a godzillion, will you destroy and uncreate it all? Right and wrong, good and bad, POD and POC, all 9, shorts, boys and beyonds.

Sometimes when people talk about a point of view, they say, "Well, when I have a point of view, I POD and POC it." It's not about POD-ing and POC-ing the point of view. In order to POD and POC a point of view, you have to make it solid and real. Interesting point of view I have this point of view is different. It's about seeing that the point of view you have only has to be an interesting point of view. It doesn't have to be solid enough to POD and POC. If you're trying to POD and POC it, you're aligning with it in order to get rid of it. That doesn't actually work.

The idea is to get clear about the fact that a point of view is just a point of view. It's not right or wrong, good or bad, real or true, it's just a point of view.

Dain: "It's not right or wrong, good or bad, real or true, it's just a point of view." You could say that 100 times a day.

What fantasy and beingness are you using to squelch and suppress the quantum entanglements that would allow you to be interesting point of view? Everything that is times a godzillion, will you destroy and uncreate it all? Right and wrong, good and bad, POD and POC, all 9, shorts, boys and beyonds.

Question: I am under contract as a consultant to a company that owes me about $9,000. I just heard from their lawyer that they are restructuring the company and probably will not be able to pay me. The thing is, I am under contract to them for a few more months, and they expect me to continue working for them, but I may not get paid for that, either.

Gary: Wait a minute. Where's interesting point of view in this story? Interesting point of view that they can control me. I would tell them, "If you're not able to pay me, I'm not going to be able to work for you" or "I'm going to slow down the amount of work I'm doing for you until I get paid for what I've already done. You can do whatever you need to do for your restructuring, but I need to live and take care of my family." You've got to go into interesting point of view. Do interesting point of view this is happening not "I am controlled by them."

But I'm worried.

Gary: No, no, no. Being worried is not interesting point of view. You've got to get in there and do interesting point of view that I'm worried.

Dain: Get in there and do interesting point of view! Get in there and do it!

Gary: When you do interesting point of view to all of the emotions, thoughts and other points of view that are going on, you open the door to the space that will show you a different possibility.

As long as you're saying, "It's this, this or this," you are functioning from conclusions. To whatever degree you align and agree with the idea that they can't pay you, that will keep you from getting paid. When you do interesting point of view and you really become interesting point of view with them, they may discover money somewhere so they can catch up with you.

Dain: Thank you for bringing up the questions you have. Often it is easier to see these things in somebody else's life, so your questions show everybody what is and is not the energy of interesting point of view. Your questions show people the way we create situations we don't desire. Once you get to interesting point of view, even if you have to do it 100 times, the charge that's creating the insanity around your situation goes away. It's a totally different way of being. It creates the possibility for a different situation as well as more peace in your life. If you're not functioning from interesting point of view, it's impossible to live at peace. How does it get any better than that?

What fantasy and beingness are you using to squelch and suppress the quantum entanglements that would allow you to be interesting point of view? Everything that is times a godzillion, will you destroy and uncreate it all? Right and wrong, good and bad, POD and POC, all 9, shorts, boys and beyonds.

Question: If I'm in a large group of people, and they all have the same point of view about something, and I do interesting point of view, is that going to be enough to change everybody's point of view?

Gary: The more you do interesting point of view, the harder it's going to be for them to hold onto their point of view. Just one person doing interesting point of view makes it less and less easy for 500 people to maintain their point of view. And if you don't align and agree with anything they say, the situation becomes easier for you instantaneously. And as long as it's easier for you, a different possibility can occur.

We get stuck if we think a point of view is actually real. A point of view is only a point of view. It's not real, nor does it create reality. If you get twenty people who align and agree with a point of view, then that becomes their point of view. But it doesn't make it real. You don't have to align and agree with it. You don't have to resist and react to it. You simply have to recognize "This is just their point of view." Their point of view does not make anything real.

Question: Gary, a couple of weeks ago I watched you on a TV show where you talked about money. The two people who were interviewing you didn't understand anything you were saying. You gave them one tool, "How does it get any better than that?" which they totally didn't get. As I watched, I thought, "Wow, how can he do that?" I kept thinking, "What's Gary seeing that I'm not seeing?" To me it seemed like a waste of time for you to talk with them.

Gary: For me nothing is a waste of time because my point of view is it's just an interesting point of view. What everybody chooses is what they choose. I will look at something and I will ask, "Okay, so what else is possible? Can I say anything that might help these people or might change something for them?"

I got calls after that show from people who said, "Thank you so much. That was great." These were not Access Consciousness people. They were surprised that they could use that little tool and it would actually do something for them.

When you have interesting point of view as a reality in your life and as your life, people cannot maintain the solidity of the fantasy of what is real to them. If you're doing interesting point of view, nobody who has a fixed point of view can maintain it.

Question: How does interesting point of view work with things that are going really well or that we're enjoying?

Gary: If you're enjoying something and you do interesting point of view, it usually gets better.

What if not doing interesting point of view creates a limitation? For example, if you say, "I've got all my money stuff handled," are you doing interesting point of view?

Dain: No, you're in conclusion.

Gary: Yeah, and once you've come to conclusion, you are limiting what can show up. Do you really want to limit how much money you can have in your life or how much fun you can have in your life—or anything else that is possible? Interesting point of view is about expanding everything in your life, not just the things you're willing to change.

So, anytime we find ourselves coming to conclusions like "This is great" or "This is awesome" or "Wow, this really sucks," interesting point of view can unlock those?

Gary: Yes, and when it unlocks something, it opens a door to another possibility.

Dain: Let's say you've got all kinds of money and there's a financial crisis. You know you're set; money is not a problem for you. You can do "It's interesting that all these other people have the point of view it's a problem."

Or let's say somebody is talking about his or her body issues and you're thinking, "My body is exactly the way I want it to be." You can be interesting point of view about everybody else's body issues and have a sense of ease with that. You create a sense of ease by being interesting point of view,

Gary: But it's even more important to do interesting point of view about what you think are your own points of view. When I started to do interesting point of view, I would think things like "I hate burkas. They are so frigging ugly." Then I would say, "Wow, interesting point of view I have that point of view, because I have never in my life had a thought about a burka. Not ever."

I realized that much of what was running in my universe was based on picking up other people's thoughts, feelings and emotions. Ninety-nine thousand percent of the thoughts, feelings and emotions people have are points of view they have taken, shared or come to conclusion about. It doesn't make them real.

Once I found myself saying, "I don't like those kinds of flowers." I said, "Wow, interesting point of view I don't like those kinds of flowers." After I said it three times, I discovered I really had no point of view about the flowers. I just thought I was supposed to have one. Why? Because other people had a point of view about those kinds of flowers.

You may realize that most of the points of view you have were created by you because you thought that's what you were supposed to do. I talk with people who say, "Blah, blah, blah," about this thing or this person.

I ask, "Is that really your point of view? Is that the point of view you actually have—or is that the point of view you think you are supposed to have?"

They say, "Oh! That was never my point of view. That's the point of view I was supposed to have."

Exactly! Once you start doing interesting point of view, you recognize "I've created almost all of my points of view because I thought they were the ones I was supposed to have."

And as you get interesting point of view, it becomes a choice: "Do I really want to hold on to this point of view? Will it contribute to my life? Or is there something else that might work a lot better?

Dain: We're talking about creating the space of interesting point of view and a sense of ease where it didn't exist before. You may not be interesting point of view right now, but by choosing it, you create ease. It's the ease you feel when you have something handled, even if somebody else has a point of view about it. What if you could have that in every area of your life?

People often hear about this tool, and they say, "I can't seem to do interesting point of view."

I say, "That's because you've never tried. That's why you can't … yet." It's something you've never been taught, and it's not considered valuable in the rest of the world. We're talking about creating a space where everything that comes up—every point of view that comes into your own head—can be whatever it is, and then it can change.

Everything becomes an interesting point of view. Think about a bad experience from your past. Get all the feelings of that and say, "Interesting point of view I have that point of view about that experience." And say it once again…

Question: Are you saying that any place you feel like you're not being you, you should immediately say interesting point of view three times?

Gary: Yes, that's the only way you have the freedom to change anything. Each one of The Ten Keys is designed to help you change areas of your life where something is locked up and not working. You apply these tools to that area and open the door to all the possibilities you were not able to see because you were fixed in a point of view. Or because you didn't think you were an infinite being. Or because you hadn't asked the question, "Who does this belong to?" This is true for each of the keys. Each key enables you to look at the situations in your life from a different direction so you can have a different choice and a different possibility, and so the universe can contribute to you in ways you never imagined.

Question: Sometimes I get awareness and point of view mixed up. I'm sad about somebody's death right now, and I have the point of view that it's really messy. Is that a point of view and an awareness?

Gary: It sounds like the first one is a point of view and the second one is a conclusion.

Sometimes I look at my car and see that it's dirty. I don't like it to be dirty. I would like to have it clean. Is that a point of view?

Dain: "I would like to have it clean" is a preference. "I don't like it dirty" is a point of view.

Gary: I don't like my house to be dirty, and I don't like things to be untidy. If my daughter has her friends over, and they leave the kitchen untidy, I don't like that. When that happens, I have a choice: I can yell at her, I can tell her what a bad girl she is, I can try to make her come and clean it up or I can take two and a half minutes and clean it up myself.

But you just said, "I don't like it." You're contradicting yourself.

Gary: I don't like it. But once I recognize that I don't like it and my point of view is, "I don't want it to be this way," I can change it.

Dain: Notice that in his not liking it, there's no resistance and reaction. We're looking for the energy of the situation. That's the crux of the matter. Gary's point of view is "I don't like this" and then he asks, "What can I do to change it?" There's no resistance and reaction. He doesn't make himself less or get pissed off at someone else. It's an awareness on his part that says, "This isn't the way I would like it to be. Okay, what can I do to change it?"

That's not a point of view?

Dain: We don't say, "Have no point of view." We're saying, "Have an interesting point of view." You can have the point of view that you'd rather not have the car be dirty, but notice that you can have that viewpoint from an "interesting point of view" place. When you have that, you'll do something to change it—or not.

Let's say you don't have time to do anything about your car for the next three days. If you're in interesting point of view, it's not something that causes consternation, judgment, pain and suffering in your world. It's "Okay, I'll get to it when I can get to it." There's an ease in your world about something when it's an interesting point of view.

Gary: Yeah, whereas when you go into resistance and reaction or alignment and agreement, you have to try to make something happen. And usually that's about trying to get somebody else to change rather than realizing the only person you can actually change is you.

It seems like a very fine line. My car was dusty and I had to leave it for a week. It annoyed the hell out of me.

Dain: That's not interesting point of view.

Gary: "It annoyed the hell out of me" is not an interesting point of view. Interesting point of view is "Okay, I've got to get my car clean." Once I go to interesting point of view, a new possibility occurs.

So, you aren't making your preferences valuable?

Gary: Well, it's not making any of it significant. It's simply "So, what can I be, do and have different here?"

Sorry, I know I'm being nit-picky here, but I'm just…

Gary: I'm glad you're being nit-picky, because this will help others too.

I am not clear about the difference between value, preference and significance.

Gary: Let's say you decide that what's really valuable is the red rosebush in your front yard. That's the most valuable thing to you. The gardener doesn't know how to trim a rosebush, and he cuts it at the wrong time of year. It's just a giant stump.

If you say, "I can't believe he just destroyed my rosebush!" what will happen? Every year the gardener will destroy the rose bush in the same way because he doesn't know any better.

But if you say, "Wow, interesting point of view. How can I get a different result here?" you'll see that you can talk to him and tell him you would like him to trim the rosebush at a different time of year. You do that, and he's fine.

By not doing interesting point of view, you're in resistance and reaction, and the gardener will be in resistance and reaction as well. Everybody tries to make things turn out the way they want them to be, because they value their point of view. When you do interesting point of view to the point of view you value, it begins to shift everyone's capacity to create a different outcome.

It's "I really like looking at my rosebush. I wish it bloomed all year-round." That's still from no point of view. It's not trying to make it bloom all year-round, nor is it assuming it has to be any particular way. It just is what it is.

Dain: Nor is it getting upset or frustrated if it doesn't bloom all year.

Gary: It's taking away the created and invented value. Invented values are values you invent. They're not actually true.

What invented value are you using to eliminate interesting point of view as a choosing? Everything that is times a godzillion, will you destroy and uncreate it all? Right and wrong, good and bad, POD and POC, all 9, shorts, boys and beyonds.

Did you notice that I said *choosing* rather than *choice?* That because I'm looking for *total choosing* not just a single, puny *choice.*

If I can change this, I know it will change my whole life. I've been feeling tearful the whole time we've talked about this, so it's obviously changing.

Gary: How much have you made your resistance to things of value to you? When you make resisting something a value, you must always resist in order to have the value. In so doing, you end up blocking your capacity to actually have something greater.

What invented value are you using to eliminate interesting point of view as a choosing? Everything that is times a godzillion, will you destroy and uncreate it all? Right and wrong, good and bad, POD and POC, all 9, shorts, boys and beyonds.

Dain and I like to have dust-free cars. We go away for two or three weeks at a time, and when we get back, our cars are dusty. So we've said, "Personal Assistant, we want these cars clean when we come home so we can have a fun time." Personal Assistant gets our cars cleaned before we get home—and we come home to totally clean cars.

It's an interesting point of view that we can't have a clean car and it's an interesting point of view that we like to have a clean car. At the same time, we're willing to do whatever it takes to get what we would like to have. We don't do it from a place of being frustrated by not having a clean car. If there's some circumstance under which Personal Assistant was not able to get it done, like it rained the day before we came home, we don't go into upset and say, "How come you didn't get the car cleaned?" We say, "Oh well, we'll get it done tomorrow."

Resistance and reaction lock you into being the effect of the situation. Whenever you get upset about something, you're always the effect of it. Interesting point of view gives you a whole range of choices that you didn't realize were available—because you had a point of view in place that kept you from seeing them.

What invented value are you using to eliminate interesting point of view as a choosing? Everything that is times a godzillion, will you destroy and uncreate it all? Right and wrong, good and bad, POD and POC, all 9, shorts, boys and beyonds.

Gary: Every point of view is just an invention; it's not a reality. When you go to interesting point of view, it becomes clear that people invent the things that are important to them. Those things are not actually important. It's just what people have made important. It's what they've made valuable. It's a totally invented point of view. It's a total creation—it's based on proving the choice they made was valuable and good—and all it does is create a limitation that they cannot overcome.

What invented value are you using to eliminate interesting point of view as a choosing? Everything that is times a godzillion, will you destroy and uncreate it all? Right and wrong, good and bad, POD and POC, all 9, shorts, boys and beyonds.

Question: I'd like to talk a little more about preference. What I think I'm hearing you say is that a preference doesn't really have any value to it. It's just a preference.

Gary: Yep, it's just a preference. When I go to my closet in the morning, I pick a shirt by preference, not because it has more value than another shirt.

So, is having to get something right, a way we block having preference?

Gary: That's where you invent that *this* has more value than *that*, which means you have to judge, which means you don't actually get to choose. You have to get it right. You have to do the right thing and that's the way it has to be—and it has to be—and it has to be—and it has to be. When in actuality, it's just "Interesting point of view that I think I have to have that point of view."

Thank you.

Question: For the emotion of anger, would you use "Would an infinite being choose anger?" or "Interesting point of view I have this anger"?

Gary: Anger is a distracter implant,* so it doesn't actually accomplish anything. It's something you use to try to overpower and override somebody else's point of view. Would an infinite being choose anger? No.

The only time anger is correct is when somebody is lying to you or telling an untruth. When somebody is lying to you, you will get angry. What you have to ask is "Is somebody lying to me here? Is there a lie here?" And if there's a lie, then you will get angry. It's okay.

Dain: The reason you're getting angry is so you can spot the lie, and once you spot the lie, the anger goes too, because you got the information and the awareness that you were looking for.

Gary: And that becomes interesting point of view.

You might want to try this: "I have this emotion. What would make this an interesting point of view? I have this thought. What would make this an interesting point of view? I have this feeling. What would make this an interesting point of view? I have this sex or no sex.* What would make this an interesting point of view?" You start to recognize that your thoughts, feelings, emotions and sex or no sex are just points of view that you create from. They're things you've invented from, things you've tried to create from. They have nothing to do with real choice.

What invented value are you using to eliminate interesting point of view as a choosing? Everything that is times a godzillion, will you

---

* See glossary for definition.

destroy and uncreate it all? Right and wrong, good and bad, POD and POC, all 9, shorts, boys and beyonds.

Question: Sometimes when I'm staying in interesting point of view, I cannot take a point of view, and people get irritated with me.

Gary: A lot of people get irritated when you're doing interesting point of view. They want you to have a point of view so they can fight it, align and agree with it or force you into something they think is appropriate.

So, what do you do?

Gary: I just say, "I know, I'm so frigging irritating."

Recently I had no point of view about where I went to eat and people were asking, "Where do you want to go?" I didn't care. Well, today I have a new point of view. I just created a new point of view right now.

Dain: What is it?

Gary: I'll go anywhere they have Don Julio Reposado margaritas with Grand Marnier!

Question: How does interesting point of view apply to grief or loss? Like when someone dies and the person is not able to get beyond...

Gary: It's interesting that you should mention this, because I received this email just before the call.

Dain (reading): *Hi Gary and Dain, this is not a question. It's an acknowledgement and a thank you. For the last week, I have been by the bedside of my dear friend, Tina, being the tools of Access Consciousness and supporting her, reassuring her and allowing her to pass on. What a gift for me, for Tina and for her friends and family. She died Sunday evening with all of us by her side. As I walked back to my car I saw how beautiful it is to be living, and yes, yes, yes, in this grand time. Thank you and gratitude for being here now and continually assisting us with all of our choices.*

Gary: So, what if death was a choice that people make?

I have no problem with that. I often help people get beyond their grief, and my question is about the way they perceive death and how to help them see it as another step and not as a loss. They seem to carry a lot of other people's energy about how that should look.

Gary: The basic point of view that everybody aligns and agrees with is that if you have a death in the family, you're supposed to grieve horribly. You're supposed to miss the person. You're supposed to talk about them nonstop for about a year. Then after that, the grief is supposed to slowly go away. That's been the point of view in the "civilized world" for the last 5,000 years.

In the past, if you lost someone, you had to wear black clothing for a year. But the clothing stores got really upset about that, so they made it six months. Then in the 1920s, they made it three months, and in the 1950s they made it three days. Now you only wear black to the funeral. You don't have to wear black after that.

There was a time when you covered the mirrors so you wouldn't invite the soul of the dearly departed to go into some other reality. These are strong viewpoints that people are stuck with. They don't do interesting point of view with them, but you can. You have to be willing to see what their point of view is.

This particular interesting point of view has to do with the fact that the person I was working with had some association with people who buy grievers. Grievers used to go around and grieve for other people. It was a service they provided. Apparently, my client had some association with that in her past—and she went on and on with her grieving. For me it was, "Okay, are you done?" I didn't want to come right out and say, "Are you done with that point of view?" It sounds cold, given her present situation. Is there a gentler way to introduce interesting point of view that wouldn't leave her feeling like she got slapped in the face?

Gary: Well, you might wish to recognize that some people aren't ever going to hear what you have to say, so don't bother to talk. That's what I do.

Dain: You realize "Wow, this person doesn't actually want to change anything." That's an interesting point of view. She has that in her universe, and for some reason, it validates the non-interesting point of view that she has chosen.

Gary: Which is why she keeps it.

Dain: If you can get to the place where you're just an interesting point of view, you can say, "Okay, this person doesn't actually desire to let this go," and it gets a lot easier in your world. And it may be that your doing interesting point of view is the only thing that will create the energy that will allow her to let go of it. She can let go because you're in allowance of her point of view.

Gary: Interesting point of view is not about *saying* it as much as it is about *being* it or *becoming* it. When you become interesting point of view, you become an energy that does not require you to align and agree with a point of view, nor resist and react to it. You are able to see more of what is and choose. The whole idea of interesting point of view is that you've got a choice.

Dain: We are asking you to say, "Interesting point of view," and see what shifts in the energy, so you can get to a place where you can begin to be interesting point of view with much greater ease. As Gary said, it's not always about *saying* it; it's about *being* it. At this point, saying it helps you see what the energy would be like if you entertained the possibility of interesting point of view. As you say it, you will start to become it.

Question: Sometimes when I do the tools of Access Consciousness in my head, and especially when I do interesting point of view, I hear or have an energy that invalidates me. It's as if I don't believe myself. It's like something is saying, "I don't believe you." Is that just another interesting point of view? Or is it an entity or a beingness?

Gary: Do you ask, "Is this mine or somebody else's?"

Oh, okay!

Gary: Until you recognize that you pick up other people's thoughts, feelings and emotions, you will immediately assume they are yours. The majority of people in the world are willing to fall apart in a heartbeat. They're willing to judge themselves. You assume the judgment is yours. You've got to come out of that and say, "Okay, interesting point of view that I have this judgment." Ninety-nine thousand percent of the time, the judgment ain't even yours.

That's such good news. Thank you.

Gary: I hope you have some awareness of what interesting point of view is now.

Question: I have done four sessions of Bars with a client over a period of about six weeks. Two weeks ago, I gave her the interesting point of view tool because she couldn't stand to sit at the table with her 80-year-old mother-in-law when the mother-in-law would talk on and on about her friends. My client then went away for a week to the mountains in North Carolina with her husband, mother-in-law and other members of the family. I saw her just two days ago, and she didn't once mention the situation with her mother-in-law. All she talked about were the mountains and the birds, the wind and the stream, and all the things she noticed that she had never seen before because she was no longer caught up in everybody's else's stuff. It was very interesting.

Dain: Thank you for sharing that. You bring up a really good point. When you *be* interesting point of view you start to perceive things in the world around you that you never knew existed.

Gary: And that you never had easy access to. Oh, that's why we call it Access!

Dain: This small statement, interesting point of view, is one of the biggest keys to the kingdom.

For a long time Gary has said that if you're willing to do: "Interesting point of view I have this point of view" for an entire year, nothing in your life would ever be a difficulty again. You would be the space that allowed total ease.

Would you be willing to institute this into your life for the next week? With every point of view that comes up, with everything you think, say, "Interesting point of view I have that point of view."

Gary: Okay, folks, we're going to end this conversation now. We love you all. And we'll talk to you again soon!

~~~

Live in Ten-Second Increments

Gary: The third key is about living in ten-second increments, which is about realizing that you have infinite choice. When you live in ten-second increments, no choice you make is right or wrong, no choice is good or bad. Choice is just choice—and you get to make a new one every ten seconds.

There's a man I know who said, "Choice creates awareness, awareness doesn't create choice." I think that was Dr. Dain Heer, but I couldn't be certain of that—because I stole it at the first opportunity.

Dain: There was someone who said that, I remember.

You hear about infinite choice in Access Consciousness, and you kind of doubt it. Then you live your life and you doubt it. Then you see what other people choose and you really doubt it. We all have the idea that infinite choice can't actually exist. Even in the face of total awareness and consciousness, you would still believe in the fantasy, the beingness and the secret agenda* point of view that infinite choice cannot actually exist.

Gary: As we speak, I'm in Texas, and Dain is in California. That's not a choice I necessarily like. However, I'm here, dealing with my horses. Am I coming to conclusion about this? No, I'm choosing every ten seconds what I'm doing with the horses, what I'm looking at with the horses and what else is possible with the horses. Every time I make a choice, I open a door to another level of awareness of choice. The whole idea of ten-second increments of choice is that once you choose something, it opens the door to infinite choices—not more limited choices.

We keep trying to come to a conclusion about the right choice or the wrong choice. We try not to make a so-called mistaken choice. We think that if we eliminate "mistakes" in choice that we will have more choice. That's not the way it works. Ten-second increments of choice give you infi-

---

* See glossary for definition.

nite choices for the infinite possibilities that could create something greater in your life than you've ever had.

Dain: Gary is saying that making a choice always leads to more choices. We misidentify the lie that once we choose something, we're screwed because we can't ever choose anything else. It's actually the opposite. You need to choose in order to have more choices available. When you don't choose, you eliminate the choices that are available to you.

Gary: In order to choose "right" or "wrong," you have to judge. And when you judge, you automatically eliminate choice. You eliminate possibility. Judgment eliminates all possibility.

What fantasy, beingness and secret agendas for never having infinite choice as a reality have you made so real that even in the face of total awareness, you absolutely will not change, choose or alter it? Everything that is times a godzillion, will you destroy and uncreate it, please? Right and wrong, good and bad, POD and POC, all 9, shorts, boys and beyonds.

Question: I had a distinct flashback of a time when I was a kid, and my mom said, "If you touch that piece of food or anything in the store, you have to keep it. That's it. That's all you get at the store, that's all you get at the dinner table." Can we process that a little bit?

Gary: That's what this process should be good for.

Okay.

Dain: Whenever we buy into the things we're told, what we buy eliminates choice from our life. In the example you just gave, you were told that if you touched something, that was it—you chose it—and that was all you could have.

The other side of this is the idea that if you can't touch something, you can never have it. This idea eliminates anything that doesn't already exist in physical reality. It's saying that if something is not in front of you (which means you can't touch it) it can never become part of your reality. This point of view would lead you to believe you couldn't ever choose anything you couldn't see—or anything you couldn't touch.

Gary: And if it had to be only something you *could* see or touch, you would be cutting off infinite choice and infinite possibility, which means you wouldn't be able to have the generative energy that could create the life you would really like to have. You'd never have as a choice all the generative energy and possibility that are available to you. You would be limited to creating and instituting from the limited choices of this reality.

What fantasy, beingness and secret agendas for never having infinite choice as a reality have you made so real that even in the face of total awareness, you absolutely will not change, choose or alter it? Everything that is times a godzillion, will you destroy and uncreate it, please? Right and wrong, good and bad, POD and POC, all 9, shorts, boys and beyonds.

I think it blends into the fact that we're multidimensional people who want everything, so we go into resisting what we can't have when what we actually want is more.

Gary: That's the whole idea behind ten-second increments of choice. All of us are infinite beings who want more. You look out in the world and you say, "This place can't be enough. If this is all there is, please God, let me off."

Until you start choosing from ten-second increments of choice, you can't open the door to infinite choice. Until you have infinite choice, you can't have total infinite being. And until you have total infinite choice and total infinite being, you can't have interesting point of view and your reality. Oops! You mean all these things are built on top of one another? Yes. The Ten Keys are like the pyramids of consciousness.

Dain: I love what you said. These things are interrelated and interlinked.

Question: I've listened to the call about key number two many times, but I seem no closer to being interesting point of view. I feel more confused than educated. For instance, if I decide to work on my impatience, I don't know if I need to use: Would an infinite being be impatient? or Who does this belong to? or Interesting point of view I have that point of view. Perhaps this is too advanced for me.

Dain: It's not too advanced. This stuff is basic, but as we've said, everything is interlinked. These are the keys to the kingdom. What happens when you go to a locked door and you have a key ring? Do you try one key and if it doesn't work, do you decide you're not going to get in the door? Or do you try every damn key on the ring until the frigging door opens? You try every key until the door opens.

These are the keys to the doors that have been locked all your life. You've always wanted to open these doors. Just keep trying the next key and the next one and the next one until something creates a lightness. As soon as you get the right key, you will feel lighter. What's true for you will always make you feel lighter.

Λ lot of people haven't yet gotten the way this works. I processed this with a few of the people that are part of the Access Consciousness team—the people we work with day in and day out—and each of them said, "Well, you know how it is when you feel there must be something else because we haven't gotten to the thing that makes me feel lighter yet? I know we're not actually at the thing that is the sticking point of the problem for me. I know that what we're dealing with right now is some part of the lie—but I also know there's some other place we need to go."

It's the same thing with these tools. When you use these keys, the one that makes you feel lighter—or the lightest—is the one that will change the situation or the thing that's out of whack. When you use it, it will put things back into whack.

What fantasy, beingness and secret agendas for never having infinite choice as a reality have you made so real that even in the face of total awareness, you absolutely will not change, choose or alter it? Everything that is times a godzillion, will you destroy and uncreate it, please? Right and wrong, good and bad, POD and POC, all 9, shorts, boys and beyonds.

Question: I've resisted the idea of living in ten-second increments because all my life, I've been told I change my mind like a toilet seat—up and down. I read energy, so I constantly change my mind. I'm trying to decide whether to become an Access Consciousness facilitator and go to Costa Rica. One day it reads light, and the next day it doesn't. I need some help with this.

Gary: What's wrong with changing your mind?

If you're constantly changing your mind, how do you actually make a choice?

Gary: You're trying to choose based on "Yes, I want to go" or "No, I don't want to go." You're not choosing from: What will this choice create? You need to ask, "If I choose this, will it expand my reality and make everything better for me?"

I see. I'm not asking the right question.

Gary: Yes. You haven't taken the next step, which is asking the question, "What will this choice create?" The whole idea of ten-second increments of choice is to get you to recognize that every choice creates something.

You've got to ask, "What will this choice create? Will it create more or less in my life?" If it will create more, then you've got your decision. But it's not really a decision; it's a level of awareness.

By the way, changing your mind all the time is a great thing, not a bad thing. You just didn't have this missing piece of the puzzle, the question, "What will this choice create in my life?"

Yeah, that's true. I've never really felt like I could be in first position where I be and choose for me. I was always choosing for everybody else.

Gary: That's part of the problem of being a humanoid. You're always aware of what everybody else needs, wants, requires and desires, and you have no clue what your needs, wants and desires are because you say, "I could choose anything!"

It's true that you could choose anything; that's because you're willing to have more than other people are. Most people spend their lives trying to eliminate choice so they only have a limited menu. They're only willing to go to McDonald's because they know the menu there. They choose not to go to other places and try new things.

Dain: Most people on the planet do not know that this way of functioning is possible. So, when you hear something, if it makes you feel lighter, you know, "Cool, maybe that's another possibility I can incorporate into my life and living and see how it might work for me."

We make infinite choice into a fantasy. We make it into a beingness. We make it into a secret agenda that we can't ever figure out. It's none of those things.

> What fantasy, beingness and secret agendas for never having infinite choice as a reality have you made so real that even in the face of total awareness, you absolutely will not change, choose or alter it? Everything that is times a godzillion, will you destroy and uncreate it, please? Right and wrong, good and bad, POD and POC, all 9, shorts, boys and beyonds.

Gary: You won't make a choice unless you know what the result is going to be or how it's going to affect somebody else. You don't ask the question, "What will this choice create in my life?" Choice is a source of creation—but instead of choosing, we try to eliminate things from our life so we won't create "bad" effects.

Dain: We end up having a tiny universe with very few things going on because we've eliminated so many of the choices that are actually possible. We limit our universe to a tiny sphere of influence that we can control rather than the infinite choices that are available.

Gary: For example, people say that right now we're in the technological revolution. If you're not technologically adept, you're suddenly not within the scope of a choose-able item. You cannot choose what is not technologically adept nor can you be a technological choice. You have limited your choice by your lack of technical capacity.

It's always a lack that limits you—never a possibility. You are never limited by a possibility.

Question: When I was younger, every choice I made was looked down upon or considered wrong, so I had to contract to figure out why it was wrong or why it didn't work for the people in my family.

Gary: Yep, that's pretty much what we're taught here. Disapproval is the primary source for the creation of choice in this reality.

The whole idea of ten-second increments is to open the door to a different possibility. You can either buy that your family is right or you can choose for you.

Dain: Oh, there's an idea! Life gets better when you start choosing for you.

Gary: Yeah, I know.

What fantasy, beingness and secret agendas for never having infinite choice as a reality (oh yeah, and never having infinite happiness either because that would be really bad) have you made so real that even in the face of total awareness, you absolutely will not change, choose or alter it? Everything that is times a godzillion, will you destroy and uncreate it, please? Right and wrong, good and bad, POD and POC, all 9, shorts, boys and beyonds.

Gary: Dain, where did you ever get the idea that happiness was on the menu of choice?

Dain: I know, exactly! As we're running this process, I'm realizing you can't have happiness if you don't have choice. If you don't get that you have choice, you can't have happiness.

Gary: That's correct.

Dain: And if we don't choose in ten-second increments, we can't get to the place where happiness is an option for us. We're stuck with the unhappiness of everything we see around us in everybody else's world. We act like it's real and true and we have to buy it and to live according to it.

Gary: I know. Amazing, isn't it?

Everything that is times a godzillion, will you destroy and uncreate it, please? Right and wrong, good and bad, POD and POC, all 9, shorts, boys and beyonds.

What fantasy, beingness and secret agendas for never having infinite choice as a reality have you made so real that even in the face of total awareness, you absolutely will not change, choose or alter it? Everything that is times a godzillion, will you destroy and uncreate it, please?

Right and wrong, good and bad, POD and POC, all 9, shorts, boys and beyonds.

Question: Would you talk about the use of the word beingness in this process?

Gary: *Being* is when you're actually just present. *Beingness* is when you're doing something in order to prove something. It's "See, I'm doing this now; therefore, I'm being this thing."

How many times have you done housecleaning? When you clean your house, do you do the beingness of a maid? Do you do the beingness of a house cleaner? Do you do the beingness of "I hate this?" Do you do the beingness of a perfect homemaker? Or do you just do the cleaning job? Are you just being present and getting through it quickly?

Thank you! That's brilliant.

Dain: What fantasy, beingness and secret agendas for never having infinite choice as a reality have you made so real that even in the face of total awareness, you absolutely will not change, choose or alter it? Everything that is times a godzillion, will you destroy and uncreate it, please? Right and wrong, good and bad, POD and POC, all 9, shorts, boys and beyonds.

Gary: Thanks for that question. It just made the process go deeper.

Dain: What fantasy, beingness and secret agendas for never having infinite choice as a reality have you made so real that even in the face of total awareness, you absolutely will not change, choose or alter it? Everything that is times a godzillion, will you destroy and uncreate it, please? Right and wrong, good and bad, POD and POC, all 9, shorts, boys and beyonds.

Question: When I clean something, I automatically want to have it clean or I think that I am a good person or that I do it very nicely. This is nearly automatic. When you gave this example, it was so clear and helpful. I want to ask you to say more about that so I can understand it more.

Gary: *Beingness* is something you are doing to prove you are being something. When you are *being* something, you don't think about it. You're just being it. You don't have any point of view about it. You just deliver whatever's necessary.

If you listen to this call a few more times after we have done some more processing, it will become clearer to you. You will understand it at a whole new level. This process will unlock you from living in "I have to prove I'm a good girl by doing this" or "I have to prove that I care about things" or "I have to prove (<u>anything</u>)." Beingness is always about trying to prove that you're being something; it's never about doing something just because you like doing it.

Before I got to ten-second increments of choice, I always felt like I somehow had to look into everybody else's negative world to determine what I needed to do or be so they would not have to deal with the negative things they had to deal with. I thought that if I could somehow take the negative out of their world, then I wouldn't have to be negative nor would they.

Dain: There's no ease in that point of view; there's a constant state of judgment in it.

Gary: Yeah, and you're always trying to choose based on other people's needs, wants, requirements or desires—and never on yours.

Question: I have no trouble choosing in ten-second increments when it's things like blowing my nose or washing my hands. There are no long-term consequences.

Gary: When you say "long-term consequences," you're agreeing with the conclusion that if you make a choice, it's going to be forever instead of for ten seconds.

Well, It's hard to imagine quitting my job or divorcing in ten-second increments.

Gary: If you divorce or quit your job in ten-second increments, you'd have to choose whether you actually wanted to be in that relationship or in that job or in that business.

Question: I get stuck on what I've decided are limited options rather than truly being open to all the possibilities. Can I apply the ten-second increment key to those areas where I'm stuck, for example, when I get stuck on ideas about how to start up my business? Can I use it to facilitate breaking the cycle of limited choices I seem to have given myself?

Dain: Try running:

> What fantasy, beingness and secret agendas for never having infinite choice as a reality have you made so real that even in the face of total awareness, you absolutely will not change, choose or alter it? Everything that is times a godzillion, will you destroy and uncreate it, please? Right and wrong, good and bad, POD and POC, all 9, shorts, boys and beyonds.

Question: There are times when I'm not sure what to choose, like when I'm buying a ticket or something like that. I look at the energy and ask, "If I choose this, what's the energy in my life going to be like in three months or six months or nine months?" Is that something you guys recommend? Is there something else I should be asking?

Gary: Do you notice that choosing in that way opens up things in different areas of your life?

Yes.

Gary: When you make a choice, you're actually choosing what your future is going to be. You're not choosing it based on somebody else's reality.

Yeah, that's what it feels like.

Dain: What generation and creation of the no-mind space of infinite choice and ten-second increments of choice as an absolute non-reality are you using to lock into existence the positional HEPADs* you're instituting to place you in the negative elements of realities that are other people's realities of choiceless non-existence? Everything that is times a godzillion, will you destroy and uncreate it, please? Right and wrong, good and bad, POD and POC, all 9, shorts, boys and beyonds.

Gary: This isn't supposed to make sense to you. It's supposed to fry your mind so that you can change and have total freedom to change.

Question: What are positional HEPADs?

Dain: Any time you take a position or a fixed point of view, you create HEPADs. H stands for handicapping, E stands for entropy, P stands for paralysis, A stands for atrophy and D stands for destruction.

Whenever you're not in interesting point of view about something, you create positional HEPADs. They're a huge part of what creates lock-ups in people's bodies, where they can't seem to be flexible anymore. HEPADs are also a contributor to the creation of disease in people's bodies and their minds.

Gary: HEPADs are all the things that create living in this limited reality. They are all the ways you stop yourself from having an unlimited reality.

I looked at living in ten-second increments and the rest of these tools as things that were so simple and so easy that I couldn't imagine people not being able to apply them. This Ten Keys class has been a great gift for me. It has allowed me to see why people can't apply what seems to me so forthright and obvious.

Dain: Having been around you for eleven years, I've seen that you function from a different place than anybody else I know or have heard of on the planet.

What I recognize with these Ten Keys calls is that we all have the capacity to function from the place of ease. That's the reality I see you functioning from. Most people probably don't even know what this is like.

---

* See glossary for definition.

For those of you who don't know Gary, I'd like to say that no matter what comes up in his life—and he has all the stuff come up in his life that we all have come up in ours—he does not choose the difficulty, the trauma or the drama of things. No matter what comes up, even if it is a trauma and drama in somebody else's world, he always has a sense of ease about dealing with it. I see him choosing things that will create a greater future even when they seem to make no sense today. Part of the reason he can do that is because he functions from these Ten Keys.

So, if you're on this call and you're thinking, "I sort of get this one—but I kind of don't, and I don't want anybody to know that I don't get it because I want to do Access Consciousness right," please don't go into that. Don't judge yourself. Just realize that this is an opportunity to choose to live from a totally different place. It is about ease and joy and exuberant expression of life. It's about allowing the difficulties of life to fade away as the ease becomes more and more present.

Gary: I talked with a lady in New Zealand who was furious because her grandson had come to live with her and he would leave the kitchen a mess every time he went in there.

I asked her, "So, what are you doing about it?"

She said, "Well, I clean up his mess and I give him my mind about it. I tell him he's bad and he shouldn't do that and he needs to stop doing that and all that stuff. But it never changes."

I asked, "Why are you cleaning the kitchen—for him or for you?"

She said, "Well, for me, of course."

I asked, "Really? Then why are you objecting? He likes it dirty. He thinks it's more fun to have it dirty. So you're cleaning it up not for him, but for you."

She said, "But I'm cleaning up after him."

I said, "No, you're not. You're cleaning it up for you. If you didn't have the point of view that you were cleaning up after him, would that change everything in the way this works?"

She called me back a week later and said, "Thank you. Once I realized I was cleaning up the kitchen for me, all the charge went away. I had no point of view. I would just say, 'Okay, it's a mess,' and clean it up. And then, all of a sudden, my grandson started cleaning up after himself."

I said, "Yeah, change your point of view; they change theirs."

Dain: What generation and creation of the no-mind space of infinite choice and ten-second increments of choice as an absolute non-reality are you using to lock into existence the positional HEPADs you're insti-tuting to place you in the negative elements of realities that are other people's realities of choiceless non-existence? Everything that is times a godzillion, will you destroy and uncreate it, please? Right and wrong, good and bad, POD and POC, all 9, shorts, boys and beyonds.

Gary: One of the reasons we talk about this ten-second increment as mindless space is because people keep saying, "Well, what about my mind? I can't wrap my mind around ten-second increments. Have I changed my mind?"

It's not about your mind. It's about creating a different reality for your-self. In the space of infinite choice, a different reality begins to be created. Do you want a different reality? This is the way to get there.

Everything that is times a godzillion, will you destroy and uncreate it, please? Right and wrong, good and bad, POD and POC, all 9, shorts, boys and beyonds.

Question: Could you elaborate a little more on that no-mind space, Gary?

Gary: We keep trying to look to our mind as a source for creation. But our mind can only define what we already know. Our mind is a pretense of being. It's a beingness. Your mind is basically a beingness that you use to try to define what you have chosen. When you have the space of no-mind, you walk into the space of total choice. Total choice comes from space. No-mind begins to create space. Choosing from space always shows you what's going to get created by the choice you make.

The choice is creating, not the mind?

Gary: That's correct. Your mind can only define; it cannot create. Your choice can create, but you only create your life and your reality when you're in the space of total choice.

Thank you.

Dain: Our mind creates beingness, so we believe we are our mind. Our mind pumps up beingness after beingness after beingness, because when we're functioning from our mind, we never get to being.

We have beingnesses that don't create anything. These beingnesses are based on the definitions our mind sets up. We put forth a beingness based on those definitions and we wonder why we don't create anything greater than what we've had in the past. You, as a being, are creative and generative and your choice is creative and generative. Your mind is always definitive and defining.

What generation and creation of the no-mind space of infinite choice and ten-second increments of choice as an absolute non-reality are you using to lock into existence the positional HEPADs you're instituting to place you in the negative elements of realities that are other people's realities of choiceless non-existence? Everything that is times a godzillion, will you destroy and uncreate it, please? Right and wrong, good and bad, POD and POC, all 9, shorts, boys and beyonds.

Gary: People try to function from their mind instead of the sense of space that no-mind is. When you get to that sense of space, then you are functioning from a ten-second increment of choice.

I was at the stables with my horses and a girl came at me. She said, "I hate you and blah, blah, blah."

I said, "Okay."

She said, "What do you mean, 'Okay'?"

I said, "Well, if you want to hate me, that's fine. I don't care. It's your choice."

She said, "I don't want to choose that."

I asked, "Then why are you choosing it?"

She stood there and said, "Uh, well, well, well…"

I asked, "Are you psychically aware?"

She said, "Yeah."

I asked, "Is that feeling of hate actually yours—or is it somebody else's?"

She said, "It's somebody else's!"

I asked, "So, do you really hate me?"

She said, "No, I love you!"

I said, "Okay good."

If I had been functioning from my mind, I wouldn't have had the choice to respond the way I did. My mind would have tried to figure out what was going on with her and why she was choosing that. All your mind does is run you into the *why's* of reality. You're always running in a circle so you can stay in the maze called your mind. It's an a-mazing mind.

Dain: And if you look at it, the mind is always a set of judgments of right or wrong, good or bad, positive and negative, on or off.

What generation and creation of the no-mind space of infinite choice and ten-second increments of choice as an absolute non-reality are you using to lock into existence the positional HEPADs you're instituting to place you in the negative elements of realities that are other people's realities of choiceless non-existence? Everything that is times a godzillion, will you destroy and uncreate it, please? Right and wrong, good and bad, POD and POC, all 9, shorts, boys and beyonds.

Question: When you find you're in the space of configuring the mind, how do you move out of that space?

Gary: You can ask, "Okay, do I want to continue to do this choice?" Yes or no? No? Okay good. Or you could ask, "Would an infinite being choose this?" Or you could say, "Interesting point of view I have this point of view." You've got choice.

Going back to what you were saying before about being present, is that the space of total choice?

Gary: Yes. When you're being totally present and you're totally aware, you're creating a space of total choice.

What would it take to constantly be that?

Gary: If you use these tools, you will start to create that. But you've got to *use* them. I found that most people doing Foundation and Level One were reading through the tools once, and saying, "Well, I read them, and they didn't do any good."

No, you're supposed to use them every day, all day long for at least six months to a year. At the end of a year, you'll have a level of freedom you never had in your entire life.

I've been continuously using interesting point of view that I have that point of view. Doing that is allowing me to move into so many more spaces. You were saying, "Just go with one tool and stay with that one." That's what I'm doing, and it's creating so much more ease.

Gary: Cool. If you take one of the tools and run with it non-stop for six months, your whole life will change. If you did each one of the tools for six months, everything in your world would change. But it's always a choice.

Can you say that again?

Gary: Take each one of the tools and run with it for six months. Let's say you did interesting point of view I have that point of view for six months. It would create a place where you would never again have the point of view that any point of view mattered to you. For most of you, doing it for three months would probably work, but it would definitely work for you if you did it for six months.

Okay! I'm choosing that. There are lots of projections all around me, and interesting point of view is…

Gary: People project stuff at us all the time. When you do interesting point of view I have that point of view, all of a sudden you'll say, "I don't care about that. Why am I making it significant?" It makes things a lot easier.

Question: You gave me a wedgie,* a big wedgie. I didn't know it was a wedgie at the time, but what I realized is that I am such a control freak that I shut down my choices and constrict my life. I just couldn't be out of control,* I couldn't have too many things going on, I couldn't have so much money that it was out of control. I made a demand yesterday that I let go of this control thing, and it seems like I'm now functioning from more from the space of no-mind. It's so different!

Gary: Isn't it fun?

Yes! Thank you!

Dain: Oh no, she's having fun! Oh no!

Gary: The thing about control freaks is they're always trying to control things so they don't have too much fun.

Gary: Let's do the process again, Dain.

Dain: What generation and creation of the no-mind space of infinite choice and ten-second increments of choice as an absolute non-reality are you using to lock into existence the positional HEPADs you're instituting to place you in the negative elements of realities that are other people's realities of choiceless non-existence? Everything that is times a godzillion, will you destroy and uncreate it, please? Right and wrong, good and bad, POD and POC, all 9, shorts, boys and beyonds.

Question: Would you please give an example of being and living in ten-second increments? Is it asking, "What else?" every ten seconds?

Dain: Okay, here's an example. I often talk with my communications coordinator about plans for a class or an event that might be six months into the future. When we first started to work together, we would go with a choice for the class based on the information we had at the time. We'd make that real and solid—and it became a conclusion. We were functioning from a conclusion that we put into the world rather than being in a constant state of question.

That started to change as we became more open to the fact that we could have other choices and that things might change as time passed. Sometimes an energy would light up in our world or we would get some new information, and we would say, "Wait a minute. There's something we need to look at here. Maybe we need to change the title, maybe we need to change the place or maybe we need to cancel the class."

---

* See glossary for definition.

At one point, I was planning to give several workshops at a conference center in Sweden. I was originally going to do the Being You and Changing the World class. A while later, I said, "You know what? We need to change this." It wasn't something people were ready for.

A while after that, my communications coordinator said to me, "Something's calling to me. What do we need to do differently here?" That's part of ten-second increments of choice. She looked at the class we had planned and said, "Whatever we were going to do isn't going to work. It needs to go back to the Being You and Changing the World class. It will work now because the universe has changed and something different is available."

So we changed the title of the class, and it feels really good now. There will be people who can get it now, whereas several months earlier, they wouldn't have been able to.

Gary: After I had been doing Access Consciousness for a long period of time, I got to the point where I didn't care what I did. I didn't care about anything. Where would you like to eat? I don't care. What would you like to do? I don't care. What would you like to watch on TV? I don't care. Nothing mattered, nothing was significant, nothing was important, nothing was demanding on me.

So I said, "Okay, I've got ten seconds to live the rest of my life. What would I choose now?" I realized that I had spent my entire life choosing based on other people's needs, wants, requires and desires because that was easy. I had never sat down and chosen for me since I had gotten married.

I said, "Okay, I'm going to walk outside. That's ten seconds. Now what am I going to do? I'm going to go smell that rose. Okay, I did that. I've got ten seconds, what would I like to do now?" I began to realize I had lost the capacity to choose more than three things.

I didn't have infinite choice as a possibility. It was not even in my world that I could have such a thing. Now I know I can have things, and I know I can get whatever I want. I know that whatever I ask for will be delivered, and as a result, that's exactly what shows up.

I still function in ten-second increments. Today I was at the ranch with my horses, and I knew I had to be on this call with everyone. I could have gone to Annie's house, where the horses are, and done this call from there. It would have been air conditioned, comfortable and nice. The other choice was to go back to my hotel. I asked, "House? Hotel?" I said, "Hotel feels lighter; I'll do that." I went back to the hotel, and it was a good thing I did, because I had a bunch of things to do between the ranch and the hotel. I would never have been able to do all of those things if I had not gone to the hotel. It was a moment of knowing that going to the hotel was the right thing to do. I knew it was right because it's the one that felt light. It was the choice that ended up opening the door to about twelve other possibilities in less than fifteen minutes.

Dain: The other thing about this is that there was no conclusion in your world. You didn't say, "I must do the call here," or "I must do it there." You were open to whatever would create the most lightness or the greatest number of possibilities. It seems like a lot of people are saying, "Give me the right conclusion so I can have the one that will be right for all eternity."

Gary: When I first put this tool out there, I used to say, "The world is filled with lions, tigers, bears and poisonous snakes, and you're going to encounter them when you walk out the door. What would you choose right now if you were going to be eaten in the next ten seconds? What if you knew you were going to die in the next ten seconds?"

My dad died when I was 17. Prior to his death, he had done something that made me angry, and I didn't talk to him for two years. He tried to "make up" to me in that two-year period, and I just wouldn't have it. My attitude was, "You've offended me, you asshole, and I'm not talking to you ever again."

He died and I realized, "Wow, that decision I made two years ago that I held onto with such vehemence lost me the opportunity to have the last minutes with my father that might have given me some clarity about what it was like to be where he was."

I found out that he had known for two years that he was dying. Could we have had a better relationship? Could I have gotten to know him better? Yes. A lot of things could have been different. I didn't tell him I loved him before he died.

For me, it was a recognition that you need to say what is true for you today, and not wait until tomorrow. What if someone died ten seconds after talking to you? Do you want the last thing you said to them to be "You're a frigging asshole?" Or do you want the last thing you said to them to be "I'm grateful to have you in my life?"

What is it you would like to say in that last ten seconds of your life? What is it you would like to hear in that last ten seconds? What is it you would like to do in that last ten seconds of your life? If you were going to die and you knew you only had ten seconds, what would be the most important thing for you? When you look at this, you begin to realize what is important to you and what isn't important, what you want to make significant and what is irrelevant.

Dain: That helps a lot.

Question: A few weeks ago, I was having lots of trouble with the school where I work and how authoritarian they were being to me. I went home and listened to the first Energetic Synthesis of Communion class, and something happened. I said, "Wow, I'm going to connect to the school and the teachers and the kids," and that's what I did. So much changed with that ten-second choice. Now people are really, really nice, and it's totally easy at school.

Gary: It's not an effort; it's not something you do. You just be and allow yourself to choose the way you did, and that changes the entire reality.

Yes, it's a different reality. It was as easy as that.

Gary: Now you have to say, "Okay, that was a good ten-second choice. What other choices do I have now? And how can I use everything I have available and everything I know, in a different way than anybody has ever used it?"

Question: What do you do when you know someone's dying and you try to live in that ten seconds or show them "Hey, there's only ten seconds," but they don't hear it?

Gary: You can't make somebody hear something they don't want to hear. We had a 92-year-old friend named Mary who lived with us. Mary was dying, and she said, "I would just like to go now."

I asked, "So, what is it that's holding you here?"

She said, "Well, I'm not sure."

I asked, "Is there something you would like to be aware of before you leave?"

She said, "Yes, I want to know where I'm going next."

I said, "Why don't you decide what you're going to have next? If you were going to your next life, what would you like it to be?"

She stated a whole bunch of things, and I said, "You can have that if you want it."

She asked, "I can?"

I said, "Yeah. It is all a matter of choice. It's your choice. If this is what you would like your life to be, do it, ask for it. Demand that it show up for you."

She said, "That's great," and about a month later she was finally able to let go. Clearing her willingness to create goals for her next lifetime enabled her to do that.

It's necessary for a lot of people, especially if they're Catholic or meta-physical, to create goals for the next lifetime. They have to do this before they can leave. Then the ten-second increment of it is: Okay, for the next ten seconds you are dying. What's next? What will you choose?

And as you say, if they don't want to change, it's their choice, right?

Gary: Yep, that's their choice. From their point of view, they don't have the ten-second increments of choice as a reality. They believe they have to make a right or wrong choice. If someone isn't willing to hear that there are ten-second increments of choice, you've got to acknowledge the fact they've chosen and say, "Interesting choice, this is your choice," not from a point of view of right or wrong—but from the point of view of "That wouldn't be the choice I would make, but go for it. Do whatever works for you."

Dain: Let me get to another process that Gary came up with, because it's another brilliant one.

What generation and creation of not being, doing, having, creating, generating and instituting anything and everything at will as the erasure of your reality are you using to lock into existence the positional HEPADs you're instituting to blame you for not fixing the world? Everything that is times a godzillion, will you destroy and uncreate it, please? Right and wrong, good and bad, POD and POC, all 9, shorts, boys and beyonds.

Gary: Do any of you recognize that you blame you for not having chosen the right thing to make the world a better place?

Yep.

Gary: Good.

Dain: What generation and creation of not being, doing, having, creating, generating and instituting anything and everything at will, as the erasure of your reality are you using to lock into existence the positional HEPADs you're instituting to blame you for not fixing the world? Everything that is times a godzillion, will you destroy and uncreate it, please? Right and wrong, good and bad, POD and POC, all 9, shorts, boys and beyonds.

Gary: If you don't choose in ten-second increments, you can't fix the world. All you can fix is the past—because when you're not in ten-second increments, you're no longer in the present.

Dain: In other words, to be present, you have to be functioning in ten-second increments.

Gary: If you're not functioning in ten-second increments, you're functioning in the past. And if you're functioning from the past, you can't fix anything, you can't make anything better and you can't generate anything at all.

Dain: If you aren't functioning in ten-second increments, you're either functioning from the past or you're projecting into the future...

Gary: Which means you're functioning from what the future *might* be.

Dain: What generation and creation of not being, doing, having, creating, generating and instituting anything and everything at will, as the erasure of your reality are you using to lock into existence the positional HEPADs you're instituting to blame you for not fixing the world? Everything that is times a godzillion, will you destroy and uncreate it, please? Right and wrong, good and bad, POD and POC, all 9, shorts, boys and beyonds.

Gary: For a long time, I tried to get people to create their own reality. I couldn't figure out why they couldn't do that. Then I realized the reason they can't is that they don't understand any of The Ten Keys. If they're not doing ten-second increments of choice, they can't create their reality. They can only create a reality based on the past that has nothing to do with them in the present.

Dain: That's the thing about functioning from the past. It has nothing to do with you in the present. You're functioning from all the other things you have put in place, the fantasies, the beingnesses, and the secret agendas. They have nothing to do with you being you. It's crazy!

Question: There are three areas where I feel limited around ten-second increments of choice. I want to get this out because I'd like to have a different experience. Number one, I get performance anxiety around functioning in ten-second increments. I'm aware that way more than ten seconds pass before I choose something else. What would it take for me to relax around that or actually have an awareness of ten seconds as they go by?

Gary: You're looking at the ten seconds as though they are a fixed amount of time. It's really just about the choice you need to make in this moment. It's "What would I like to choose right now?" You have to practice using this question. Say you're getting in the bathtub. You ask, "Okay, what would I like to choose right now? I want the water hotter." Okay, good. Those ten seconds have passed. Then it's "This isn't hot enough." Okay, I'll do another ten seconds of hot water. "Not quite hot enough yet." Okay, I'll do another ten seconds.

You keep trying to come to a conclusion about what ten seconds is rather than seeing that it is about learning to choose. You have never been taught to choose; you've been taught to do what is right. So, your performance anxiety around ten-second increments is not abnormal. It's normal because you've never been taught to choose.

Thank you. I see I've been operating out of a predominantly no-choice universe. That brings me to part two. What is actual choosing or real choice? When you give an example, it's always something that is an action or a something you can do, like adjusting the water temperature. But if these were my last ten seconds and I asked myself what I would choose, my first thought would be "I would love to be in the ocean, swimming with the dolphins." But that's not going to happen in ten seconds.

Gary: You've got to start where you are and learn to choose. The whole idea of this is learning to choose. You're still trying to make the best choices.

The choices I would prefer.

Gary: No, not the choices you would prefer. You've got to learn to choose in ten-second increments. You're doing, "This would be the best choice." That's a conclusion; it's not a choice. You've misidentified and misapplied conclusion as choice. How many of you have misidentified and misapplied choice as conclusion and conclusion as choice?

> Everything that is times a godzillion, will you destroy and uncreate it, please? Right and wrong, good and bad, POD and POC, all 9, shorts, boys and beyonds.

The last part of my question is about choosing from space, because most of the time I feel like I'm choosing inside an energetic straightjacket. I really like having that sense of space.

Gary: In order to get a sense of space, all you have to do is walk outside the door and ask, "Okay, do I want to put my right foot in front of my left foot, or my left foot in front of my right foot?" Give yourself simple steps. You have been taught to jump to conclusion, to get it right and to only do the right thing. That is not choice. That's judgment. That's the other thing you have misidentified and misapplied about choice. You believe judgment is choice and choice is judgment.

> Everything that is times a godzillion, will you destroy and uncreate it, please? Right and wrong, good and bad, POD and POC, all 9, shorts, boys and beyonds.

This is about learning how to choose. I've got ten seconds to choose the rest of my life, what am I going to choose? Okay, those ten seconds are up. I've got ten seconds to choose the rest of my life, what would I choose?

You learn how to choose. The purpose of this is to get you to learn how to choose, not to make the right choice.

Are you saying that you choose something you can actually do in those ten seconds?

Gary: Yeah, because that's the only way you're going to learn to choose.

Okay, thank you.

Gary: Your version is something like "What would be the best thing to do?" That's based on judgment and what you would like to do that you haven't done.

Dain: It's not about getting it right. It's about learning how to choose. What if you looked at The Ten Keys from this point of view: "I should be doing The Ten Keys perfectly already, so let me get on the call."

Now, what if you looked at it this way: "It's time to learn about these Ten Keys and how I can choose them, institute them and use them in my life."

One of Gary's daughters wanted to take ballet lessons, but before she would take the class, she wanted to have private tutoring in ballet. She wanted to know how to do ballet before she signed up for the class. We do this to ourselves all the time. We think that somehow we're supposed to be perfect at something we don't yet know how to do. Before you went to school, did you know how to read? Or did you go to school so you could hopefully learn a thing or two?

Everything you've done to buy that you're supposed to be perfect with these Ten Keys, which is why you're on the call, will you destroy and uncreate it, please, and allow yourself to learn all these things and how to choose and institute them? Right and wrong, good and bad, POD and POC, all 9, shorts, boys and beyonds.

Gary: All of this is about learning to be an infinite being. Would an infinite being truly choose this? It's about learning to see what an infinite being would choose. Interesting point of view I have this point of view is about recognizing that ninety percent of what I perceive isn't mine.

Dealing in ten-second increments is about coming out of judgment. It's about learning to choose without judgment. It's a great gift. It will make your life so much easier. It will blow your mind. But you've got to do it without judgment. You've got to just choose.

And get over the fear of making a mistake.

Gary: If you only choose for ten seconds, you can't really make a mistake. You say, "Okay, bad choice. What do I want to choose now?" You can't judge in ten-second increments. You can only choose.

Dain: In other words, choosing in ten-second increments eliminates judgment. If you truly get that you can choose something else ten seconds from now, why would you judge that choice? You'd just move on to something else. Within the tool itself is the way out of the limitation that you're using it for.

That's beautiful.

Dain: What generation and creation of not being, doing, having, creating and generating and instituting anything and everything at will, including choosing in ten seconds, as the erasure of your reality are you using to lock into existence the positional HEPADs you're instituting to blame you for not fixing the world? Everything that is times a godzillion, will you destroy and uncreate it, please? Right and wrong, good and bad, POD and POC, all 9, shorts, boys and beyonds.

I just had an interesting awareness show up here. If you believe that each of your choices in itself is not enough to fix the world, does that somehow negate your willingness, your capacity, your ability and the value of choice?

Gary: Only absolutely, completely and irrevocably.

Dain: Everything you've done to buy that each choice is too tiny to actually make the world a different place, and everything you've done to buy that all the choices that we can make together, added up, would change the world but can't ever come into existence, will you destroy and uncreate it, please? Right and wrong, good and bad, POD and POC, all 9, shorts, boys and beyonds.

Gary: So Dain, this brilliance, is one of the reasons I adore you.

Every time you choose, every single solitary time you choose, you open a door to greater possibilities. Your choice is actually a gift to the universe. You've got to choose—and learn to choose—so that every choice you make opens a door to more possibilities, which helps the world.

Dain: That's the potency we've been refusing to be.

Gary: When you get that your choice opens a door, you can make a choice and then say, "Oh, that choice didn't work! Next choice." You do this without judgment. You don't stick that choice in the world as something that can't be changed. You open the door to a different possibility by choosing again.

Dain: What generation and creation of not being, doing, having, creating, generating and instituting anything and everything at will, as the erasure of your reality are you using to lock into existence the positional HEPADs you're instituting to blame you for not fixing the world? Everything that is times a godzillion, will you destroy and uncreate it, please? Right and wrong, good and bad, POD and POC, all 9, shorts, boys and beyonds.

Gary: If you want to fix the world, learn to choose—not from judgment but from choice.

Dain: Choose from choice, just because you can. After you've used these tools for a while and your judgments aren't pulling at you any more, you may think, "What's wrong?" What's happening is that you've gotten to that place Gary was describing, where you don't care about where you eat. You could just sit on the couch all day and watch TV. It feels weird because you're not being pushed and pulled in all different directions in the way you used to be. You used to think this indicated that you needed to choose something, but actually this is the space where true choice begins.

Choice comes from this space, not from a solidity that hits you in the head, which you're trying to put into the world. It's a space that has none of the solidities, none of the mental constructs and none of the heaviness you may be used to.

What generation and creation of not being, doing, having, creating, generating and instituting anything and everything at will, like The Ten Keys, as the erasure of your reality are you using to lock into existence the positional HEPADs you're instituting to blame you for not fixing the world? Everything that is times a godzillion, will you destroy and uncreate it, please? Right and wrong, good and bad, POD and POC, all 9, shorts, boys and beyonds.

Gary: We have to go now. I'm very grateful for your questions and I hope you see the whole purpose of learning to choose is to not have to choose the same problem over and over again but to have a different choice. You can choose differently every ten seconds. This is the most important concept you can get in life.

Dain: It really is about practice. This is something you're learning and something I'm learning more every day. It's not something you're supposed to be perfect at already. Maybe you haven't been choosing. You may not even know what choice is right now—but if you keep practicing, you'll start to get what choice is.

This is not something you've learned to do before. That's all right. It doesn't mean there's something wrong with you. Please keep choosing, please keep practising and please keep enjoying this cool adventure of functioning from a place that almost no one on the planet has ever functioned from before. The planet needs you. And now is our time.

~~~

THE FOURTH KEY TO TOTAL FREEDOM

Live as the Question

Gary: Hello everyone. Tonight we're going to talk about the fourth key: Live as the question.

Dain: In this reality, we've all been taught not to live as the question. We've been taught specifically not to function as the question. We're supposed to be the answer.

Gary: It's all about having the answer. We're taught to seek the answer, find the answer and do the answer—because if we get the right answer, we'll have everything right in our life. This, by the way, is not true.

Dain: We've been sold the lie that we are wrong if we have to ask a question—you can't be right if you've had to ask a question. This is absolute crap.

Gary: The first step toward living as the question is to ask questions.

If you keep asking questions, you'll get to a point where you're being the question and suddenly the need for questions ceases because you are functioning from the question called absolute awareness. Absolute awareness is always a question. You no longer have to ask a question because your whole life is about being the question.

That's what we mean by living in the question.

Question: From the time I was a child until I became a young adult, it was innate for me to ask questions. As I got older, I was ridiculed or ignored for asking too many questions, and I gradually stopped doing it. I stopped being in the question, which was where I felt the most joy, growth and expansion. Could you please give us a process to undo the judgment of many years of taking on the feeling of being stupid, dumb, slow or not smart enough?

Gary: What generation and creation of question as innate wrongness are you using to validate the positional HEPADs* you are choosing that make answers the reality and questions the embodiment of stupid-

---

* See glossary for definition.

ity, dumbness and slowness? Everything that is times a godzillion, will you destroy and uncreate it all? Right and wrong, good and bad, POD and POC, all 9, shorts, boys and beyonds.

Question: What do you mean by dumbness?

Gary: Dumbness is the idea that you're not bright enough to know what's true. It's not having awareness. You actually aren't dumb—but you can pretend you are if you want to! Dumbness is where you actually use energy to make you less than aware.

Have you used massive amounts of energy to make yourself dumb enough to live in this reality? Oops, did I say that? Will you destroy and uncreate it all? Right and wrong, good and bad, POD and POC, all 9, shorts, boys and beyonds.

What generation and creation of question as innate wrongness are you using to validate the positional HEPADs you are choosing that make answers the reality and questions the embodiment of stupidity, dumbness and slowness? Everything that is times a godzillion, will you destroy and uncreate it all? Right and wrong, good and bad, POD and POC, all 9, shorts, boys and beyonds

Question: When I was a child and I asked a question, my family would say, "Curiosity is the ultimate crime. Don't ask questions."

Gary: Yeah, in my family, they said, "Curiosity killed the cat. Will it please kill you?" How's that for fun?

I discovered that the reason they tried to stop me from asking questions was because they never had an answer that made any sense. I would ask another question until something made sense to me and then I would stop asking questions. Since they couldn't make their answers reasonable enough to get me to stop, they tried to stop me from asking questions. Did you experience anything like that?

Everything that is times a godzillion, will you destroy and uncreate it all? Right and wrong, good and bad, POD and POC, all 9, shorts, boys and beyonds.

People give you stupid answers that make no sense, and you think, "How can that be the answer?" If you have an ounce of awareness, you realize that the answers you're given are stupid and worthless.

Why couldn't you get your question answered? It was because you have twenty ounces of awareness and everybody else has one ounce of awareness. Your question was too bright for them to answer!

A lady said to me, "I was the dumbest person in my family."

I asked, "You made that decision based on what?"

She said, "Well, when I was five they told me I was an overachiever."

I asked, "Do you know what an overachiever is?"

She stopped in her tracks and said, "It's somebody who has to try harder because they're dumber."

I said, "No, it's somebody who's so smart they have to do more than anybody else can do!"

She said, "What? I wasn't stupid?"

This happened when she was five years old and she is now a woman of fifty. For the last forty-five years, she has thought she was the dumbest member of her family because she was an overachiever—but she didn't know what that was.

People tell you things like this when you're a kid and you have no idea what they mean, so you put your own spin on what they say. You assume that being an overachiever is a bad thing. So, if I'm bad, I must be wrong and if I'm wrong, I must be stupid.

> Everywhere you have decided that, would you please destroy and uncreate it all times a godzillion? Right and wrong, good and bad, POD and POC, all 9, shorts, boys and beyonds.

> What generation and creation of question as innate wrongness are you using to validate the positional HEPADs you are instituting that make answers the reality and questions the embodiment of stupidity, dumbness and slowness? Everything that is times a godzillion, will you destroy and uncreate it all? Right and wrong, good and bad, POD and POC, all 9, shorts, boys and beyonds.

Question: I feel like I got stopped when you were talking about overachieving. I had a huge emotional reaction to it. It brought back the experience of my parents being tremendously threatened every time I asked a question. I still feel like I'm about to commit a crime when I ask a question. It seems like a big deal and my palms sweat. What could I do to destroy and uncreate that as an automatic response to asking a question?

> **Gary:** How many lies did you buy about the wrongness of asking questions? Everything that is times a godzillion, will you destroy and uncreate it all? Right and wrong, good and bad, POD and POC, all 9, shorts, boys and beyonds.

> Did you buy a lie about the wrongness of asking questions? How many lies are you using to make it wrong for you to ask or be the question you truly are? Everything that is times a godzillion, will you

destroy and uncreate it all? Right and wrong, good and bad, POD and POC, all 9, shorts, boys and beyonds.

You were talking about being smart. My family did acknowledge and celebrate that I was smart, but this left me feeling impotent, because despite my awareness, despite my smartness, I didn't seem able to have a positive impact. What can I do to shift out of this identity of no matter what, no matter how smart or aware I am, I'm still going to be stuck in that failure?

Gary: You might have to do something terrible.

Like what?

Gary: Choose against your family.

Ah...

Gary: My father died when I was seventeen. I wanted to go into the Army. I wanted to become a Marine. My mother said, "You need to go to college. If you don't go to college, your father will roll over in his grave. It was the only thing he wanted you to do." So I went to college.

I had been in college for three years. I went home for a visit, and my younger sister had become a holy roller. These are people who roll down the aisle in the church screaming, "Yes, Jesus! Yes, Jesus!"

I was about twenty at the time. My sister said to me, "If you don't believe in Jesus, you're going to hell!"

I said, "Well, to be honest with you, I'm not sure I believe in God." She ran into the house screaming and yelling because I didn't believe in God.

My mother said to her, "Don't worry, honey. That's just some silly idea he picked up in college."

My mother had forced me to go to college based on the idea that my dad was going to turn over in his grave if I didn't go, but her point of view was that I just picked up silly ideas in college.

I looked at it and said, "That's crazy. You're telling my sister that it's a stupid idea I learned in college and you're telling me I need to go to college because otherwise I'm stupid. I'm sorry, this is stupid!"

I started flunking out of college just to prove her wrong. I finally looked at that and said, "You know what? That's stupid too! Why am I trying to prove my mother is right by proving I'm stupid for going to school and that I'm stupid by not going to school and that I'm stupid for flunking out of school and what the hell am I trying to believe here?"

So, would any of you who are still trying to please your living or long-dead parents, stop doing that and instead ask the question:

How stupid were my parents? Everything that is times a godzillion, will you destroy and uncreate it all? Right and wrong, good and bad, POD and POC, all 9, shorts, boys and beyonds.

Question: The first time I experienced being in the question, it felt like nothing at all. It didn't feel like what you guys are saying. When I ask questions, it seems like I'm in the mud. It feels like I'm in the mind.

Dain: Everything you've decided that living as the question is—and everything that you think it's going to feel like when you do it—is a projection from a point of view. It's not a question.

Gary: Everything you've decided living as the question is going to be and what it's going to look like, will you destroy and uncreate it all times a godzillion? Right and wrong, good and bad, POD and POC, all 9, shorts, boys and beyonds.

Dain: When you have a way of being that is about this reality, you function from answer. You twist you out of the willingness to be the question as though that's an abhorrence.

When you do that, you're setting up your body to be the physical embodiment of this reality and to carry that burden for you so you don't have to twist yourself out of the question every moment of every day.

Gary: Your body has to go along for the ride of consciousness as much as you do. It's amazing, the changes that can occur in your body and in your connection with everything around you when you live as the question. Your body is a sensory organ that gives you information. It tells you what's going on around you. If you're not willing to be in communion with it, you cut off ninety percent of what you're capable of perceiving, knowing, being and receiving. Is that where you want to live?

Dain: Your body is a contribution to the sum total of energy you perceive yourself to be in this reality.

Gary: It's what you create yourself as. That's why we're running this process—it will help you to live as the question. Doing the Advanced Body Class will also help.

Dain: People ask, "What the hell would an Advanced Body Class have to do with being able to live as the question?"

The Advanced Body Class processes unlock things, so rather than having a super-heavy elephant called "this reality" sitting on your shoulders, your elephant starts losing weight. It becomes easier to be the things we've been talking about.

Question: I was at the Advanced Body Class, which was beyond amazing, and I realized that my questions used to come from the mind. Now they seem to come from a different space.

Gary: Yes. That's exactly how it works. Your body has to go on the same ride you do. So, you do Bars, Foundation, Level One, Level Two, Level Three and the Basic Body Class, which you need to do at least twice in order to come to the Advanced Body Class, because if you haven't had enough bodywork, the results that you get are half as good as those somebody else will get. And then the Energetic Synthesis of Being Class. With all of those, you have a chance of choosing a totally different reality—if that's what you would like to have. So there, I've said it. I've given my thirty-second spot.

Question: I was listening to a class from way back about how Gary went into Dain's office for network chiropractic. It was the first time they met. Dain worked on Gary's body without touching him, and Gary had a great result.

Believing that would be something like blind faith for me. I don't believe anything until I see it. It's kind of like when I was a kid. I used to cry when I went to bed at night because I didn't believe in Jesus. I was told I was going to hell if I didn't believe in him, so I made sure I thought I believed even though I knew deep down that I didn't.

So, if I don't believe it, then why did I go to Dain's Energetic Synthesis of Being class last month? Why do I try to believe in things that I don't believe? I get a lot from energetic clearings and bodywork, and I'm a bodyworker myself. I believe in the healing of energy. But unless I can feel it, or see it or touch it, I can't believe it. Is it a lack of trust and rightness of my point of view about blind faith? What is it about this story that I am so resistant to?

Gary: What if the idea of blind faith is how you blind yourself to the faith in you? Oops.

> Everything that is times a godzillion, will you destroy and uncreate it all? Right and wrong, good and bad, POD and POC, all 9, shorts, boys and beyonds.

I'm in resistance to receiving and to Energetic Synthesis of Being.* Is this about not being able to receive something I can't understand? Is it a control issue? Do I need more information? What else is possible here?

Gary: When you ask, "Is it a control issue?" is that a question, or is that an answer you're putting a question mark at the end of, as though it's going to give you clarity?

---

* See glossary for definition.

Dain: This is something a lot of people do. They have an answer or a conclusion and they tack a question mark on the end of it. They act like they're asking a question and wonder why it doesn't open any doors. A question will always open up doors of awareness. An answer will always give you more of what you've decided is.

Gary: And answer keeps you on the same track you've been functioning from—the one that didn't work in the first place.

Dain: A question opens doors off the track you are on.

Gary: "Do I need more information?" is not a question. If you are confused or frustrated or if you feel like something is not quite right, you need more information. It's not "Do I need information?" It's "Where do I get the information I need that will get me greater clarity and ease?"

Try asking, "What else is possible here?" This is a true question. What else is possible here that I have not yet been willing to perceive, know, be and receive? What have you decided you have to believe, that if you don't believe it, you can't be it?

What if you were so great that having to believe in your greatness was what you had defined as the necessity of being greatness? Have you bought that you can be it only if you can define it? Everything that is times a godzillion, will you destroy and uncreate it all? Right and wrong, good and bad, POD and POC, all 9, shorts, boys and beyonds.

Dain: You said you have to define your greatness in order to be it, but apparently what this question is bringing to light is that in order to believe something, you have to define it before you can believe in it, before you can have it, before you can be it.

Gary: Everything that is times a godzillion, will you destroy and uncreate it all? Right and wrong, good and bad, POD and POC, all 9, shorts, boys and beyonds.

Dain: What if you didn't have to believe or define something in order to be it?

Gary: Dain, when I first came to your office, did you believe that I knew what I was talking about?

Dain: Uh, no.

Gary: Did you think I was nuts?

Dain: Yes, moderately so. We traded sessions, and I knew that when you worked on me, something was happening. I could feel my reality changing. But I didn't believe in my ability to gift or contribute to you at all. That didn't matter. Belief had nothing to do with it.

Gary: So what if it wasn't about belief? What if it's about you choosing something? In that first session, I said to you, "Just trust what you know and ask my body what you can do for it." Right?

Dain: Yeah, you said, "You'll know what to do." There was a part of me that came from the old place of belief and doubt, but there was also a part that was enticed and excited. That part of me said, "Really? I'll know what to do?" It went beyond the belief that I had no ability and no contribution to make to someone.

Gary: That's the most important aspect of this. You've got to be willing to ask the question and go beyond your limited beliefs. The only way you're going to go beyond what you believe is by asking a question.

Dain: What's beyond what you believe is what is actually possible. What's beyond what you believe is what you actually know. It's what you can perceive, what you can receive and what you can be.

Gary: Living in ten-second increments of choice is the beginning of recognizing you have infinite choice. Unfortunately, most people don't get that. They try to create the conclusion, judgment or answer that will make everything work for them, as though that's actually possible. What I'm suggesting you do is ask the question, "If I make this choice, what will I create?" Do you have any examples of that in your life, Dain?

Dain: Were you thinking of something in particular, my friend?

Gary: There was a woman who wanted to come and spend the night with you and you looked at it and you asked…

Dain: Right. I asked, "If I choose this, will it be a contribution to my life and living? Will it create more for me—or less?" Asking this question was very different than functioning from my usual conclusion, which was "Sex? Yes. Women? Yes. Definitely."

So, I asked the question and I got a totally different awareness than I had been willing to have previously. It's the energy that you're looking at. When you ask, "If I choose this, will it be a contribution to my life and living?" you will get a sense or a feeling of how it's going to be if you choose that thing.

I saw that being with that woman was not going to create an energy I wished to have in my life. Having sex with her was not going to be a contribution to my life. It felt much more like it was going to be a drain on my life. I said, "You know what? Even for sex, I'm not willing to choose that."

That is a major change for me. It seems like we all have at least one area where we seem to negate our willingness to ask questions, to look at things and to choose what will contribute to us. Whatever that area is for you, you can look at it and ask, "Would choosing this be a contribution?"

Be willing to ask that question. If you ask it and function according to the awareness you get, you will get even greater awareness of what it's like to be the question.

Question: When I ask questions, I feel that I have to take care of the things that come into my awareness. It's as if I have a responsibility to fix those things.

Gary: That's an assumed point of view. It's not about asking questions. Asking questions is about having greater awareness. When you get greater awareness, a different possibility is available. You have to be willing to look at something and ask, "Okay, what's actually possible here that I'm not perceiving, knowing, being or receiving?"

Everything that Access Consciousness is expands your awareness. You have to get over the idea that you're responsible for everything that occurs and that you have to do something about every awareness you have. You'll drive yourself crazy.

Being aware of something doesn't mean you have to do anything with it. What you do have to do is ask a question, "Is there anything I need to do, have to do or could do here?"

Ninety percent of the time you'll find that there's nothing to be done. For instance, I see very easily when people have chosen to die. I'll ask, "Can I do anything about this? Yes? No? No, okay. Is there anything I can change here? Yes? No? No, okay. Is this what they want? Yes or no? Yes, okay."

At that point, I stop trying to do anything. I recognize that I simply have an awareness. Then I ask, "When are they going to die?" When you ask a question like that, you become aware of the energy of death and when that will occur. You can't define it by a calendar or a clock. You just know that death is going to occur. It makes a huge difference to understand this.

Dain: If you're not functioning as the question or if you're not asking an actual question, you're headed in one direction. It's as if you have walls to the left of you and walls to the right. You can't see over the walls, you can't see around them, you can't see through them, you can't see between them. You can only go in that one direction.

Once you ask a question, doors open to the left and the right, and you see possibilities that you never considered before. The question is the thing that opens up those possibilities. The question is the key to allowing those possibilities to exist.

We walk around acting like we don't have other choices and possibilities available. We're not willing to be the question—and the way to get there is to start asking questions. You're walking down a narrow corridor called your life. You have walls to either side and you can't see any other possibilities. If you ask a question, doors open to the left and the right. If you be the question, there are no walls to limit your awareness of what you can have or be. The walls cease to exist. And isn't it the walls you've been bumping your head up against your whole life, while wondering, "How do I get through this wall? How do I get through this wall? How do I get through this wall?"

You get through the wall by being the question, which starts by asking a question.

Question: What's the difference between intuitive knowing and societal knowing? Like when you know the answer in an intuitive way and when you know the answer in terms of society?

Gary: Intuition, in and of itself, is a lie. It's not intuition that you have; it's awareness.

You define intuition as something that comes and goes rather than awareness, which is something that is always there. Intuition is the idea that something comes to you as if by magic. But awareness is not something that comes to you as if by magic; it's something that is a part of who you are. As long as you define awareness as intuition, you are seeing it as something that's not instantly available to you at all times.

You've got to be willing to have everything that occurs be something that's available to you at all times. The question is "How do I expand this awareness?" Every time you have an intuition, acknowledge it as awareness. Ask, "How do I expand this awareness until it's here all the time?"

Question: My mother passed away last week and I received a small inheritance. Now my family wants some of it. I don't know what to do. I've been trying to come up with a question to figure this out...

Gary: The question is "What kind of stupid people think they deserve it?" Your mother left it to you. Did she leave it to them?

No.

Gary: Why do they deserve anything?

They don't have any money.

Gary: All people who have no money think they deserve everything from anybody who has money.

All you have to do is say, "I'm sorry, I'm so poor I have to use all this money to pay my bills" or "I've already used the money to pay my bills."

My sister said to me, "If it's a lot of money, you have to share with me."

Gary: And did you ask, "Why?"

Yeah, and then I had a bunch of guilt.

Gary: That guilt is not yours. It's being projected at you, darling. How many people in your family are trying to make you feel guilty because you got it?

All of them.

Gary: Did you get it because you were a bad kid or because you were a good kid? Did they not get it because they were bad kids or good kids?

I don't know.

Gary: Yes, you do. They didn't get it because they kept trying to take it from your mother before it was time.

They did.

Gary: They've been trying to get it their whole life. "You should die so I can have your money" is not a nice thing to project on a poor old lady. You, on the other hand, loved her regardless of whether she gave you money or not.

Right.

Gary: Were you someone who actually cared?

Yes, I think so.

Gary: You don't think, you know. Cut that out. As long as you're doing *think*, you're not in the question. Get to the question, "Was I caring?" Did you really care about her money? Truth?

No. Yes, no.

Gary: No, you didn't just care about her money. You liked her for who she was. Everybody else liked her for her money. You'd think she might have been aware enough to know that and to say, "Screw them, I'm not going to leave them anything."

Yes.

Gary: Or did she just want to leave you everything so she could torture you to death?

Dain: Or maybe she left you everything so she could torture you and them.

(Laughing) I thought of that possibility too.

Gary: Everything you're unwilling to perceive, know, be and receive about all that, will you destroy and uncreate it all, times a godzillion? Right and wrong, good and bad, POD and POC, all 9, shorts, boys and beyonds.

Dain: When I said, "She left you everything so she could torture you *and* them," you laughed. That's the way it feels when you get the awareness that comes from being in the question or from asking the question. It's the awareness of what's true. It makes you feel lighter and it often makes you laugh.

Gary: If it makes you feel lighter or it makes you laugh, it's true. If it makes you feel heavy and awful, it isn't true.

I think it's great that she handed you the reins to torture the rest of your family. Now you can torture them if you wish to. Or you can lie and pretend that you were so deeply in debt that you had to use it all to pay your bills. You can say that you totally understand how they're also deeply in debt and can't pay their bills—but you're sorry, it's all gone.

And why would you not lie to ugly people? So all the ugly people in your life that you're not willing to lie to and not have a question about, will that actually create or generate something in their world?

And if you gave them money, would it truly generate or create something greater in their world? Or would it just be the solution that they had been waiting for their entire lives? Would it actually accomplish anything? Truth?

No.

Gary: Okay, then, screw them.

Everything that is times a godzillion, will you destroy and uncreate it all? Right and wrong, good and bad, POD and POC, all 9, shorts, boys and beyonds.

Question: I was in unhappiness so long that there was no question in my universe about there being any other possibility. Then I started doing the processes in the Advanced Body Class and I woke up one morning in an incredible state of happiness. It was "What is this?" I had gotten so used to all the unhappiness or pain and punishment that I thought, "Well, that's just the way things are." I didn't know anything else.

Gary: What question is "That's just the way things are?"

Exactly, there was no question in my world about it. Until that point, I wasn't aware that there was a question I could ask like "How could I be happier?"

Gary: Like you said, it's about asking the question. You could ask, "Am I happy?" But that's not a question. It's a right or wrong point of view. It should be an open-ended possibility.

An open-ended question would be "What would it take for me to be happy?"

Everything that you made right or wrong about your happiness times a godzillion, will you destroy and uncreate it all? Right and wrong, good and bad, POD and POC, all 9, shorts, boys and beyonds.

Question: I have a dilemma about whether I should ask a question or just let something be. I spoke with someone a couple of times and he said, "I would like to come to your Access Consciousness Bars class." A friend called me today and said, "I spoke with him today, and he said he's not going to your class because you are too exuberant." I thought, "Should I ask a question about this?" Then I got, "No, I will just let it go."

Gary: Was he in question, conclusion or answer?

He was in conclusion. But do I have to do something about it?

Gary: No. I'm sorry, who loses if he doesn't come to your class? Him or you?

Both of us. I lose a client.

Gary: No, no, no. You're assuming the money he would pay you for the class would handle things for you. You're not looking at the fact that his choice to not live, which is what he's choosing by not going, somehow means you lose. You've got to see that some people are willing to choose only what allows them to lose. I see it happen all the time.

Everything that is times a godzillion, will you destroy and uncreate it all? Right and wrong, good and bad, POD and POC, all 9, shorts, boys and beyonds.

What question can you be that you refuse to be that if you would be it, would change all realities? Everything that is times a godzillion, will you destroy and uncreate it all? Right and wrong, good and bad, POD and POC, all 9, shorts, boys and beyonds.

Dain: How much anti-consciousness does it require to take you out of being the question that you naturally are, to where it feels unnatural for you now?

Gary: It was part of what was beaten out of you as a kid when they said, "Be quiet and don't ask that question." You were taught not to question. Your innate capacity is to question.

Dain: My mom put Band-Aids on my mouth when I was a kid because I was always asking questions. Do you think it worked? Of course not! I found a way to talk with Band-Aids on my mouth. You just have to separate them a little bit to get enough air out so you can still talk.

Gary: That's very funny.

Everything that is times a godzillion, will you destroy and uncreate it all? Right and wrong, good and bad, POD and POC, all 9, shorts, boys and beyonds.

Dain: So here's the deal: If Band-Aids didn't kill the question in me, and if I can still be as annoyingly in question as I am, so can you.

Gary: The thing that made Dain different from anybody else who has come to Access Consciousness is that he would ask a question about something, we'd come up with a process, we'd clear him on some major issue in his life—and thirty seconds later, he would say, "Well, now that we got that, what about this?"

I'd say, "Can't you enjoy the peace and the possibility of the thing you created for just a moment?"

He would say, "No, there's other stuff to clear." That willingness to seek always for more is living as the question. When you stop seeking for more is when you die. If you don't believe me, check out people who are really old and still active and doing things. They have an active mind; they're still looking for more. More is the basic operative state of someone who is willing to be a question.

Question: My whole life as a child, I was told not to be more, not to ask for more, not to expect more, so was I basically being told to be a zombie?

Gary: You were being told not to be.

Dain: More, more, more. Being more, receiving more and asking for more, is actually the state of being. You, as a being, are always desiring more, creating more, and generating more.

Gary: If you are truly willing to be, is there ever a place where you are not in question about how to have more perceiving, knowing, being or receiving?

It's like a new concept. My old way of being just got turned on its head. That's amazing.

Gary: That's what we're trying to do here. The Ten Keys, by themselves, will create for you a sense of looking for what else is possible in your life, of having more and of being the question.

Dain: I've noticed that sometimes when we talk about The Ten Keys, if people have trouble understanding something, they go into judgment of themselves. It's as though they think we're telling them, "You're stupid. You're not conscious."

That's all stuff from this reality's point of view. It's stuff we were handed. It's a place we function from—we buy into that stuff and continue creating the wrongness of us.

Gary: You have to ask the question, "What's right about me that I'm not getting?"

You've been made wrong for asking questions, you've been made wrong for wanting more, you've been made wrong for having a sense that there's got to be something greater and for desiring to have a life greater than most people have.

At one point in my life, I had what my mother thought was the perfect 1400-square-foot tract home. It was in a bad section of town, but I had a 1400-square-foot house. My mother's point of view was "What more would anybody want?"

I sold that house and moved into a broken-down wreck in the best part of town. The great thing about living in the best section of town is you have the "right" address to tell people who think they're better than you are.

My mother's point of view was "You've got a perfectly good tract house here. Why are you moving?"

My point of view was "Because it's not enough. I want more in my life."

Her point of view was "You should be satisfied with what you've got."

I could never have that point of view because I was living as the question at all moments in my entire life.

And as it turned out, I sold the wreck for more money than I paid for it and made money on it, too.

Question: What are some questions and clearings that may serve those of us who have the desire to do things we don't seem able to afford.

Gary: When people can't afford something, it's a solution they made about never being more.

What solution have you created to never being more to make sure you can never be the more you could truly be? Everything that is times a godzillion, will you destroy and uncreate it all? Right and wrong, good and bad, POD and POC, all 9, shorts, boys and beyonds.

That's the process for people who say they can't afford more.

Question: As I become more sensitive, I perceive the feelings, emotions and thoughts of people around me. I don't exactly want to perceive everything. What can I do about this?

Gary: Why not?

Because I get pain in my body. I was speaking on the phone this morning with a friend who was ill, and I could perceive everything that was going on in her body.

Dain: Wait! When you say you don't want to perceive everything, you're taking yourself out of the capacity to have and be everything you've been asking for. You've misidentified and misapplied that your perception is creating the problem.

The problem comes from the fixed points of view you have and the things you're doing with your perception. Gary can perceive everything and not be the effect of it. I'm getting to the place where I can perceive everything and not be the effect of it. It's a different way of being that hasn't been able to show up until now. You have to go into the question.

Gary: A friend's husband is getting dementia. He's angry beyond his wildest dreams, and he has a lot of guns. My perception was that if she didn't change something major in her life quickly, he was going to shoot her. Is that what I would like to have happen? No. Can I stop it? No. Only she can. Can I tell her? No. What do I do about that? Be aware. That's the sum total of what you can do with a whole lot of the information that you have.

You think that because you have this awareness, you have to experience the pain, change the pain and do something for the people who have the pain. Who made you God? Having total awareness does not make you God. It makes you a person with God's abilities—not God's responsibility.

> Everything you keep trying to make yourself responsible for as the god of awareness, will you destroy and uncreate it all? Right and wrong, good and bad, POD and POC, all 9, shorts, boys and beyonds.

Question: Every time you say create, I realize I don't know what create is. Or what it feels like. I know what generating is, but I don't know what creating is.

Gary: *Create* is the place where you take the generative energy you're aware of and you turn it into something. You're willing to be aware of the energy and willing to do the steps required to bring what you desire into fruition. You could say, "This is a generative energy. What I desire should just come into existence." Yeah, it should, but it won't. You have to do something to create it. You have to bring it into existence.

Generative energy is a good thing to understand, but unless you're willing to take that generative energy and to create something—to bring it into reality—the generative energy, by itself, won't actually create anything in your life. What creative energy in your life would you like to have? You have to ask, "How do I use this? How do I take advantage of this? How do I make this work for me?"

I hear your words and I understand them, but I still don't get it. I just don't get it. I could ask, "What's it going to take for me to get what creating is?" Or...

Gary: Ask, "What am I refusing to be that I truly could be that if I would be it would change all realities?"

You're refusing to be something so that you don't have to create a different reality. Most of us have a place where we know we should just get the energy of something, and it should then fall in our lap. We know that should be a reality. But that's not how it works.

How do we get you to the place where you realize how to take this generative energy and bring it into fruition as something that actually shows up in this reality? That's creation—something that shows up in this reality from the energy you're capable of using, controlling, changing and instituting.

I get it in the context of creating a class. I know how to do that.

Gary: It's similar, but your whole life should be that, not just a class.

Question: How can we be the question—and until we get to that point—what questions can we ask?

Gary: This would probably apply to your question about creating:

What energies am I aware of that I could use to create something that would be valuable to me?

Once you feel and become aware of what would be valuable to you, then you start instituting. You ask, "What would I need to institute today in order to create this right away?"

Here's an example: I was talking to somebody the other day who was interested in creating a class. I said, "You want to create a class. What's the purpose of the class? "

She said, "To get people interested in this, this and this."

I asked, "What's the platform off of which you're building?"

She asked, "What do you mean?"

I said, "You have to have a platform off of which you create something." I explained that when they constructed buildings in the city of Venice, they put pylons into the mud and then they built a platform across the pylons. Then they constructed a house with two interior walls to hold up the main structure and two other walls going in a different direction. They leaned the outside walls of the house against the structure of the internal walls. The houses didn't have a foundation. They had a platform off of which they built everything. That platform would withstand anything. The platform would stand even if the structure fell.

The platform is the creation part of it. You have the generation of it, which is the energy of what you would like to create, you have the platform and then you can institute the parts that will work and what needs to happen next based on the platform. The platform is the creation.

Once you have the generation, the creation is the platform off of which you will institute what you're trying to create. Does that help?

Yes, thank you.

Gary: You're welcome. Great questions, by the way. Consider the possibility of asking a few real questions instead of "When is my BMW coming?" or "When is my partner coming?" Those are not questions. Those are decisions with a question mark attached.

You have to look at "What can I generate that will create the platform off of which I can institute everything I would like to create in and as my life?" Please use open-ended questions.

Dain: Or you might look at it this way: "If I were no longer wrong for anything, what questions could I ask? What choices would I have that I didn't have before?"

Gary: Okay, folks, I hope this explains some things for you. Please know that every time you ask a question, you create a different choice. When you create a different choice, you create a different awareness. Dr. Dain said it: "Choice creates awareness, awareness does not create choice." Live that.

Dain: So there!

Gary: So there! We love you lots and look forward to talking with you about the fifth key. Take care.

Dain: Bye ya'll.

~~~

No Form, No Structure, No Significance

Gary: Hello everyone. Tonight we're going to talk about the fifth key. This key is: No form, no structure, no significance.

Form is the shape or outline of something. It is also the way something is done or a way of acting.

Structure is a manner of organizing, building or constructing something that makes sure everything runs in a specific manner. It's something that everyone agrees exists in a particular way and that you don't have the right to change.

Significance is importance or meaning. We make something significant when we make it meaningful, important or consequential.

Suppose you have a new relationship and you say, "I now have a relationship with someone who is the love of my life. Our relationship is going to be perfect."

Relationship is a form.

A *perfect relationship* is a structure you're trying to make real and rigid and true that may not be those things.

The love of my life is a significance. Seriously.

These are all just interesting points of view. There is no necessity of having form (a relationship), no necessity of creating a structure (the perfect relationship), and no necessity of having a significance (that person is the love of your life).

What would no form, no structure and no significance look like in this example? It would be "This relationship is great today."

If you're going to do a relationship, you do it from the point of view of "What can I create today? What do I desire today? What can I enjoy today? And how about making more of this?"

Most of us are not willing to have a relationship that is not based on the form, structure or significance that we've all seen, heard about and been told we're supposed to have.

When you start to create a relationship from no form, no structure and no significance, you give up being Cinderella, the prince on the white horse or the dwarf that only gets to kiss the dead meat.

When you create a relationship from no form, no structure and no significance, you can give up the relationship—or you can also create it, desire it, enjoy it and seek it. Do you see the freedom this gives you? Contrast this to the form, structure and significance version of relationship: "I have to have a perfect relationship with the person who is the love of my life."

Dain: When you have no form, no structure and no significance, there is no judgment attached to anything. Every judgment you use creates a form, a structure and a significance. It puts up walls around you. You try to beat your head against the walls or to go around them—but you can't.

With no form, no structure and no significance, there's no judgment. It's the embodiment of interesting point of view.

Gary: Do you see how this works?

Question: I understand what not making something significant is, but I am not clear about what form and structure are. For example, I thought that there was form and structure in a Bars class because there are things you need to do in order for it to be a "correct" Bars Class. You said that wasn't form or structure, and I don't get that. Could you say some more about this, please?

Gary: What you're talking about in the Bars class is a system that will make something work.

There's a difference between a system and a structure. A *system* is something you can change and alter when it does not work. A *structure* is something that is fixed in place. You have a structure when you try to make everything work around it, as if you have no other choice.

Often teachers will say, "You have to learn this way. You have to do it this way." That becomes a rigid format under which no change can occur and no awareness can increase. They have turned the *system* into a *structure*.

A significance would be, "This is the only way it is. This is the way it has to be and this is the way you have to do it. This is the only way that works. This is the best way. This is the right way."

Any time you say, "This is the only way," "This is the right way" or "This is the answer," you have created a significance, which creates the structure that holds in place what you cannot change—that is the form that is the source for all limitation.

Dain: That was brilliant.

Gary: I have my moments. They are few and far between—but I do have them.

Let's say you are going to clean the toilet.

The form of cleaning a toilet is: I have to get the brush, I have to get the cleanser, I have to scrub it diligently and I have to use some kind of chemical or else it won't be clean. The structure of cleaning a toilet is: Scrub, scrub, scrub until everything is "clean." The significance of a clean toilet is: Nobody will judge me for having a dirty toilet.

If there was no form, no structure and no significance, you could clean the toilet any way you wanted to—because no form, no structure and no significance create total choice.

Question: First a small acknowledgement. I have been in a state of indescribable peace for weeks since the San Francisco class. I have a feeling of freedom, and I have moments when I just want to scream, "Hello! I am free." I am so light and happy. Thank you, thank you, thank you.

Please explain about this physical form that we have. Is this real—or is it an illusion created by consciousness? How do we create forms? What does a life form look like outside the box of the way we think it looks?

Gary: You create your physical form from the form, structure and significance of this reality. You create it and then you say things like, "I'm fourteen years old now, so I'm too old to run around and play like a kid. I must do everything sedately and beautifully and be the swan flying through the water of this life." That's form.

When you do structure, you look at your body and say, "I am not athletic because I can't do this."

Significance would be "Now I'm old, and that means I've got to get fat like all of my friends." That is the form, structure and significance of this body.

Dain: I love the question about how form gets created—because you have choice about how it gets created. You can choose to create from the form, structure and significance of everything in this reality—or you can choose to create from a different place. When you create it from a different space, things are not fixed in place. Everything is malleable.

Gary: This is where life is about the *system* of creation instead of the *structure* of creation—because the system is adjustable. If you looked at your body and said, "I'm really fat. What structure do I have to use to change this?" or "What form do I have to take to change this?" you'll be required to do a diet and exercise and all that.

A system would be, "Okay, Body, what, if we did it, would change all this?" And then your body begins to tell you, "Do this, this and this." All of a sudden, you stop doing things by the form, structure and significance that you have been taught and you begin to create a system that works for your body.

Dain: When you create something from no form, no structure and no significance, you can change it in ten-second increments. You can't do this when you create from form, structure and significance. In other words, you've made your form the way it is with the significance you attribute to it, which gives you no place to change anything.

Gary, it's interesting that you mentioned being fourteen years old. That is the time when form, structure and significance actually start coming into reality for us.

Gary: Before kids are fourteen, they expect every day to be different. They don't have the idea that anything is supposed to be a certain way or that they have to act a certain way or look a certain way. But at about fourteen, the time of puberty, they suddenly think, "I have to start acting like an adult. I've got to start acting like...." instead of "What would I like to choose today? What would be fun for me and my body?" The fun goes out of life and living and the drudgery of adulthood comes in.

When you do the form, structure and significance of something, you start to lock up the parts of your body, and it doesn't work as well.

It's been very interesting to watch Dain change and morph his body before my very eyes in ways I never knew people could do. He does this when he functions from no form, no structure and no significance. Then, when he gets into form, structure and significance, he diminishes his body. He has gotten shorter than I in a heartbeat just because he had form, structure and significance about something.

Dain: Normally Gary and I stand eye-to-eye, but it sometimes happened that we were no longer at eye level. I would suddenly be looking at his mouth. It was "What the hell just happened?" And then I would change back to my usual height, or sometimes become taller than Gary. It wasn't ever cognitive. It was never "I'm now going to shrink my body and feel like a pile of poo." It always happened when I was choosing form, structure and significance.

As you read this, you may be thinking, "Oh, I don't get it. I don't under-stand this!" That's fine. As we talk about this, your awareness will change. You'll say, "Wait a minute. This is something that can be different in my life. There's a different way to create."

It may not become part of your reality in totality at this moment, but each key opens a door for things to be different for you.

Gary: I was talking with my daughter this morning. She said that when she saw me at the Advanced Body Class, I was stiff, and she noticed that I couldn't bend forward.

I looked at that and said, "Wow, I made it significant that I am the age I am. I have created the structure of my body to fit my age. I have made the form of my body appear to be the form of the age that my body is. Enough of that! No form, no structure and no significance on that today."

I went in to take a shower, and as I bent down I could only bend over far enough to reach my knees. I said:

> All the form, structure and significance I've used to create this, right and wrong, good and bad, POD and POC, all 9, shorts, boys and beyonds.

I kept doing that, and within ten minutes, I could bend over so my hands were within one inch of the floor. I have not been able to get that close to the floor for a long time because I've been doing form, structure and significance about the age I am and the shape I'm in and whether I do enough exercise. I said, "You know what? That's frigging nuts!"

A lot of people I know create their bodies like this. They say, "I've put on twenty extra pounds. That's because I'm not exercising." That's the form, structure and significance of how we create our body as it is.

Dain: We take a point of view and then we use that point of view to create a solid reality, whether it's our body or anything else.

I started doing a super-intense fitness program called Insanity, which was supposed to get you the insanely fit, buff body you wanted in sixty days. I had done it for three days when Gary looked at me and said, "Do you really think you need to do that program for sixty days?"

I asked, "What are you talking about?"

He asked, "Have you looked at your body in the mirror lately?"

I asked, "What do you mean?"

He said, "It looks like you already got the result in three days that they said you were supposed to get in sixty days." I said, "Oh." I hadn't noticed that I had already gotten what they said you're supposed to get. I was trying to put their form, structure and significance in place: "You need to do this for sixty days."

We're used to functioning according to the form, structure and significance of this reality as it relates to time, bodies, the results we can create and what other people tell us we have to do or be. What if we didn't have those? If we had no form, no structure, no significance and no point of view about what could or could not be created, imagine what we could create with our body.

Gary: Let's go back to the second part of the last question: *What does a life form look like outside the box of the way we think it looks?*

First of all, the way you think a life form looks is the form, structure and significance you create on it. When you start creating from outside the box, all of a sudden everything starts to melt away and things change.

Recently I was planning to go to Auckland, New Zealand, and I decided to hire a driver to take me to the airport.

The driver asked me, "What time do you need to leave?"

I said, "I don't know. What do you think? I would like to be at the L.A. Airport some time between 9:00 and 9:30."

He said, "We should probably leave at seven o'clock."

I said, "Okay, let's go at seven." He got to my house at five minutes to seven, and we were loaded and out of there in five minutes. That's the kind of thing that happens when you do no form, no structure and no significance.

I got to the airport in less than two hours, which never happens, even though it was during rush hour and there was heavy traffic. How did that occur? Oh yeah, no form, no structure and no significance.

So, I was very early. I went to the Qantas desk to get checked in, and they said, "We've cancelled that flight."

I said, "What!"

Then they said, "But we have another one that's leaving in half an hour. If you can get through security, we'll give you a seat on it."

I said, "What!"

They said, "This flight is going to Sydney, Australia, so once you get there, you'll have to take another flight on to Auckland."

I said, "Okay."

They rebooked me and had everything in place in a heartbeat. I was on the plane mere minutes before it was ready to take off. Had I not been at the airport early, I would have been waiting around Los Angeles forever, because a volcano in Chile had erupted, and flights were being cancelled.

That's what a life form looks like when you function from no form, no structure and no significance.

Dain: People keep asking things like, "How do things like that come into existence?"

When Gary talked with the driver about what time they should leave, and the driver suggested seven, that felt light. It matched the energy of the lightness Gary was being. He didn't go into thinking about what time was best. In other words, he didn't do form, structure and significance, which would have been: "Oh it takes exactly one and a half hours if there's no traffic, and two-plus hours if it's during rush hour. Therefore we should leave at such-and-such a time." Instead, Gary went with the energy.

Following the energy allowed that result to occur. If Gary had gone with form, structure and significance, the structure would have been "It takes this long to get to the airport." If he had done that, he would have missed his plane, because he would not have been there early enough to catch the flight they offered him. He didn't place any significance on the idea of how long it supposedly takes to get to the airport; he just allowed the information to be there.

Gary: And I also had no significance on it when I got to the airport three and half hours early. I thought, "I'll just go check in" not "Oh no, I'm so early and my plane doesn't leave for hours!"

If I had been there five minutes later, there wouldn't have been time for me to board the flight. I would have missed the plane.

Dain: And it's not cognitive—ever. It's the interaction of the energy of you and your life and the choices that come up.

So, when Gary's driver said, "Seven," and Gary said, "Okay, cool," and the driver arrived at five to seven—none of that was cognitive. If the energy hadn't matched, Gary would have asked a question. He would have said, "Okay. Earlier or later? Earlier. Okay. I need to go earlier. I don't know why, but let's go a little earlier."

We've done that a hundred times. The driver will ask, "Shall I pick you up at this time?" and one of us will say, "Hm, let's do it a little earlier." We don't know why we're choosing that—but as a result, we end up missing traffic jams and accidents.

Question: I would like my body to be less significant.

Dain: When you're trying to get out of significance with something, you've already made it significant. Otherwise, you wouldn't have to try to get out of significance with it.

Gary: All your body can do is create the structure you've judged it to be. That's the only choice it has. Judgment is the structure that you use to create the limitations of your body. Whatever you judge your body to be, it has to create that structure and that form. When you look in the mirror, you automatically create a significance about how your body looks.

If you judge that you're fat, the body will create more fat. If you judge that you're too skinny, your body will create more skinniness. If you judge that you have too many wrinkles, your body will create more wrinkles. Whatever you judge is what your body will create.

Dain: And how important is it to most people when they're overweight? Or when they have wrinkles? Or when kids have zits? It's the most important thing in their lives! When you try to button your pants, and the pants won't button, it's so important. That's making it significant—rather than "Interesting point of view that I have this point of view" or "That's interesting! I wonder what it's going to take to change this."

You don't have that freedom when something is significant because that solid energy is the only thing that can be there.

Gary: Significance solidifies things into existence.

Question: I made a demand that I do the body processes from the Advanced Body Class, and I've done a few. Here's where I get confused: The processes have a form and a structure, and I have a certain number of them to do. How is that not form and structure?

Dain: People have misidentified and misapplied structure and what it is. There is an unchangeability that is inherent in structure. This is a key point. The body processes are not unchangeable. We change them all the time. In the Advanced Body Class, Gary recently got rid of all kinds of body processes that we had been coming up with because he found that two other processes were what everything else was building up to. So, the body processes are not a structure; they're a system, which is a totally different way of being with things. It's changeable and it's malleable, which is what you have when you don't have structure.

So, it's not about the form, structure and significance of the processes? It's just an awareness of what's required to get the result you desire? It's not about getting all caught up in the energy of having to do them? If there's an ease to something, is that a clue that it's no form, no structure and no significance?

Gary: Yeah, when you have a sense of ease with something, it means you're coming out of form, structure and significance. When you're using force or feel the need to do something, you are doing form, structure and significance.

So, it's not what the action or the statement is; it's the energy around it?

Gary: Yes.

Dain: We're not saying that nothing in the world should have a structure. The important thing is the way you're choosing to live your life and create yourself and whether you are in communion with everything that's in your life and in the world.

Gary: If there is a structure, and you can have communion with it, then it has no significance. Its form is malleable or changeable for you, even if it isn't for somebody else.

One of the things we've run into is the idea of necessity. When you decide that something is a necessity, you have no choice. And when you create no choice, you usually get angry. Everybody takes that anger and does something different with it. Some people build more fat cells in their body. Some people make themselves slower in the head. Some people make themselves stiff and rigid. Necessity becomes a giant lock-up in our body. Some people make themselves emotional basket cases.

It's all about the places where they think they have no choice, which comes from the idea that it's a necessity—not a choice. You have to learn to function from choice and recognize the choice you have.

When you are doing form, structure and significance, you are sitting in the no-choice universe. You're saying, "This is necessary. This is the way it's supposed to be. This is what I have to do."

When you have choice, you ask, "What else is possible? What choices do I have? What other contributions are there? What question can I be or receive that would change all that?"

One of the things that keeps us in the form, structure and significance of this reality is the idea that there is no choice; there is only necessity and you must do what you must do—because you must do it.

There are things that are priorities and things you are required to do. For example, there are things you do because you're a member of your family. You have to do them. It's not really a necessity; it's just a choice that you made a long time ago when you decided to go to that family. You created some choices. It's not that you have no choice; it's that you have to choose to do what's going to make things easy for you. Most people try to avoid what's going to be easy for them because they want the other people to change.

Dain: When you find yourself resenting something, you can ask, "How many necessities do I have creating this?"—and POD and POC it. Or when you find yourself getting slow or messing things up, ask, "How many necessities for doing this do I have?" and destroy and uncreate them. Look at it and cognitively acknowledge, "Wait a minute. I'm actually making a choice to do this. It's not a necessity. I'm making a choice to do it."

Recently, I had some writing I wanted to do. Gary and I were leaving town and the next day was fully booked and I still had a million things to do. Gary said, "I'm going to meet with the editor to work on the book. Do you want to come?"

I said, "Yes." Before this necessity thing came up, I would have been resentful of going with him because I had so many things I needed to do, but I said, "This is a choice I'm making. Doing this will contribute to a greater future for everyone."

Understanding that there is no necessity changes the places you've ever resented anything.

Gary: And we lock all that resentment into our bodies.

Dain: We stiffen them up and we make them ugly.

Question: Is being in the question, for example, always asking what else is possible with the body, an antidote to form, structure and significance? Is that how it works?

Gary: Yes. Good call. When you function from no form, no structure and no significance, things happen with great ease—and very quickly. Things that other people have difficulty with, you will have no difficulty with.

Every judgment you make locks you into a form, structure or significance. As Dain said earlier, if you're doing no form, no structure and no significance about anything, you can't have judgment.

If anything "means" anything, it's significance. Significance creates structure and it creates form.

Question: Could you give an example of no form, no structure and no significance related to creating revenue, wealth and abundance in my life and living?

Gary: An example would be when somebody gives me an opportunity and I'm willing to trust my awareness and ask a question like, "If I buy you, will you make me money?"

You can also ask:

- What would it take to create wealth, money and abundance in my life?

- What form, structure and significance have I made so important that I can't have that?

That process will show you the places where you haven't been willing to create wealth, money and abundance.

You said, "No form, no structure, no significance means nothing," so does this mean I can create and generate my way, and all the laws of this reality don't apply?

Gary: Yes and no. Does physical reality have particular laws it abides by? Sort of—but not always. Everybody thinks you have no choice when it comes to physical reality, but when you're into no choice, you're into the necessity point of view.

We're never taught to ask the questions:

- What's really possible here?
- What choices do I really have?
- What question could I ask and what would that question create?
- What kind of contribution can I be or receive here?

Contribution is a two-way street; it goes in both directions. You can be and receive simultaneously. If you have no form, no structure and no significance about how you create and generate money, for instance, instead of saying, "Oh, I get all my money by doing x, y or z," ask, "What possibilities are out here today?"

You've got to function from the question:

- Where else can I make money?
- Where else can money come from?
- What else is possible?

As long as you continuously do "What else?" you will have a continuing expansiveness about the way you create and generate money.

If you say, "I can only earn money by babysitting or going to work every day," you'll get a different result. You've bought into the significance that work equals money. This is very different from "How do I create and generate money beyond my wildest dreams?"

What would it be like if you didn't do "I have to do x number of hours in order to create this?" Instead what if you asked, "How quickly could I get this done and get a ton of money?"

You can create it your way if you're willing to have no form, no structure and no significance about whether you have money, wealth and abundance. You can create anything if you have the willingness to function as the question and see what else is possible.

Dain: You also have to be in no form, no structure and no significance about whether or not you create it your way.

Gary: There are lots of good ways to make money, so why not use them?

Dain: Hey, there you go. Why re-invent the wheel if you don't have to? Then you can add what you have to it.

Question: Can you please assist me here? I have been calling all the people who have attended my Bars class to invite them to the class Dain is going to give. One of the ladies I called said, "I'm not choosing Access Consciousness because you are not doing a higher state of consciousness. It is only about the money." I want to defend myself and Access Consciousness in this situation. I really don't know what to say...

Gary: You can say, "You're probably right. I'm glad that you are more aware and much further along than I am. You actually do not need Access Consciousness. You are correct."

Thank you. I made her comment very significant, and I got frustrated about it.

Dain: No form, no structure and no significance can come in at any point along the way, and it will change everything after that point.

If you didn't do form, structure and significance, you could be in a place where you could say just what Gary said. But because it became significant, you made the lady's judgment valuable and real. When you do that, it sits there like a rock that you can't do anything with. The only way to deal with a situation like that is to take it out of the significance you are trying to place it in. Find a way to undo that significance. Dissolve the rock that's there in front of you and then you get free.

If you don't make it significant whether this lady comes to Access Consciousness, whether she goes to my class or someone else's class, whether she gets conscious or anything else, then you'll be willing to say, "Okay, enough of making this lady significant, enough of making her point of view about Access Consciousness or anything else significant. Enough of making her judgments significant." Whenever you have form, structure and significance, you've got judgment.

Gary: No form, no structure and no significance means you don't have to get anybody to come to the class. It's "You don't want to come? Good idea, don't come. Bye, see you later! Thanks for your judgment, by the way."

Dain: "Thank you very much for your judgment, thanks for sharing, have a nice day, don't let the door hit you on the butt on the way out!"

Question: Is deciding that something has value the same thing as making it significant?

Gary: Yes. You create significance as a way of not having whatever you have decided is significant.

If you keep trying to look at the form of it or the structure of it and the significance of whether you have it or you don't have it, then you have to lose it. This applies to everything in life, including money.

Dain: All the things in consciousness, including you, have a space that they are. If you try to put a form and a structure on them, you're undoing the consciousness of them. You are trying to fit them into this reality—and the beauty of what they are goes away.

When you put form to something, when you try to put structure to something, you ensure that you will lose it. When you make anything significant, you will either lose it or judge it so you can't receive it.

Question: This brings tears to my eyes. I see that by valuing you and my experiences with you and the growth and expansion I've had, that I was touching something infinite and trying to make it finite. It's like putting a butterfly in a jar.

Dain: Yes.

Gary: It's like making Dain into a specimen that you put in a frame and look at every day.

Yes, I realize that putting form, structure and significance on something takes it out of the freedom of the newness it can be in any ten-second increment.

Gary: Yep.

Question: I would love to have a process that could destroy and uncreate the place where I feel that I am stuck. If I'm with somebody who has shared a point of view that is the opposite of mine, I go into paralysis because…

Gary: Whoa! "I go into paralysis because…" is the significance of why you go into paralysis. Instead ask the question, "What is it that generates and creates this paralysis?"

Maybe you go into paralysis because the person can't hear what you have to say. Maybe going into paralysis is one of the smartest things you ever did!

Hmm… so, how do I get out of the paralysis?

Gary: You don't want to get out of the paralysis. You want to recognize that the paralysis most likely occurs when somebody can't hear what you have to say—so just shut up and listen. That's no form, no structure and no significance.

You're creating structure and significance. "I'm paralyzed" is the structure. "I need to tell them my truth" is the significance. You don't need to tell them your truth.

The form in which it is coming is a sense of paralysis. Perhaps you're aware enough to know the other person is totally paralyzed with the rightness of their point of view, and talking to them is going to do no good. So why would you bother?

Let's say I'm in a business setting and the situation requires resolution or action.

Gary: Whenever you're in a business situation, you have to ask, "Okay, what's the deal here? What do you deliver and what do I deliver? And exactly what does that look like?"

Keep asking until you get an exact answer. When you do this, people cannot be convoluted about what they're saying. They have to be succinct about what they're stating. Keep going until you get the succinctness and the awareness of exactly what they're asking for and exactly what you have to deliver and exactly what they're going to deliver.

And what if they say one thing about what they're going to deliver and then they deliver the opposite?

Gary: If you ask, "Exactly what does that look like?" and get an exact answer, then they can't deliver the opposite.

You've got to ask, "Exactly what does that look like? Exactly what does that mean? Exactly what do you require of me? Exactly what are you going to deliver?"

When you do that, they have to get clear and succinct about what it's going to be.

Don't try to understand, validate or confront. None of those things work. You get paralyzed because confrontation doesn't work. You let them get away with crap and then they don't deliver what they said they were going to deliver.

The other thing is you're making form, structure and significance about the business deal. You create the form, structure and significance before you go into it. You say, "Oh, this is going to work" or "This will be good" or "I think this one is the right one."

Can I ask you about another piece of my situation? Someone I work with said she was going to rectify a situation, and then ten seconds later, she claimed she never said that. I didn't know how to handle this. I got stuck in trying to alter the situation then I realized I was trying to fix her insanity, which doesn't work—and I just went into silence, which also doesn't work.

Gary: Well, it does work.

Really? How?

Gary: Because going into silence can give you awareness. You've got awareness, but you're trying to get her to align and agree with your point of view and make up for the damage she has done from your point of view. You're trying to confront her and make her change. Is that really going to work?

No.

Gary: So, why would you do that? You've created a form, structure and significance in your world about how things are supposed to be rather than being in the question about how they are.

Here's an example. Think about your family, which is a form. There's you, the father, the mother, the sisters, the brothers, right?

Now think about the structure of your family and how really wonderful and amazing they were (or were not).

Now think about the significance of having your family or losing your family. Does that give you space and allowance or does it do something else? Actually, get the significance of never being able to get rid of them.

(Laughing) Okay.

Gary: Now how does that feel? Does that make you feel light and airy?

No, not when I landed on the awareness of how contracted that feels.

Gary: That's the idea. I wanted you to get the awareness of what it's like when something feels contractive.

Dain: And notice that you laughed. When Gary said, "Get the significance of never being able to get rid of them," it was "Ha-ha! I've been making that so frigging significant—that's funny!" So, you can change it now. Now you have a different choice. The thing with all these Ten Keys is that they're based on awareness. Once you become aware of something, the lie comes off of it. It can change right in front of you in the moment you become aware of it.

I see. Making something significant is going to be the very energy that will keep it away from me.

Gary: That is correct. Then you have to look at the form, structure and significance of whatever it is, and say, "This is not working. Let's try something else."

A lady called me from New Zealand the other day and said, "I want to come and do your class but I only have $4,000 left."

I asked, "What do you mean, you only have $4,000?"

She said, "Well, I've been out of work for a year, and I only have $4,000 left."

I asked, "Why don't you start looking at a different reality? What if, instead of saying, 'I *only* have $4,000 left,' you said, 'I *still* have $4,000'? Do you feel the difference in the energy of those two statements? 'I only have $4,000 left' means you're going to lose all of it. If you say, 'I still have $4,000,' you can ask, 'How can I hold onto that?' It's a completely different energy."

She said, "I go out for job interviews, and they offer me $15 an hour, but I don't perceive that it's nurturing to me and my body."

I said, "You're out of money. Get a frigging job. No work is going to feel honoring of you until you get in there and produce something and someone says, 'I'm so grateful for you,' or they get that you are a gift—or you get that you want to go do another job. You've got to stop trying to create form, structure and significance. Your structure is that it has to be a job you love, where they love you. Get over yourself. It's a job. You're getting money for doing a job. Deliver the job and shut up."

Dain: So, you think she might have been making that a little significant?

Gary: Yeah, just a tad! She said, "But if I do that, I can't come to your class."

Then don't come to the class. Keep your $4,000. Are you crazy? I should have said, "Do you realize you're crazy?" That would have been a more appropriate response.

Question: For the last couple of days, I've been asking for the energy of caring, and I've had way more caring for the Earth and for bodies. This morning I woke up and couldn't get that energy; I couldn't be it, and I couldn't find it. I said, "Where is this energy? I'm asking for it. Where is it?" and I got stressed about it.

I find this happens when I make something significant or when I'm asking for something and I just don't seem to be able to be it or... What I'm hearing you guys say is "It doesn't matter. Let it go." Then I say, "But that feels like I don't care."

Gary: You've created the form of caring as though you can care for the Earth or you can care for bodies. That's less than what caring is and more than you're willing to be.

You've made the structure of caring appear to come from a particular place or to be a certain way. And you've made your feelings a significance.

With the form, structure and significance of what you have defined as caring, you have created a limitation in what caring is. You have limited what caring is, in order to have the significance of what you feel, the structure of how you feel it or experience it, and the form in which it must come to you for you to know that you've got it.

Once you *achieve* caring, you cannot *feel* it. Once you *are* caring, it has no form, it has no structure, it has no significance; it just is. And it just is what you are.

Dain: Gary, would you suggest as a tool: What is the form of this? What's the structure? What am I making significant here?

Gary: That's a good beginning. I also have a process here:

> What fantasy, beingness and secret agenda for the creation of form, structure and significance have I made so real that even in the face of total awareness and consciousness I cannot and will not change, choose and cure it? Everything that is times a godzillion, will you destroy and uncreate it all? Right and wrong, good and bad, POD and POC, all 9, shorts, boys and beyonds.

Question: It was always reinforced on me through my childhood that I had to get an education, get a job and get experience in order to earn a good living. How can I destroy and uncreate the ladder and stairway to success?

Gary: You don't have to destroy it. You just have to look at it to see if it is significant. Your parents tried to give you the form, structure and significance of how they thought it was supposed to be. Most of them didn't follow that, and because they didn't do it, they thought it had to be right.

In my family, it was "You've got to get an education, you've got to get a job, you've got to earn a good living. Go to school"—but going to school meant nothing because that was not what my mother did.

For me, all of that was okay, but it just wasn't a life I wished to have. It was not the form, structure and significance I wanted to live with. As it turned out, I actually wanted to live with no form, no structure and no significance.

When you have no form, no structure and no significance about anything, you have total choice. It is not based on "The form is this, the structure is this, the significance is this, so that's what I've got to do." It's more like "Okay, what choice do I have here?" No form, no structure and no significance give you total choice.

Question: There's a saying, "Ignorance is bliss." I believe that if you don't know about something and you don't think about it, you can't make it significant. However, since Access Consciousness, I'm starting to become aware of everything, so how can I apply this key to my advantage?

You actually make something significant by making yourself ignorant of it. You can apply this key to your advantage by recognizing that total awareness gives you total choice. When there's no form, structure or significance about what you should know or shouldn't know, you get to know everything and then you can take advantage of everything and get anything you wish in life.

Question: My mom makes everything significant. Everything is a fact and all the stories she creates are real. It's an interesting point of view; but what is a nice, blistering wedgie I can put into her universe, just for fun?

Gary: She's a mother. What part of that don't you get? All mothers know all facts. Tell her she's right—and you're so grateful. Say, "I'm so grateful that I have you to guide me, Mother."

Dain: This is a brilliant wedgie. Tell your parents how grateful you are for them, for how much they have taught you and for the way they have guided you. Then everything you do is the result of what they have given you, so they can't make you wrong for it anymore.

Gary: Oops! If you express gratitude, they don't know what to do because they can't complain any more. And they can't make everything significant and factual and believe all their stories, because the purpose of the stories is to give you awareness. When you tell them you're grateful because they have given you awareness, they will stop trying to give you awareness.

Question: If there is no form, no structure and no significance, then what about the human tendency to want to form a connection with another living creature, human or animal? To want to feel the love and connection with another as pure and caring and giving?

Gary: Wow, talk about a frigging fantasy. I love you, but that is just total frigging fantasy.

Dain: The interesting part about that is, there's a form, structure and significance in the idea that we're already not oneness and not already totally connected.

I have lived my life outside the normal structure and always had relationships where I didn't feel like I belonged. I was the black sheep, the Hunchback of Notre Dame, and at times, it was okay with me. But at other times, I so wanted to belong, to have some significance, to yell from the bell tower and be seen.

Gary: Is that form, structure and significance? Totally. It's the significance that caring is real, when in actuality, most humans cannot care. Caring in a human reality means you get to kill the person. So, screaming from the tower to get people to see that you're there, that you care, that you can be cared for and that you would give that kind of caring to somebody is a sure-fire way of getting yourself killed. I would not do that if I were you. That's the no form, no structure and no significance of how it is supposed to be.

I am one of those Latin women who got entrenched in the emotional telenovela [Spanish for soap opera] and rebelled against all of that, yet I hung onto the emotional drama of deeply felt love.

Gary: The whole idea of love is form, structure and significance. You've got to go to gratitude instead of love. Ask, "What am I grateful for with this person?"

Love allows judgment. People say, "I have total loving allowance for this person," until that person pisses them off, then the moment they're pissed off, their love suddenly becomes conditional. I've watched this repeatedly in every church, cult and religion I've gone to. You can have love and judgment in the same universe—but you can't have gratitude and judgment at the same time.

Dain: Love is one of the huge forms, structures and significances. It is designed to take you out of the space that gratitude is. Love makes sure that you always have to rail against or fight for something or someone.

Gary: In gratitude there is no form, no structure and no significance.

Question: Sometimes I've wondered how you and Dain live in your connection or in oneness without making it significant. I've heard you say you adore each other, which I think is truly lovely. Clearly you're not making it significant. I'd like to understand more about how you do that. Could you expand on this?

Gary: I can say I adore Dain, but I would not give up me for him. Most people have the point of view that adoration means you worship the other person. Adoration is a form of worship and you worship the other person and you make him or her more significant than you.

Now Dain, you've had people adore you. Do you like to be worshiped that way?

Dain: No, I don't.

Gary: Why?

Dain: Because, as you've pointed out, when someone worships you, you have to serve him or her. It's not fun. There's so much form, structure and significance attached to it, that it is not a place of ease.

The other part of adoration is that the other person doesn't actually receive any part of me. They only receive the fantasy of what they're projecting that I'm going to be or do. They won't receive the change or the gift of possibility that I would like to facilitate for them.

I see that all of that is a real limitation. It seems like we forget that we're infinite beings. If I adore someone, I would have to go to a lesser definition of who I think I am in relation to that person. That would limit both of us.

Gary: Yes, when you adore someone in terms of this reality's definition, you make yourself less than they are. You have judged them as better than you, and at some time or another, you will automatically have to separate yourself from them and go away, either physically or energetically. You will have to believe that somehow you and/or the other person wanted that. You will get to the point where you resist and react to the idea that you're making somebody else greater than you. You have to resist and react to this in order to have you.

It's similar to what teenagers do. As children, they made mom and dad the end-all and be-all of everything, and then all of a sudden, they said, "Screw this! I don't want to be like these people. I want to have me."

What if you didn't have to go down that path at all? What if you didn't have to have the form, the structure and the significance of the adoration or worship of someone, and you could simply ask, "Okay, what do they have that I actually like? What do they have that I wouldn't want to have? What would it take to have more of what I would actually like to have? End of story, let's go. Let's move on."

That's choice and communion you're talking about. You just helped me understand my entire childhood. My mom absolutely adored me, but it was such a burden. There was such a heaviness to that energy. She was like a fire hydrant of love that flowed in my direction, but it always missed me by about five feet because it was never real. It never really addressed me, so I always felt unloved or love-starved, while everything she was saying and doing seemed to say I was the best thing on the planet. It was all just a reflection on her, because I was her creation. She never got that she created a separate person who had freedom of her own choice.

Gary: She never realized what a monster she created.

Yeah, that was a whole mess. And then my sister, who put me on a pedestal, completely rejected me when I didn't meet her expectations anymore.

Gary: They adored a fantasy, not you. In the 1950s and 1960s, a book by Khalil Gibran called *The Prophet* was very popular. He says that if you let go of that which you love, it will return. But if you hold on to that which you love, it must die. It's like holding onto a bird. You love it so much that you love it to death. The no form, no structure and no significance of loving somebody is a place where you let it go. You let it fly, and if it wishes to be with you, it will return.

When I read that book forty years ago, I said, "Wow, that actually makes sense!" Since that time, I have functioned from the idea that if it loves you, it will return. Letting something be free because you love it is the only way for it to be who it is.

Dain: I'd like to say something about love, gratitude and significance. A long time ago, I was going out with a girl. I really liked her. I was "I love her, I love her and I love her." She started telling lies about me to everybody I knew. She badmouthed me in every way possible.

I asked Gary, "How is this happening? I love this person."

Gary asked, "Well, how's this love thing working for you in this situation?"

I said, "I'm killing myself over it!"

He said, "Let me ask you a question. Can you still have gratitude for what she's doing?"

I said, "Yes, because I'm getting a lot of awareness from it. I'm realizing that it's not significant. It doesn't have to mean anything. People who buy the lies are just people who buy lies. They were looking for a reason to go into judgment anyway."

Gary asked, "And can you still have gratitude for her and everything you received from her and all the fun you had when you were having fun, before she started hating you?"

I realized I could have total gratitude for her. I saw that trying to maintain that place called love was killing me. There's such form, structure and significance about what that looks like to all of us. Each of us are handed our forms, structures and significances as we grow up—and each person's look different from everybody else's.

Question: You said love is about huge form, structure and significance—and gratitude takes you out of it. Why is gratitude so freeing and so joyful? How does that come about?

Gary: Love has been the form, structure and significance for all songs, all drama, all trauma, all upset, all intrigue, all bad television shows, all good television shows, all movies and just about everything else.

But why is gratitude so freeing and so wonderful?

Dain: Because gratitude acknowledges and puts you in connection with others. It allows you to become one of the aspects and the spaces of being that's available.

Love, from my weird point of view, is like taking everything that gratitude, caring, kindness and possibility could be and twisting them so you always have to attach form, structure and significance to them. You would always be out of the caring, out of the gratitude, out of the kindness and out of the possibility. You'd always be trying to head for those things, but you'd never be able to actually, right now, be those things.

Question: Do you have any other clearing processes we can do around no form, no structure, no significance? My head feels like a football.

Gary: Run the one I gave you:

What fantasy, beingness and secret agenda for the creation of form, structure and significance have I made so real that even in the face of total awareness and consciousness I cannot, and will not change, choose and cure it? Everything that is times a godzillion, will you destroy and uncreate it all? Right and wrong, good and bad, POD and POC, all 9, shorts, boys and beyonds.

You might want to run this process a lot. It will start to disintegrate all the things you've made as form, structure and significance and start to give you a new possibility.

All right, folks, it's time for us to end our conversation about no form, no structure and no significance. We'll talk to you next week!

~~~

No Judgment, No Discrimination, No Discernment

Gary: Hello, everyone. Tonight we're going to talk about the sixth key: No judgment, no discrimination, no discernment. Dain's on the phone with us, but he's having trouble with his voice, so he'll be listening in and not saying much.

I'd like to read an email that came in. I think it would be helpful for everybody if we talked about it upfront:

Many of us have been taught that discernment is very important. I couldn't get the idea of no discernment until I realized that discernment is judgment and discrimination, and that knowingness replaces discernment. It is through know-ingness as the infinite being that we be, know, perceive and receive that we may be without judgment, discrimination and discernment. Do you agree with this? And if so, would you please elaborate on it?

Gary: This is exactly correct. As long as you're doing no judgment, no discrimination, no discernment, you can be an infinite being of perceiving, knowing, being and receiving.

When you do judgment, discrimination or discernment of any kind, you eliminate your capacity to be, know, perceive and receive.

Judgment is "I don't eat pork on Wednesdays." You're saying, "Any other time pork would be good, but I can't eat it on Wednesdays." That's your judgment. It's a conclusion you've come to.

Discrimination is the way we try to create something as not quite right.

Discernment is the idea that you must choose something. Discernment is "I don't like this; this is terrible. It's bad and it tastes awful." It is a milder form of judgment. For example, people talk about discerning taste. That's a judgment. Discerning taste means, "I judge that this is so." Discernment is a conclusion you come to. Choice and awareness are a possibility you become aware of.

Choice is "I'm not going to eat this."

Awareness is "I don't want to eat cauliflower. I don't care for it."

Preference is "I prefer delicious food over ordinary food, but I don't discriminate against the ordinary stuff because occasionally I eat it or drink it, depending on the circumstances—because I always have choice.

What all this is really about, though, is the way you see things. Are you in choice and awareness? Or are you doing some form of judgment?

Question: The word intensity came up for me one morning as I woke up. It seems that the denser I become, the more human I am, the more earthbound I feel, the more emotions I pick up from humans around me and the more judgmental I become.

The less dense I am, by which I mean the more expanded I am, the more judgment drops away. When I thought about this, I felt a sense of freedom all around me. Is this where we find no judgment, no discrimination and no discernment?

Gary: It's not where you *find* no judgment; it's how you become it. When you are space, it is very difficult to do the form, structure and significance that's required to create judgment, discrimination, and discernment.

Question: Would you please say more about last week's comment: Once you become something, say peace or love or caring, you don't feel it, you are it. Does that equate to being in a very still space? For example, when you are witnessing the drama of an event and experiencing compassion, are you a detached observer that remains a still point?

Gary: This question is perfect because the last person just said that if you become density, you feel it. Density is always a feeling, and feeling is always a density. When you become space, all of that drops away. So when you become space, all the density that is required to create the "feeling" of something ceases. It is eliminated and goes away.

The second part of the question asks about being a still point. Could an infinite being truly be still? No, infinite beings can only be totally expanded, so expanded that there is only infinite choice available to them. In those cases where there's infinite choice, they cannot come to conclusion, they cannot come to judgment and they cannot go into discrimination, discernment or judgment in any way, shape or form. That's why talking about it as a still point is incorrect. *Still point* is a concept that was designed to make us as little as possible and bring us as close to nothing as it is possible to do.

So everywhere any of you bought *still* point as a way to get to awareness, will you destroy and uncreate all that please? Right and wrong, good and bad, POD and POC, all 9, shorts, boys and beyonds.

Question: Is judgment an attachment? Is it the associations we have with things from the past that we recall? Is it the energy, be it good or bad, that we attach to things like food, music and places?

Gary: Judgment is something you attach to other judgments. It's not something you have as an awareness. If you danced with somebody and you had a good time and then later you heard that old song again and the memory of dancing came back, that is not judgment, discernment or discrimination. That is awareness. It's the recall that gives you access to everything that is possible in the world. Unfortunately, we recall memories rather than awareness. So, what awareness did you have during that song that you didn't acknowledge that got you to recall it, remember it and have it available to you? You've got to start looking to that.

Question: Why is it easier to give up judgment of others and so much harder to give up judgment of self? How amazing would I be without the judgment that ekes out, sticking me in place?

Gary: That's the reason you have to apply this key.

One of the things you need to look at when you are doing judgment of yourself is: Is this mine? Let's say you have blond hair and blue eyes, and you are standing next to somebody who also has blond hair and blue eyes. All of a sudden you start thinking, "My hair looks terrible today!"

What's happening? The person next to you is thinking that her hair looks terrible today. You always assume the thoughts, feelings and emotions you experience are yours. You assume that every judgment must be yours. You've got to ask the question, "Is this mine?" It's the only way you're going to get through and over this.

Question: It seems to me that we mostly judge ourselves, which limits us. I made a demand last year to change this, whatever it took. Funny, what happens when you make a demand—you start to become aware of all the places that you're choosing the very thing that you're working on changing.

So, then you get to put the tools into action. You get to ask questions like "What would I like to have different here?" You POD and POC things and you make different choices, which allows for something else to show up. How does it get easier than that?

Gary: With no discrimination, no judgment and no discernment, you're moving toward choice and away from conclusion. Judgment, discrimination and discernment are sources for creating conclusions so you can get something right. But if you never had to be right and you never had to be wrong, what choice would you actually have?

The less I judge myself, the easier and more expansive my life gets. One area where I still have difficulty is going into the wrongness of me, even though I don't stay there as long as I used to.

Gary: As you begin to apply these tools and use them, changes occur a little bit at a time. This is all you can ask for. You have been shown your whole life that you're wrong. You've been taught to judge you and you've been told you need to be discerning and discriminating. What if none of those things were true? What if all of that was a lie? I've got a process I think will help this, which I'll give to you in a few minutes.

My life is expanding and my business is growing. I have more peace and joy, and my kids are happy, but it's still like it's not big enough and I'm not reaching enough to make a change. What is that? And what would it take to change it?

Gary: You've got to realize that all it takes to change the world is to change one person. Every person you touch with the change you create for them creates them creating change for two others, which creates change for two others, which creates change for two others—and will it ever be enough? No. Why? Because the world is not the place you know it could be. You came here because you wanted to change the world. So what would it take? Keep practicing; keep doing it. And stop looking for what you're still doing. That's the problem with being a still point. We say, "I'm still (whatever it may be)," which means you are going back to that finite point in which you don't exist and in which you are not the infinite being you are.

Question: What's the difference between observation and judgment? I find it difficult to apply no judgment, no discrimination and no discernment, especially with family and close friends.

Gary: If I do it, it's observation. If you do it, it's judgment. (That's a joke.)

Let's say that your mother tells you your dress is ugly. "That's such an ugly dress; I wish you wouldn't wear that." Is that discrimination, discernment, or judgment?

Then you say, "My mother is such a bitch." Is that discrimination, discernment, or judgment?

Most people have the point of view that if it's a positive comment, it's not a judgment, and if it's a negative remark, it is a judgment. They think that when your mother tells you that your dress is ugly, and you say, "My mom's a bitch," that it's judgment.

It could be an observation, even though it's negative. Maybe the dress is ugly. Maybe your mother is being a bitch at that particular moment. The difference between a judgment and an observation is primarily the way the energy feels. When you say something that is a judgment, it increases the density. When you say something that is an awareness, it decreases the density.

Your family and friends believe that their purpose in life is to judge you. You, of course, would not pick up those judgments at all, would you? Oh yes, you would! You do it nonstop. So, again, you have to ask, "Is this mine? Is this my point of view?"

Question: Could you please say a bit more about caring?

Gary: Caring is when you do not have any judgment. As long as you're doing judgment of anything, you're not caring. You cannot care *and* judge. You can only judge and not care—or care and not judge. Those are the only choices you have.

When you try to put caring into a form, structure or significance, you limit it. So it's caring *for* rather than just being caring. Does the Earth have a form that it cares for or does it just care all the time? The Earth gifts to us all the time. It gifts its caring to the birds and the bees, and the flowers and the trees. It gives us everything without any point of view. It doesn't have the idea that caring is to care for people (which is a form). It cares for everything. It doesn't have the point of view that it needs to care for an individual (which is a significance). It cares for everyone and everything equally. It cares for death as much as it cares for life. If we can get to the place where we can care that way, we have lost the form, structure and significance of caring. We have become the allowance and the caring that the Earth is.

Is that what stands between us and infinite space? Is that what prevents us from being the infinite beings we are? It's judgment and discrimination, isn't it?

Gary: Yep, it is. But there are also the rest of the keys, as well. I'll show you how those work as we go through them. I'm sorry I can't do all of them at once. It takes a little while for some of this to settle in. And then you sometimes come up with questions that indicate what didn't get handled and what additional explanations and processes are necessary.

> What creation and generation of judgment, discrimination and discernment as the absolute necessity for the creation of life are you using to lock into existence the positional HEPADs* you are instituting as the source for the wrongness of you, the rightness of your point of view and the necessity of never losing? Everything that is times a godzillion, will you destroy and uncreate it all? Right and wrong, good and bad, POD and POC, all 9, shorts, boys and beyonds.

The good news is you may all give up judgment. (Joking) Nah, not in a million years. You couldn't give up judgment if your life depended on it.

---

* See glossary for definition.

Watch me!

Question: Recently within two days of having someone work on me, I gained five pounds. This person worked on me again two weeks later, and I gained 10 more pounds. At first I thought something was going on with me, but this person has in the past made comments about my being too thin. Could this be an example of someone putting their point of view into the session? And if this is the case, how is it reversed?

Gary: It's her judgment that you are thin—and you are trying to judge, discriminate and discern whether she is right or wrong. Are you too thin? You've got to go to the question. You've got to ask, "Body, what do you want to look like?"

This is an example of judgment being impelled at you. If you impel judgments at your body, you will increase the amount of thinness or fatness you have, based on your judgment, because judgment creates density. What does the body feel? Density. When the body feels density, it becomes more of that density because it assumes you desire it. If you are willing to be in total awareness and total caring without discrimination, judgment or discernment, you can create a different possibility both for you and your body.

Question: I seem to be making choices, yet there's a density to the choices I make. When I ask, "Will this be rewarding?" or "Would this add to my life?" I get a yes, but there seems to be something not quite right. Is there an interweaving of discrimination with choice—like do we choose and then go back to discriminating?

Gary: Yes, because that's what you've been taught to do. People ask you, "How could you make that choice?" When I was a kid and I would make a choice that my parents didn't agree with, they would ask, "How did you come to that conclusion?" or "Why did you make that choice? That was not a good choice." When that happens, you begin to doubt all the choices you make. This process may help you.

What have you defined as discrimination, judgment and discernment that actually *isn't?* Everything that is times a godzillion, will you destroy and uncreate it all? Right and wrong, good and bad, POD and POC, all 9, shorts, boys and beyonds.

Question: It's as if my very being is judgment, discernment and discrimination. That's what I grew up with. Everything I was, was judgment, discernment and discrimination.

Gary: That's everything that was validated as you that wasn't actually you. It's what your family validated.

Dain: One of the things I've become aware of is that people do conclusion dynamically all the time and they don't even recognize it. Is that based on this judgment, discrimination and discernment point of view as though it's us?

Gary: We function as though judgment is actually the way we define us. You define you by your judgment, your discernment and your discrimination. People say all the time, "I have discriminating taste. I like champagne even though I have a beer budget." That's not discriminating taste; that's judgment defined as "This other thing would be better than what I'm choosing." It's a judgment of you. This is how this stuff interweaves and keeps us from a place in which we actually have true choice.

We've been taught that you only have one choice—or there's only one good choice. Or you only have two choices and you need to choose between this and this. Infinite choice is the ability to choose it all. The question you should be asking is "Okay, I'm going to choose all of this, and how will I do that?"

When you have a choice and you see five different possibilities, you can choose to have all five possibilities. You just have to determine—not judge—which one you would like to choose first.

That's the way we should work in everything we do in life. All you have to do is put order into which way you bring things into your life. You just have to keep practicing this.

Question: I remember getting lost because I thought I had to make one choice.

Gary: You become lost when you discriminate. You say, "I have to choose this," which requires you to cut off your awareness, which will then create a sense of loss. When you cut off any awareness, you lose the capacity to continue to move or go someplace.

> What have you decided is not judgment, discrimination or discernment that actually is? Besides everything your parents say. Everything that is times a godzillion, will you destroy and uncreate it all? Right and wrong, good and bad, POD and POC, all 9, shorts, boys and beyonds.

Judgments have always come at me from the point of view, "I'm just doing this because I love you and I want to help you."

Gary: No, people do judgment because they want to do judgment, not because they're trying to help anybody. Judgment is just judgment. Dain and I were recently in Boerne, Texas. We were eating breakfast in our low-class hotel. A woman who was very short and very heavy was there with her daughter, who was also very short and very heavy. They were with a skinny little girl who was the woman's niece. The woman said to the girl, "You need to eat more because you're way too skinny. Don't you want to grow up and be as beautiful as we are?" The girl got really big eyes and didn't say a word.

I'm sure in her universe, she was saying, "No, I don't want to be like you. Please, don't make me do that!"

The woman's comment was discrimination, judgment and discernment. The girl was having an awareness: "No, I don't want to be like that."

You've been told that something is judgment when it *isn't,* and you've been told something *isn't* judgment when it is and you have created an incredible confusion in your world as to whether you're being judgmental or not. You assume that if you say something negative, you are definitely judgmental—and if you say something positive, you are definitely not judgmental. But it ain't necessarily so.

What have you decided *is not* judgment, discrimination or discernment that actually *is?* Everything that is times a godzillion, will you destroy and uncreate it all? Right and wrong, good and bad, POD and POC, all 9, shorts, boys and beyonds.

What have you decided *is* judgment, discrimination or discernment that actually *isn't?* Everything that is times a godzillion, will you destroy and uncreate it all? Right and wrong, good and bad, POD and POC, all 9, shorts, boys and beyonds.

If you are having any form of judgment that keeps coming up for you, put these two processes on a loop and run them all night and all day for about ten to fifteen days. See what changes with that.

What have you defined *is not* judgmental, not discriminating and not discerning that actually *is?* Everything that is times a godzillion, will you destroy and uncreate it all? Right and wrong, good and bad, POD and POC, all 9, shorts, boys and beyonds.

What have you decided *is* judgment, discrimination or discernment that actually *isn't?* Everything that is times a godzillion, will you destroy and uncreate it all? Right and wrong, good and bad, POD and POC, all 9, shorts, boys and beyonds.

Dain: Can you talk more about being aware of something that is negative and how that is not necessarily being in judgment—and how a positive judgment about something is not necessarily being in awareness?

Gary: At one time a friend of mine decided his fiancée was the most beautiful woman in the world. That's a judgment that sounds positive, right? The judgment, "She's the most beautiful woman in the world" kept him feeling like a piece of crap all the time because whenever she did something that was mean or unkind, he could not see it—because of the judgment and conclusion he had come to—that she was the most beautiful woman in the world.

We have the discernment, discrimination and judgment that if it's beautiful, it's right, and if it's not beautiful, it's wrong. Both of these are judgments.

> What have you defined *is not* judgmental, not discriminating and not discerning that actually *is*? Everything that is times a godzillion, will you destroy and uncreate it all? Right and wrong, good and bad, POD and POC, all 9, shorts, boys and beyonds.

> What have you defined as judgment, discrimination and discernment that actually *isn't*? Everything that is times a godzillion, will you destroy and uncreate it all? Right and wrong, good and bad, POD and POC, all 9, shorts, boys and beyonds.

Question: I've realized that I have misapplied and misunderstood making a choice as drawing a conclusion. When you were talking about buying candy, if I said, "Okay, I'm going to have a Snickers," I would create a closed energy about that because that's my conclusion: I want a Snickers now. The other piece of this is I judge myself unendingly about every choice I make.

Gary: We've been taught that we have to choose as though there is only one choice. This gives us the idea that choice is a finite reality instead of an infinite reality. We have the idea that we have to choose as though the conclusion is choice. Conclusion is never choice—and choice never requires conclusion. Choice only opens the door to other possibilities and other choices.

It goes back to ten-second increments of choice. For these ten seconds, you'd like a Snickers. Then it's "Okay, I had one bite of that. I don't want any more." Then you can go on to another. "Now I'd like a Three Musketeers."

It's removing the stigma from changing my mind. I was indoctrinated in my childhood that changing my mind was some sort of horrific crime.

Gary: Once when my youngest daughter was two years old, I said, "Grace, make up your mind."

She said, "Daddy, it's a girl's prerogative to change her mind."

When she graduated from high school, she bought four prom dresses. The last one is the one she wore, but for ten seconds, each one of those dresses was beautiful and the one she wanted to wear.

And you can do that with ease? You can do that without creating confusion or drama?

Gary: Well, it only creates confusion and drama for others.

Yes, that's what I was asking. For the people around you, it's "Oh, my God!"

Gary: So, what are they doing when they go into the drama and the confusion? They're doing discrimination, discernment and judgment.

Right.

Gary: They could have the observation, "She's just nuts in this area," and that would not be a judgment. That would be an observation. They're saying, "The prerogative of changing your mind, by my discernment, discrimination and judgment, is nuts."

Then it's about not getting involved in a mental ping-pong game with other people?

Gary: That doesn't do any good. If someone says anything to Grace about her choices, she says, "Well, I'm a girl. I get to change my mind. I like being a girl."

Thank you.

Question: I talked with someone the other day who was confusing judgment and awareness. Every time she had an awareness, she made it a judgment. I would appreciate it if you would address the difference.

This is a person who has made an effort to work with Access Consciousness and use the tools, yet it seemed that she was using every single key against herself. For example, if she was not happy with where she was living—instead of that being an awareness—she said, "Well, is an infinite being able to live anywhere?"

Can you also talk about the difference between using the keys for expansion and using them against ourselves?

Gary: Most people use the keys against others—not against themselves. It sounds like the person you're talking about is using "Would an infinite being truly choose this?" as a sword, not as a question.

"An infinite being should be able to live anywhere" is a conclusion. The conclusion that you should be able to live anywhere or everywhere is not a choice at all.

What's a different approach? You ask, "What would I really like to choose?" And you keep it out of the density category. You have to recognize whether it feels light or heavy when you say something.

Right.

Gary: Yes, you can use these tools as weapons against yourself or against others—or you can use them as they are meant to be applied, which is to give you total choice and total freedom. That's what you're looking for.

What was your first question again?

I asked about the difference between judgment and awareness. How do you know when it's an awareness? I couldn't seem to explain this in a way that really worked.

Gary: Awareness is something that creates a lightness in your world—and judgment is what you try to do to solidify something into existence.

For example, I can have the awareness that I like horses and I would like to create the Costarricense breed. If I did this as a conclusion or a judgment, it would be "I've got to do this."

Right now I'm in a quandary as to what to do because things are not working out the way I would like them to. I have an awareness of all the things that need to change for this to actually work, and I'm also willing to look at everything and ask, "Okay, do I continue or do I stop? What do I do here?"

A question always leaves you with a sense of choice. So, I can come to one conclusion for ten seconds and I can come to another conclusion for another ten seconds—or I can be aware and say, "I've got this choice, this choice, this choice and this choice available."

If you feel confused about a choice, it's because you don't have sufficient data to make the "decision." In this case, for me, it is a decision that will affect me and a lot of other people, so I need to look at it from a different place.

How do I need to look at it differently? I need to question it, I need to be in the question and live as the question and not come to discernment, discrimination or judgment.

You could run this as a process:

> What awareness have you defined as conclusion that actually isn't and what conclusion have you defined as awareness that actually isn't? Everything that is times a godzillion, will you destroy and uncreate it all? Right and wrong, good and bad, POD and POC, all 9, shorts, boys and beyonds.

That's a great process, Gary. You can run that with anything.

Gary: Yep, anything.

You could run: What have you defined as an infinite being that actually isn't and what have you defined as not an infinite being that actually is?

Gary: Exactly.

Thank you.

Gary: This came up when I was dealing with somebody who was having a wealth issue. I asked her, "What have you defined as wealth?"

She said, "Paying my bills."

I asked, "Wow, that's wealth?"

She said, "That's insane, isn't it?"

I said, "Yes, because if you really want to be wealthy, you have to get more bills."

Question: I was trying to find signs that tell me when I have moved into judgment, and a couple of things stood out for me. It's when I say what I feel or think and I hear the words coming out of my head or my mouth.

Gary: Yep, those are two of the major ones.

So I started substituting, "I perceive this information coming to me" and from there, I began to use The Ten Keys and ask questions like, "Would an infinite being act on this?" or "Is this anything I need?" Is that a good technique or am I just leading myself down a path?

Gary: That's a good technique. That's the beginning. When we get to some of our other calls, I will give you some other tools you can use to make this easier.

So, "I feel" and "I think" are signs you've gone into judgment. Are there any other words you would indicate you've gone into judgment?

Gary: Every time I hear somebody say, "I feel that ____," I notice the energy they're delivering. When somebody delivers anything with force, that's judgment, discrimination and discernment.

Some people have the idea that being objective is the way out of being judgmental. They think they're being objective when they stand outside of something, look at it and come to a conclusion or decision or judgment. They think that being objective proves the choice they make is correct.

It's not about objectivity. You don't want to be objective. You don't want to stand outside of something and look at it. You want to look at things with awareness. You want to *observe*, not be *objective*.

To be objective requires you to become something else, stand outside of it and come to a conclusion.

When you are observing, it's just an interesting point of view. It's "Wow, that's an interesting choice" or "Wow, I'm glad I didn't choose that" or whatever point of view you came up with.

So, when you're going to make a decision, you use your body to see if you get lighter with your decision?

Gary: You're not necessarily going to use your body. When you ask, "Which choice feels lighter?" you're trying to use judgment to come to conclusion. A better question is "Which one of these would I really like to choose?"

Two things occur when you use that question. You start to move out of the *me* and into the *we,* because what you'd really like to choose is something that expands you and everybody around you. You don't know how to be selfish even though you have been accused of it, even though you've tried to make yourself selfish, even though you've tried to make yourself number one in the scheme of things.

When you are being a different space, then everything you do that you have always done works out differently. It's kind of cool. You benefit, other people benefit and the world benefits. That's called win-win-win.

> What have you defined as *not* judgment, *not* discrimination and *not* discernment that actually *is?* Everything that is times a godzillion, will you destroy and uncreate it all? Right and wrong, good and bad, POD and POC, all 9, shorts, boys and beyonds.

> What have you defined as judgment, discrimination and discernment that actually *isn't?* Everything that is times a godzillion, will you destroy and uncreate it all? Right and wrong, good and bad, POD and POC, all 9, shorts, boys and beyonds.

> What have you defined as *not* judgment, *not* discrimination and *not* discernment that actually is? Everything that is times a godzillion, will you destroy and uncreate it all? Right and wrong, good and bad, POD and POC, all 9, shorts, boys and beyonds.

As we did that, it was getting heavier and heavier.

> Do any of you believe that the purpose of life is to have judgment, discrimination and discernment in order to get it right? Everything that is times a godzillion, will you destroy and uncreate it all? Right and wrong, good and bad, POD and POC, all 9, shorts, boys and beyonds.

Question: I've been realizing that every identity and non-identity I have is based on some kind of judgment, discrimination or discernment. That's what I've been using to have an identity.

Gary: It's not really your identity; it's your individuation. It's the way you make yourself an individual. *Identity* is being, *individuation* is how you keep yourself separate from others and how you keep yourself separate from you, by judging you.

Thank you. That's great.

Gary: Every form of individuation requires a judgment, which may be why this came up.

> What have you defined as *not* judgment, *not* discrimination and *not* discernment that actually *is?* Everything that is times a godzillion, will

you destroy and uncreate it all? Right and wrong, good and bad, POD and POC, all 9, shorts, boys and beyonds.

What have you defined as judgment, discrimination and discernment that actually *isn't?* Everything that is times a godzillion, will you destroy and uncreate it all? Right and wrong, good and bad, POD and POC, all 9, shorts, boys and beyonds.

Question: Is individuation the way I keep myself separate from others—by judging myself and them?

Gary: Yes. We use judgment as a way to separate ourselves from others, but we also do it as a way to separate ourselves from the infinite potency and power we are. When you finally begin to realize "Wait a minute! I've got enough potency to knock over a bull at a dead run," then you have to ask, "How the hell am I so pathetic in the rest of my life?"

You have the potency to call the rain, but you say, "I can't do anything. I'm pathetic." No, you're not. You just aren't using the tools and you're not using your potency. You've got to get to a place where you're willing to have all that. These Ten Keys are the basis for everything that will give you that freedom. It won't be instantaneous, but it will occur. It's going to take you six months to a year of using them all the time, and then all of a sudden, you'll find yourself in a totally different universe in which everything you ask for comes to fruition. But you've got to use the tools. You have to apply them. Reading them over in the Foundation and Level One manuals does not equal application.

Question: I just had an awareness of something I was taught about not being a loser. I was always told I had to have good judgment.

Gary: Yes, with not being a loser, you're going into the seventh key about no competition. Competition is always about who wins and who loses. You compete with others to see which one of you is better than the other one.

We make a discrimination, a discernment or a judgment then we go to conclusion on it in order to make it right or wrong. We move directly from choice to judgment, discernment and discrimination and from there, we automatically go into competition. Competition is going to turn out to be a much bigger thing than you think it is.

And is that all an entrainment?

Gary: Yes, it's everything we're entrained into in this reality. My mother used to say, "You can choose either this or this."

I would ask, "Why can't I have them both?"

She would say, "You can only have one or the other, you cannot have both."

I would say, "But I want both."

She would say, "You're being a brat. Now, cut that out. You have a choice of this or this—or you're getting nothing."

I'd say, "Okay fine, I'll take that one." But it was only when I was forced into choosing and forced into judging which thing I wanted that I got into trying to choose according to the judgment my mother had. Her point of view was "You're a brat if you try to choose anything other than the two options you've been given."

This is pretty much what we're given as we grow up, and then of course, we have the multiple-choice test of life. You're given four things to choose from on your multiple-choice test. You have to discern and discriminate which two are definitely wrong so that you can guess which one of the other two is right.

And you're on a time limit.

Gary: Yeah, and you have a time limit, so you're in a rush to come to a conclusion. You try to decide and determine which are the two worst answers so you can choose from the two best answers. This is how we're entrained and taught from the time we are young.

Were you entrained and taught that way? Everything that was taught that way that actually didn't work for you, everything you tried to make you be, do, have, create and generate and everywhere you bent, stapled, folded, mutilated and stuffed yourself into that box of somebody else's reality, will you destroy and uncreate it all? Right and wrong, good and bad, POD and POC, all 9, shorts, boys and beyonds.

Question: I wonder, with consciousness that includes everything and judges nothing—including judgment—how does that work?

Gary: You have to be willing to see when somebody's doing judgment, otherwise you become the effect of their judgment.

If you can see "Oh, that's a judgment," then there's no judgment of the judgment. It's just awareness of the judgment. You can choose whatever you want. Most people use their judgments to try and convince you that they're right and you're wrong.

I recently met a man who kept telling me he was very open-minded. From my interesting point of view, being with him was like being with somebody who was in a tiny little box. He wasn't open at all. I thought, "Well, it's relative. His point of view is that he's open-minded, but from what I'm aware of, it looks like he's very constrained."

I just realized I was judging him. I wonder how I could have been different with him.

Gary: This is not about judgment; this is about seeing what you see. He said he was open-minded. Okay, good. Is that true? Is that real? Or is that his judgment of what he's supposed to be?

The last one.

Gary: Yeah, you have to get that this is the way people function. "If I'm going to impress this person, then I have to appear to be open minded, so therefore I will tell her I am open minded, even though I'm totally closed minded."

Correct.

Gary: You have to look at what is—and the way you get there is by not doing discrimination, discernment or judgment. You get there by using awareness. When he said he was open-minded, it didn't make you feel light, did it?

Correct, it was heavy.

Gary: So, it was a lie. So you've just got to say to yourself, "That's not true." "That's not true" is not a judgment; it's an awareness.

So, how could I have been more expanded in that situation? How could I have been more infinite so I could have been more joyful for myself, whether or not I had an impact on him?

Gary: You've got to start listening to your head. When you started talking to me about this, you said, "He did this and this and this, and I did this and this and this." You wound yourself up in your head to try and figure out things. Figuring out is another form of discriminating, discerning and judging that you've been taught.

Yes. That's a beautiful lead-in to part two of my question. When you talked about getting it right, the energy that came up for me was "This is so stressful. It's living with the sword of Damocles over my head, because if I don't get it right then that sword will drop. I'm going to get it wrong and then..."

Gary: Hold, hold, hold! You just did it again.

(Laughing) How do I get off this treadmill?

Gary: That's the problem, you are on a treadmill. It's a treadmill of trying to figure it out. You're trying to figure out why it is and what it is and how to get out of it based on what it is that it isn't that you already decided it must be because you're already doing it.

This is the way huge numbers of us have developed our "minds." We try to figure out, "What the hell am I really supposed to be choosing?" rather than asking, "What would I really like to choose?" Rather than being in question, you're trying to figure it out.

So all the places where figuring it out is the judgment, the discrimination and the discernment you're trying to use to get it right, will you destroy and uncreate it all? Right and wrong, good and bad, POD and POC, all 9, shorts, boys and beyonds.

Yes.

Gary: Luckily, you're the only one who does that.

(Laughing) Thank you, that was a very joyful process.

Question: A colleague of mine has been judging me for the last month. I could feel it, and I didn't know how to react to it. I tried to ignore it, but it built up so much that she almost got me sacked today. I don't know how to handle it when someone is judging me. I'm getting so sensitive that I can feel it now.

Gary: Okay, you're doing it now, too. You're going on and on in your head in an attempt to figure it out. It isn't working. Did you ask the question, "Is this person an ELF or a rattlesnake?"

Dain: These are people who actually enjoy injecting as much misery as possible into the lives of others. They're rattlesnakes. The term rattlesnake speaks for itself. A rattlesnake is actually proud of its rattle and potentially lethal ferocity. It's not necessary to judge the rattlesnake—but you want to identify it for what it is. If you see a rattlesnake on the road can you admire its beauty? Yes. Would you pick it up and take it home? Probably not.

ELF is an acronym for an evil little f---. ELFs have the same malicious intent as rattlesnakes. The difference between them, however, is that rattlesnakes will only bite you if you get within eight feet of them, whereas elves are so committed to their nefarious intent that they will seek you out to see what damage they can create in your life.

I'm getting to the point where I see that she is an ELF, but what do I do with that?

Gary: Hold, hold, hold, you're doing it again. You're going back to the story to try to make it work for you, so you can justify something and figure out what to do.

No, you've got to ask a question, "Is this person an ELF or a rattlesnake?" Oh, she's an ELF. So, when she does something nasty, you walk up to her and you say, "You're such an ELF," and walk away. Don't tell her what it means—ever. You acknowledge somebody for being an ELF...

But what do I do if...

Gary: Darling! You're not listening! You're talking in your head again! You went right back to your head to try to figure this out instead of asking a question.

You keep trying to figure things out in your head. You ask, "What's going to happen if I do that?" before it happens.

A better question would be "What would that look like?" What it would look like is this: You'll say, "You're such an ELF," and she'll say, "Thank you." Then she'll say, "Wait a minute! What did that mean?" You will have walked away by that time if you're smart.

When you acknowledge that somebody is an ELF, they usually stop being an ELF. But when you try to handle their ELF-dom, they never give it up.

Okay. But I can't walk away from these people. It's not…

Gary: In truth, you can't actually walk away from anybody, but you can vacate the premises. You can't really walk away, but you can control a situation. Acknowledgement of what is, is the way to control something.

Okay.

Gary: Try it. If you think that I'm full of crap, then you have to pay me a dollar when you discover I'm not.

All right.

Twenty-five minutes to go? I'm bored. I already want to move on. Is that an observation, a judgment, a discrimination or a discernment?

It's an awareness.

Gary: (Joking) Well, of course, when it's me, it's always awareness. No, actually, it's judgment, discernment and discrimination.

What have you defined as judgment, discrimination and discernment that actually isn't? Everything that is times a godzillion, will you destroy and uncreate it all? Right and wrong, good and bad, POD and POC, all 9, shorts, boys and beyonds.

Earlier I talked about the way you go into the right or wrong point of view, the winner or loser point of view. When you do that, you have moved from judgment, discrimination and discernment into competition. If you don't acknowledge what you've moved into, you will continue to play with the same judgment over and over again as though you're going to get a different result.

What have you defined as *not* judgment, *not* discrimination and *not* discernment that actually *is*? Everything that is times a godzillion, will you destroy and uncreate it all? Right and wrong, good and bad, POD and POC, all 9, shorts, boys and beyonds.

Question: Thank you, first of all, for the clarity of this call. It's been great. I'd like to ask about competition. Can you talk about competing with ourselves?

Gary: When you're trying to make something right or wrong in your universe, you're trying to find out whether you're going to win or lose. We compete with ourselves and we judge ourselves because we're trying to get everything right so we'll win. This is the competition we do with ourselves. And it's also the competition we do with others.

When you recognize that you have total, infinite choice, can you actually lose? Or can you just make a different choice if the first choice you make doesn't work?

Winning and losing are the elements that create competition. That is what competition is about. There are so many ways we do this. Recently I was talking with someone and I said, "You've got to stop being so competitive."

She said, "I don't perceive that I'm competitive."

I said, "That is competition, darling, because 'I don't perceive' cannot be argued with, which means you win and I lose in this argument."

It's about the willingness to recognize that the universe is infinite.

Gary: Yes, and that there is no winning or losing. There is only choice. Discrimination, judgment and discernment are the predecessors of competition. They go hand-in-hand.

What have you defined as judgment, discrimination and discernment that actually *isn't?* Everything that is times a godzillion, will you destroy and uncreate it all? Right and wrong, good and bad, POD and POC, all 9, shorts, boys and beyonds.

What have you defined as *not* judgment, *not* discrimination and *not* discernment that actually *is?* Everything that is times a godzillion, will you destroy and uncreate it all? Right and wrong, good and bad, POD and POC, all 9, shorts, boys and beyonds.

Question: When you were talking about candy, you said, "Choose what you like." How can I identify—or how can I have the awareness of—what I would like without discernment, judgment and conclusion? Or without having an attachment to results?

Gary: You go to the candy store and you ask, "Which of these would be something I'd like?" And then you buy all of them. You go home and you set them on the table and then you ask the candy bars to tell you when they want to be eaten.

Mmm…

Gary: If you did that with your lovers, you'd be in much better shape.

(Laughing) You read my mind. I'm already going there, that's great!

Question: There's something about choice that I'm trying to figure out. You're talking about buying all the candies and letting them tell you when they want to be eaten. I trip myself up around timing. I get stuck in trying to discriminate or discern the timing that would allow me the choice.

Gary: So, is time real? Or is it a construct?

It's a construct.

Gary: When I go to the store and buy all the candies, I stick them in the drawer. Sometimes I never even eat them.

Sometimes you never eat them?

Gary: Now, why don't I eat them? Once I've made the choice, I don't have to eat them. Most of us are taught that once we make a choice then we have to live with that choice. That's not true. We don't!

We're taught that once you choose something, you have to continue to choose that. No, it's "Do I want to eat this? Or do I not want to eat this?" You have to start by recognizing you have choice. When I was married, I would bring home a box of candy—and my ex-wife would eat it all until it was gone.

I could bring a box of candy into the house, eat one piece and not have another one for three to five days. Then I'd eat another one and wait another two or three days. I didn't have to eat them all at once. My ex-wife's point of view was that you were supposed to eat them all at once because you chose to buy them.

This is how we're taught to create relationship: I've chosen to be with this person so therefore I must eat them.

I resonate with that, but I don't know how to unhook it.

Gary: You unhook it by practicing. That's the reason you buy the candy and practice this. It comes a little bit at a time. Let's try another process here for you:

> What creation and generation of judgment, discrimination and discernment as the absolute necessity for the creation of life are you using to lock into existence the positional HEPADs you are instituting as the source for the wrongness of you, the rightness of your point of view and the necessity of never losing? Everything that is times a godzillion, will you destroy and uncreate it all? Right and wrong, good and bad, POD and POC, all 9, shorts, boys and beyonds.

This is a good one.

Question: When I was little, my mom would say to me, "Just make up your mind!" There was a finality in that. It's almost as if it locked up my being or brain or my mind so that once I chose something, that was it. I could never change my mind. It was, "Make up your mind and don't change it."

Gary: Yes, that's the way we're taught here. You aren't told that you have to be able to change your mind in every ten seconds or else you're going to go the wrong way in the disaster.

During 9/11, there were some people in the towers who were told to go upstairs. Half of them said, "This is stupid. I should be going downstairs," but because it was drilled into them to make up their mind and stick with it, they stuck with it—and died.

Do you want to stick with your point of view, which is guaranteed death? Everything that is times a godzillion, will you destroy and uncreate it all? Right and wrong, good and bad, POD and POC, all 9, shorts, boys and beyonds.

I would like to change your mind, okay? Is it okay if I change your mind?

Yes, please do.

Gary: Okay, I would like you to look at something here. Was your mother an idiot?

Yes.

Gary: Was your mother less aware than you are?

Yes.

Gary: You would listen to an idiot who was less aware than you for what reason? I can answer that for you. Would you like me to answer that for you?

Yes.

Gary: You listened to her because you loved her and you thought that if you observed things for yourself, that it was judgment.

Correct.

Gary: And in order to love her, you couldn't do judgment, because in your world, judgment and love could not co-exist.

You've locked yourself up, honey. Go ahead and cry, because there are a lot of places where you have locked yourself up when you tried to make your awareness less valuable than the judgment that if you loved the person, you couldn't have that awareness.

Thank you for that. I feel like my being is in a different space.

Gary: Yay! That's what we're looking for.

Question: This fits in perfectly. I have an awareness then I judge it and then I evacuate. It's awareness, judgment and evacuation. Can you talk a little bit more about why we evacuate?

Gary: You actually stop being—you don't evacuate. When you have the awareness of something, you go into "I'm being judgmental" because that's what has been given to you your whole life. You weren't being judgmental; you were actually being aware, but when you judge yourself, you feel like you have no choice.

Is it true that you have no choice? Or is it that you have so much awareness and that in recognizing the choices available, you have to try to discriminate and discern which is the best choice, in order not to lose?

Yes, that's it.

Gary: You would rather give up being than lose?

Everything that is times a godzillion, will you destroy and uncreate it all? Right and wrong, good and bad, POD and POC, all 9, shorts, boys and beyonds.

Question: I want to ask about bypassing the mind and coming from the heart. Is that what these processes are helping us to do—to come from the heart or that which we truly be?

Gary: Let me ask you a question. Is the heart a limitation?

It can be, yes.

Gary: So, you don't want to come from the heart. You want to come from total awareness and total being.

We have to be clear about the meanings of the words we use.

Gary: Yes, whatever you create form, structure and significance about, you are defining and limiting you with the meaning of words. You say, "It's got to come from the heart," then you have to define *the heart* based on your point of view, other people's points of view, and what you were taught as a point of view or an awareness of an infinite heart.

I was coming from the awareness of the infinite being we be, the heart of that.

Gary: But that's infinite being; that's not heart.

Thank you.

Gary: People use heart to define where they must feel this stuff in their body. That's not it. It's about having total awareness of something throughout the entirety of your body. It's a much bigger possibility.

Much bigger! And what about bypassing the mind?

Gary: The mind is a construct that was created to define the limitations of what you already know and to keep you in constant connection with the limitations of what you already know. It's not that you should try to bypass the mind. You simply realize that the mind, too, is a limitation.

And do we have to choose that limitation or can we have something greater?

Always something greater.

Gary: We were talking about how a mother told her daughter she had to make up her mind and stick with it. That was the place of trying to control her rather than allowing her to be the infinite being she is. When people do that, they discount the being and discourage it from having the infinite space of total awareness, total perceiving, total knowing and total being, plus the heart, the soul, the mind and the whole of who they are.

Unless somebody else has a question, I'm going to end off here, because there's nothing else I can do with you guys right now. Thank you all. Please get this: You have never been as discriminating, judgmental or discerning as you have tried to make yourself.

If you'll step into infinite perceiving, knowing, being and receiving, then judgment, discrimination and discernment will disappear like the scales off a fish that's being gutted. Nice image, eh?

Dain: Thanks for taking over tonight, Gary. Sorry about the voice. Thanks, everybody.

Gary: We love you anyway, Dr. Dain. You're awesome.

All right folks, this has been great. I hope it will help you dynamically. The next key is about competition. That's the one that has to be dealt with next. Thanks, everybody. Love you lots! Have a good day!

~~~

No Competition

Gary: Hello everyone. Tonight we're going to talk about the seventh key: No competition.

The elements of competition are *right* and *wrong, win* and *lose*. If you're doing "I need to be right" or "I need to not be wrong," you're doing competition.

Dain: Any time you need to be right or you need to win or you need to not lose—you are doing competition. Any time you want to be right or you are trying to be right, you're trying to win and not lose—and that's competition.

Gary: Not losing is sometimes more important to people than winning.

Whenever you have to make something wrong or you have to make something right, you are doing competition. If you say, "I perceive he's competing with me," it means *you're* doing competition.

No competition is completely different. It is being in the question. It's "What's going on here? How do I handle this?"

I got a call last week from an Access Consciousness facilitator who had been co-facilitating a class with another person. This facilitator felt like she wasn't sufficiently involved in the co-facilitation of the class, so she made something wrong about it. She became upset about what occurred. She then went out to lunch with one of the class participants and had the participant facilitate her on her upset. Getting upset is a form of competition. She was trying to make the other facilitator look bad and wrong and trying to make herself look right. You think that making yourself look right and the other person look wrong is the way not to lose.

Dain: This is an example of what goes on in all of our lives. Whenever you try to get somebody to side with you against somebody else, for whatever reason, whether it's someone you work with or someone you're in relationship with—you're doing competition.

You feel totally justified in what you're doing. It seems necessary or appropriate. But in actuality, when you do this, you're killing your creative capacity. You're killing what you could receive in the world and you end up creating a lot of crap in your own universe.

Gary: And at the same time you're killing your business and your future. Doing competition is the way people kill their businesses. When you're in business, you need to be the best you can be and provide the best you can provide at all times. But you're not going to provide that if you need to be right or not be wrong or if you need to win or not lose.

Dain: You need to get that your point of view creates your reality. Reality doesn't create your point of view.

When you badmouth somebody else or get another person to align and agree with you about the wrongness of somebody else and the rightness of you, what's your point of view? Is your point of view that you have value, or that you don't? That you have a contribution you can receive or that you can't? You're taking the point of view that you have no value. You screw up your life based on that point of view, because your point of view creates your reality.

As Gary said, the antidote to doing competition is to ask a question. Any time you're doing conclusion, you're doing competition.

Gary: Dain, let's talk for just a moment about how you and I co-facilitate. In the beginning when I started to co-facilitate with you, I tended to take control of things. What did that create in your universe?

Dain: Well, it created a place where I felt like I was shrinking. I felt like people were looking at me and asking, "What's this idiot doing onstage with Gary?"

Gary: Hold just a minute. "I feel like, blah, blah, blah" is the beginning of competition. You're going into right or wrong or you're trying not to lose.

Dain: That is brilliant. Making the choice to go into "I feel this way" is the beginning of competition. That's the point where you can nip competition in the bud. If you take one more step down that road, you're not going to end up anywhere you want to be, because all you can see is the conclusion that you've already come to: "I feel like this" and "I feel like that." You're going to try to make the way you feel right.

You need to go to the moment where you first said, "I feel like ____" and realize that's the place where you locked yourself into a limited point of view. That's the place you started the competitive process.

Gary: So Dain, whenever you "felt" like that, did you go to somebody else or did you come to me?

Dain: I went to you and I said, "Here is what's coming up for me." I know that if anything makes me feel heavy or less-than, there's something to be undone with Access Consciousness tools. Period. I know that I'm buying somebody else's point of view or I'm going to an old place or I'm doing competition or whatever it is.

I would go to you and I would say, "Okay, this is what's going on for me. What can we do about this? This is not making me feel lighter—and lightness is the place I would like to function from."

Gary: You always came to me because we were co-facilitating. You didn't go to anybody else. When you are a facilitator, your job is to be present and ask questions and nothing else. When you do that, you can deal with anything.

Question: When I become aware that someone is doing competition with me, I tend to diminish myself so the other person doesn't feel the need to be competitive. Obviously, that doesn't work. What can I do when someone is being competitive with me? Is it just having that awareness and saying, "Interesting point of view"?

Gary: That somebody is in competition with you is not an awareness. It's a judgment. You've got to look at the situation and ask, "What am I doing or being to create this? What am I aware of that I'm not willing to have total awareness of?"

You could do interesting point of view, but you've got to acknowledge that the other person is feeling the need to be right or not be wrong—or the need to win or to not lose. You've got to look at it and ask, "What am I creating or generating that's contributing to their feeling any of those things?"

That's what I would do with Dain. He would say, "Well, I feel like blah, blah, blah," and I'd ask, "How can I change this? What am I doing that I need to change?"

You ask:

- How can I change this?
- What is it you need from me?

You find out what the other person needs from you. If they say, "I need to talk more when we're co-facilitating," you can turn the floor over to them and let them talk more.

Dain: When that would come up for me, and it came up many times in different ways over the years that we co-facilitated, the feeling diminished after I talked with Gary—except when I didn't really have a sense of the value of me. I'd be thinking, "Why am I up here with this guy who's got so much brilliant stuff to say?"

Yet Gary was like, "Dude, I wouldn't have you up here if you weren't contributing." As I became more willing to get the contribution that I was by being me—and not by trying to have a version of Gary's point of view—I started to recognize that I could create a greater contribution. That wasn't possible when I was functioning from the place of competition that I had learned I had to function from in this reality.

Gary: Now, that's frigging brilliant. If you go into competition, you can't be the contribution you could be. When you compete with someone, you have to adjust yourself to their universe, so you can't show up as you. You have to buy someone else's reality in order to do competition.

Dain: It's when you don't recognize that you are a contribution that you go to the side of competition.

Gary: And that's where you create the real competition with yourself. When you see yourself as less-than, you create competition with yourself and others. Competition is about never seeing the contribution you are.

Question: I find that whenever I have a conversation with anyone in my daughter's presence she interrupts us and demands attention. Is this an example of competition? How would you suggest I could handle this? My daughter is four years old.

Gary: Every four year old in the universe wishes to be included in the conversation. When you exclude children from a conversation, they feel they have to get in their two cents. Whenever you're having a conversation with another adult, rather than ignoring your child, include him or her as part of the conversation. Children are aware and they are present, so why not include them? You could ask, "So, what do you think about this?" After you do this three or four times in any conversation, they will get bored and go away. They get bored with adult conversation almost instantaneously.

Dain: Their contribution has been acknowledged and they've had their say, and that's what they're looking for.

I wonder how many people are stuck in some younger age when all this competition stuff comes up; for example, when they're trying to learn things other people are doing and they don't really understand them. They get stuck there and try to figure it out—and they can't seem to go beyond it.

Gary: Well one of the difficulties is that you think you're being excluded. That's part of the "I feel bad" or "I feel left out." It is one of the triggers for all this competitive stuff that goes on.

Competition assumes that nobody else sees the contribution you are, which is why little kids want to be included in the conversation. It doesn't matter whether they understand the subject you're talking about. They want to make a contribution.

What if you just asked them, "What is it you can add to this that would make it clear to people?" Ninety percent of the people are going to say, "Bu-bu-bu... I'm cute." Okay, good. That's fine, being cute is a contribution too.

Dain: That was my greatest contribution for several years. When you believe you're not a contribution, you put it on somebody else. You say, "You don't see me as a contribution."

If you see you as a contribution, most other people can't help but see you as a contribution as well. However, if they don't see themselves as a contribution, they may see you as competition.

When you're in a situation where you think somebody doesn't see the contribution you are, it's because you have that point of view about yourself. If you know you're a contribution, other people can have any point of view they want, and it doesn't affect you.

Gary: Exactly!

Question: If you see someone being a great contribution, but they don't see it, how do you deal with that?

Gary: You ignore it, because you can't give something to someone that they're not willing to receive. All you can do is say, "You know what? You're an amazing contribution to my life. Thanks for being in my life." Treat them as if you're a man admiring a woman. Say, "Knowing you are here makes it all better."

Can gifting and receiving exist when competition is involved?

Gary: Yes, when somebody is competing with you, the gift is to acknowledge their sense of being less-than and the receiving is acknowledging the fact that they don't have to be less-than. It is their choice. If that's what they want, it's their choice.

Apart from in nature, where does gifting and receiving exist?

Dain: It occurs with animals. It occurs with babies. Have you ever been with a baby, where you were just touching them and acknowledging them as a being—and they received your acknowledgements? It seemed like it opened up their world as well as yours. That's an example of that gifting and receiving.

There was a lady at the Being You class in Stockholm who had a child just the month before. The baby would not sleep on his own. She had to be there with him all the time. I held the little guy and put his head in my hands. I just said hi and acknowledged everything I perceived in him as a being.

The next day, the mother came in to class and said, "Last night was the first night I've been able to leave him on his own, and he was just fine."

I realized that gifting and receiving is an acknowledgement of the being that's there. That's the thing that's missing in competition.

In other words, babies don't do that kind of competition. They naturally acknowledge the being in somebody, and we have to acknowledge them as a being—not as a valuable product based on what they do, what they say, what they think, how pretty they are or anything else. We have to acknowledge them just for the fact that they *be*. The absence of that acknowledgement is one of the things that leads us to go into competition. We try to prove we have value that we don't believe we actually have. We are not willing to acknowledge our value as a being because we were never acknowledged just for being.

Gary: Are you saying that if you actually acknowledged people as the amazing person they are, that might be enough to stop them competing as if something was wrong or something wasn't right or they had to win or they were going to lose?

Dain: Yes.

Gary: That's a very cool example. Please recognize that's all you've got to do with big people too, because big people like to be acknowledged as much as little tiny people.

Dain: Yeah.

Gary: The thing is, it's easier to acknowledge a tiny person because they don't require anything of you. You think that if you acknowledge big people, they're going to require something of you, which is not necessarily true.

Question: I notice that gratitude is completely missing when I am doing competition. Am I correct, or is it something else? Could you talk about that?

Gary: Yes, you are correct. Gratitude cannot exist in the face of competition, because competition is always about win, lose, right or wrong. It's never about what you're grateful for with the person.

When Dain and I would have a difficulty with competition, I would say, "Wow, you're kidding. You feel like you're less-than? I am so grateful to have you up there with me because you have a brilliant way of looking at things in a slightly different way than I do, and it allows people to see things I can't give them."

It's wonderful when you are able to have gratitude for what someone is contributing. Go to gratitude and watch the competition fade away.

Anywhere I'm going into lack of consciousness based on my fear of losing...

Gary: It's not a fear. You have no fear. I love you, but if you talk about fear of losing again, I'm going to punch you directly in the face, because you have no fear. That's a lie. Get over it.

Dain: If you do that, we will have somebody who does competition urinate on you. Carry on, Gary.

What message am I sending through the general community by withdrawing my support of other facilitators or getting pissy, nit-picky or nasty with someone who doesn't include me?

Gary: If you're an Access Consciousness facilitator and you do that, you're saying Access Consciousness is a lie. And if you think Access Consciousness is a lie, then you probably should not be a facilitator. You should go find something else to do to make money, because you have decided that Access Consciousness is your system for making money. It's a system you're going to use and abuse, not something you're going to contribute to, in order to create something greater for everyone.

Dain: Brilliant.

Gary: You need to get to the point where it is not about the competition. It's about the way we all contribute to consciousness—then consciousness can contribute to us. When you do competition, you exclude the contribution of the entire molecular structure that the Earth wishes to be for you.

I don't compete; instead I contribute to many of my colleagues by telling people about their classes and mine as well, of course. People I invite to do classes with me often choose to do courses taught by other Access Consciousness facilitators. Lately I've had classes with few or no participants. This is not working for me any longer. What can I do differently?

Gary: You've got to understand that this is not about competition. You need to ask, "What's the generative energy of competition I'm not using?"

Here's another aspect of competition that plays out in the world—and it also plays out in Access Consciousness. At times you may have the awareness that someone is either doing competition or doing dis-empowerment. You will see people go to them and it creates a place in your world that feels like competition. You've got to realize that people need to do exactly what they need to do. They're attracted to a person, whether it's a facilitator or a realtor or a dentist, for a reason. There's a reason they want to go there. And they'll get whatever it is they're there to get.

Dain: I was recently at Angsbacka, a conference center in Sweden, doing Access Consciousness. There were all kinds of people doing every spiritual modality under the sun, and they were doing huge amounts of competition with me and Access Consciousness. My point of view was "Well, that's entertaining."

Gary: What you do is totally different from what other people do. If someone is attracted to you and they need what you offer, they should have it. Why can't they do mine, why can't they do yours and why can't they choose to do either, both or none as they see fit? If you go into competition, you're basically saying that consciousness does not exist. People know what they require.

Sometimes people know how to get where they're going—and where they're going is not up to you. It has nothing to do with you. They will do other things with other people, as they see fit, because those things work for them. Rather than making the judgment call that another facilitator is bad for them, recognize that if they're in front of another facilitator, there's a reason for it. Your job is not to save the world; your job is to empower people to choose in the same way you empower yourself to choose. And then to ask, "What contribution can I be?"

Now let's talk about generative competition. There was a lady who came to an Access Consciousness class we did in Costa Rica. She got angry at Dain because he wouldn't do something for her that she thought he should do—like give up all other women for her.

Dain was planning to go to Florida to do an Access Consciousness class, and this woman found a facilitator who hated Dain, and she made arrangements with the facilitator to go to Florida to do a class the week before Dain's class.

Dain said, "If that facilitator gives a class a week before mine, nobody will come to my class!"

I said, "It's doing competition to feel that you will lose. You know what? You've got to be willing to out-create her."

The facilitator was going to Florida because she hated Dain. She wasn't going for Access Consciousness or to create more consciousness for people. She was going because she wanted to "get" Dain. What kind of deal is that?

He asked me, "How do I out-create this woman?"

I said, "Out-creating her is creating a greater invitation to a greater possibility. She's angry. She's going there because she believes she can take something away from you. People will sense that energy. When you compete against somebody, you usually end up screwing yourself.

Be a bigger invitation than she is. When you out-create somebody, you don't do competition. You don't compete against the person directly. You ask, "What's going to make me stand out? What's going to make me and what I have to offer, something greater?"

When you function from competition, the size of your classes begins to diminish—and when you try to function from no competition, the size of your classes also diminishes, because you're still stuck in competition; you're just doing anti-competition. You're trying to prove you're more right than the other person because you're not doing competition.

So, Dain out-created the facilitator. He went to Florida, and he had something like fifteen or nineteen people in his class. It turned out that the other facilitator had nine people in her class.

Dain: You have to perceive the competition—and do what you're doing anyway. In other words, perceive the competition that others are choosing and be the contribution you are. And no matter what you're offering to people, when you do that, you become the invitation they've been looking for their whole life. That's because no matter how you're interacting with them, the energy you create allows them to know a different possibility is available in every area of their life. When you be that, it changes it for them too.

Gary: When somebody is doing competition, they're going against you. When you get into generative competition, you out-create the person. Rather than going into anger, rage, fury and hate about them having something you think you lack, you look at their competition and you ask, "How can I use this situation as a source of energy for being a contribution?"

Dain: When I was at Angsbacka with a crew from Access Consciousness, we got to practice using these tools. There were lots of other groups at the center, and huge amounts of judgment were directed at me and Access Consciousness. At one point I was giving an Energetic Synthesis of Being taster, and one of the processes we did made all kinds of noise.

Some people in other classes got upset that we were so noisy. There was a big board in the hall where all the classes were posted, and someone took down my sign so others would not know that I was giving this class.

People came up to me and asked, "Is your class cancelled?"

I said, "Nope."

They said, "Oh, really? Well cool, I'm going to tell everybody it's happening."

So, my class was full. And interestingly, there was another group who was making a huge amount of noise. They were making as much noise as they could. I said to my class, "You may notice you're getting distracted by that noise. Don't let it distract you. Just let that energy contribute to your body. They're making all kinds of noise and having all kinds of energy over there. Cool, that's awesome. Let that contribute to your body and wake it up more. Don't try to shut it out, don't try to compete with it, just be here and allow yourself to be aware and receive from it. Allow it to contribute to you and your body." They did, and everybody got more present and more awake. And it stopped the separation that other people were trying to create. It eliminated it totally.

Gary: What you just described are the quantum entanglements* of all the energy you're willing to receive and the way it contributes to you. You just described that beautifully.

Quantum entanglements are, in essence, your connection with the creative, generative elements of the universe. Quantum entanglements are what allow you to receive communication from other people. If you didn't have quantum entanglements, you would not have psychic awareness, intuition or the capacity to hear somebody else's thoughts.

I was at a restaurant eating pâté the other night. It was not like when I eat pâté with Dain. When I eat pâté with Dain, he so loves it that the energy he is and the energy that he gets from eating it, makes it taste so frigging good you almost have an orgasm.

It's the quantum entanglements that do that. I have noticed that when I go out to dinner with people who really enjoy food and experience all the sensations of it, their enjoyment is a contribution to everything that goes on in the room and to everyone who's eating dinner in that place. On those occasions, the food is always great—for everyone.

I can go to the same restaurant with another person who doesn't have that sensory joy, and their food is never quite right. Nothing is ever quite the way they want it to be, nothing is as good as they would like it to be, and they always talk about other restaurants being better. Under those circumstances, the food never tastes great.

But when I go out to dinner with somebody who has the sense of the greatness of food and they get all the energies of it, it creates a contribution to my taste buds. That's the way the quantum entanglements work. It's about the way all energies are connected to one another. It doesn't matter what the energy is. If you have the energy of anger or upset, that contributes more anger and upset to the world. If you have the energy of joy and pleasure, that contributes to more joy and pleasure in the world.

You want to use the quantum entanglements to contribute to what you're creating. So here we go:

What generative capacity for the solidification of the elementals* into reality by request of the quantum entanglements fulfilled as always

---

* See glossary for definition.

out-creating all competition are you refusing to create and institute? Everything that is times a godzillion, will you destroy and uncreate it all? Right and wrong, good and bad, POD and POC, all 9, shorts, boys and beyonds.

I'm hoping this will get you to stop competing with yourself by making yourself less-than in order to compete with others, because you literally have to choose to make yourself less-than in order to have something to compete about.

Question: Are you saying that everything is like apples and oranges and grapefruit and watermelon, but in order to do competition, you have to see everybody as an apple?

Gary: In order to do competition, you have to not see what people are, and you have to not see what is possible. You cannot see what is possible and you cannot see what is as long as you have an ounce of competition in your universe. You go into the rightness or the wrongness or the winning or the losing—and how you lack something and how you're not going to lack if you win.

I asked that because competition is always about comparison, and you can't compare two disparate things.

Gary: Disparate things cannot be compared, exactly. Is an Aussie like an American? No. Is an Italian like anybody? No.

Question: I can't think of anything in this reality that's not asking us to compete.

Gary: That's right, everything in this reality is asking you to compete. But if you're willing to out-create this reality, then this reality cannot be a place where you lack anything.

It's a constant state of generation.

Gary: Yes, and a constant state of possibility instead of a constant state of lack. Right now you're all competing to be in the lead in the column of lack. You're saying, "I'm a leader in a red column of no money. I'm the leader in the red column of emotions." What you've got to be is someone who out-creates everybody.

You can't compare apples to oranges, that's true, but what if you're an apple and you think being an orange is better than being an apple?

Gary: If you think one is better than the other, then you are seeing yourself in a competitive role. Instead of that, you have to be like the cartoon character, Popeye, and say, "I yam what I yam and tha's all what I yam."

Dain: When you choose against you, when you do that thing of "I'm an orange but I see an apple as valuable," you're choosing against you. It's a form of competition. To do competition, you're always choosing against you.

Gary: Any time you're doing competition, you're choosing against you. You can't compete with anybody but you, and competition is always against you, not for you.

Question: Let's say nobody else is involved in a situation. You're looking at something to do with yourself and you're thinking it's right or wrong or win or lose—is that competition with yourself?

Gary: Yes, although there is a slight variation on competition with self.

You are the only person you can actually compete with. There is an element within each of us where we know we want to be better than we were yesterday. That's not actually a manifestation of competition—but if you are abusing yourself, it becomes something like competition. When you are doing self-degradation, you are doing competition with yourself in relationship to people that are not even present.

Dain: You are the only person you can actually compete with and the only person you can match up to. Looking to be greater today than you were yesterday will create a generative possibility. But that's not really competition; it's awareness.

Gary: Well, it is competition, but it's competition without judgment or conclusion. There's a generative energy in it. It's a generative competition, and you've got to see the difference between that and when you're doing something to make yourself right or to make yourself not wrong or to make yourself win or to make yourself not lose. Those are the elements of competition in a negative form.

Here's where you ask, "How can I use this need to be a contribution to take advantage of everything and contribute to everything and to make that an advantage for me and everyone else?" It's a slightly different point of view.

When I play sports, sometimes I will let the opposition win so they can have a new possibility of winning, whereas winning and losing don't matter to me.

Gary: If you're truly in no competition, it doesn't matter to you whether you win or lose. It's not about winning or losing. It's about the contribution you can be, which is why you let people win. You know it's more important to them than it is to you.

When I was a kid I used to come in second in the spelling bee because I knew the kid who felt he had to win it. I knew it would devastate him if he didn't win. It didn't matter to me, so I would come in second. I was always the second best, even though I could spell all the words. I knew which words the other guy didn't know, and I wasn't willing to let him be destroyed by not winning. You could say I was being a little bit superior, but at nine years old, it's good to have a little superiority.

When I am playing sports or anything that requires a winner and a loser, how can I apply this key? Everyone in this reality is so competitive. How do you play with people without competing?

Gary: When you're playing sports, it's a game. It's not living. You can play any game to win and not lose, as long as you know it's a game. The problem is, you make it part of life and living.

If you play chess with me, I will win or you will die. Those are the two choices you get. I really like to win. When I play bridge, I also like to win, so I will do everything I can to make sure I do. Am I competitive in those areas? Yeah. But I know it's a game. I know it's not life.

In a game, it's always generative to do the win or lose thing because it challenges the other person to be greater than they already are. There's nothing wrong with challenging a person to be greater than they already are. The problem comes when you do competition in life and living. That's not the place to do competition.

Is competition a polarized viewpoint of this reality?

Gary: Yeah, and that's the reason I said there's a generative element to it. There is generative competition and there is destructive competition. Whenever you're looking to win, not lose and to be right, not wrong, you are looking for the destructive portion of competition, because the person that always has to be destroyed under those circumstances is you.

Question: Just imagine how the planet would look if all the schools around the world would talk about these keys! I have a few questions about no competition. I find it difficult to play games with people who are competitive. For me, it's just a game. It's for fun. As long as we are having fun and enjoying the game, I have no point of view about losing.

Gary: Oh no, you've got to play for the fun of winning! That's not a problem, okay? I'm just kidding when I talk about the winning thing, but try it. You might win next time.

In my younger days, I was involved in classical ballet for about fifteen years, so I know what competition looks like. In my day-to-day life now, if competition is present, it gets heavy for me. I often simply give up and go away from whatever it is. I wonder if I've become a doormat here.

Gary: Yes, you have.

Often when competition is being directed at me, I go into super-nice mode with the person in the hope that being friendly will dissipate it. It usually doesn't work.

Gary: It never works!

When that happens, I can feel my barriers go up and the energy gets weird. Sometimes it even feels like the person would like to kill me and vice versa. What else is possible? How do you and Dain deal with this?

Gary: We kill each other!

Dain: Let me give you an example from the class this weekend. There was a guy in the class who raised his hand and acted like he was asking a question. He said, "You're telling us all kinds of stuff that we already know. Why are we here?"

I thought, "Really? That's interesting," because I had said all kinds of things that people hadn't known.

I said to him, "Of course you already know everything, but have you heard it put in these words? And how's your life looking? Is what you know actually showing up in your life? Or is something else showing up as though you don't actually know what you already know?"

He said, "Okay."

Later on, I said to him, "You talk about being open, but you've been sitting here in judgment of me the entire time. That's fine. I don't have a judgment of that because I already have your money. You can judge me all you want, and you don't ever have to change if you don't want to."

I knew that he was trying to make an issue of the money. He was competing with me as though he knew more than I did. I was okay with that. My attitude was "You can know more than I do. I don't care." But he was standing in the way of other people being aware of what they could have. I acknowledged what he was doing so he could look at it and choose to hold onto it or choose to move on. Doing that created freedom for everybody else in the class, because they could perceive the energy of it.

So, rather than buying his competition and resisting and reacting and trying to prove "Hey, I'm so cool. Everybody should listen to me," I said, "You know what? You know a lot of stuff. And how is what you're choosing working for you? Are you aware that this is what you're choosing?"

He may never get it, but everybody else in the class did. They saw where they had done that sort of thing and they said, "Wow, you know what? I don't want to judge you or me or anybody else. Let's move on here." And that's what occurred.

So, going into super-nice mode doesn't work very often in the face of competition.

Gary: It never works.

Dain: But if being super-nice is the only tool you've ever been given, how do you know it doesn't work? The thing is, nobody has ever shown us a different way of being, which is why we're having this conversation about The Ten Keys. When somebody is going into competition with you, and you can be totally present, you can acknowledge what's going on in your own universe.

Talking about it with the other person doesn't often work, but you can acknowledge in your own universe that there's competition. You can say, "I'm just going to be here with this and see where it goes." That can create a different result.

Question: I am aware that there are energetic forms of competition that people may not even consider to be competition. I can't even tell you what they are. It's just an energetic sense that there are subtle ways competition occurs that would not be generally identified as competition.

I avoid competition. I tend to back away from things when I think I will lose in the face of competition.

Gary: You can't avoid anything. You've got to be present for everything.

Withdrawing is competitive. Thinking that you would lose in the face of competition is being competitive. The place of not wanting to lose is competitive. The purpose of competition is to get someone to withdraw so that they will lose and you can win.

Question: I don't think of myself as competitive overall, but I have had the experience of competition rearing its ugly head unexpectedly, and when it does, I try to fight it back. Of course, resisting and reacting just makes it bigger.

Also, what would it take to have capacities and gifts that people would be drawn to?

Gary: You have those gifts—but you're not choosing them because you are still worrying about whether you're right or wrong or whether you're winning or losing.

Competition is whenever we're looking to win. It is also when you're looking to not lose, when you're looking to be right and when you're looking not to be wrong.

Question: Gary, you talked about a conversation you had with a facilitator. You said you told her she was being competitive. She said she wasn't. You said that in itself was competition. Is it competition any time someone has to prove they're right? Is it competition every time someone has to have the last word?

Gary: Yes. I called her and I said, "You've got to stop the frigging competition." She said, "I don't perceive that I'm competitive."

I said, "That is competition right there. You just made sure I had no place to go—so that makes you the winner." That's what competition is. She had to have the last word. It's always making sure that you are the winner by never giving anyone else any question to speak from. No question equals competition.

Question: Earlier you were talking about "nice" as the only option some people choose when they feel competition. I tend to do the opposite. I say, "I don't want to deal with you," and just walk away. I know that's not generative, either.

Gary: Yeah, you're trying to do "no competition" as though it is better-than. That's being superior to, which is judgment, which is separation, which is not contributive. If you want to "get" somebody really good, instead of saying, "F--- you, I'm going away," try asking, "How can I contribute to your class so you can get more people?" or "How can I contribute to what you're doing so you get more?"

If they're competing, they're thinking they don't have enough. People think they don't have enough of something in their life—not enough money, not enough accolades, not enough something else. They do competition to get more of what they think they lack. Offering to contribute to them in the area where they feel they lack will discharge the competition quicker than anything you can possibly do.

Thank you.

Dain: Brilliant.

Question: Could you say that again?

Gary: You say it, Dain.

Dain: People feel like they have to do competition in order to be contributed to or to get what they want. When you offer to contribute to someone who's doing competition, it immediately fries all their circuits, busts all their paradigms and takes them out of competition.

Be aware, though, that some people do competition simply because they do competition. But even in that case, when you offer to contribute to them, it fries all of their circuits and eliminates their competition with you. They can't hold it in place any longer. You've just gone around to the back door they didn't even know they had.

Gary: And by contributing to them, you have also created generative competition, which means they then have to contribute to you. They have to stop being as needy as they've been making themselves be, which is why they were doing competition in the first place. When you contribute to them, it's an invitation to get them to go into contribution instead of competition.

Dain: Brilliant. That's a great question: What contribution can I be to get them into contribution or to get myself into contribution rather than competition? You're either doing contribution or you're doing competition. It's your choice.

Question: I heard you say a couple of different things. One was "What am I doing to create competition in that person?" That could be a factor. The other thing was that the other person could be feeling needy or less-than and doing competition as a result. Could it go both ways? Is it one way or is it always both?

Gary: We're trying to give you the awareness of what competition is all about. We're also trying to give you awareness of how you change it—and to get you to ask questions. Everything you just asked was a question. Once you go into question, you can't do competition any longer. You cannot do competition from question. You can only do competition from conclusion and feeling.

So, you're present and you acknowledge there's competition. You are curious about whether you're creating it or whether there's something going on in their world that's creating it and you offer to be a contribution, which is a competition blaster.

Gary: Yeah, you ask, "How can I contribute to this?" When you ask that question, you start to change the energy.

Dain: And if you stay in the question, competition won't exist in your world. In other words, as long as you are in the question, competition won't exist for you.

Okay. So, if I stay in the question, competition can't exist in my world even if somebody else is doing it?

Gary: That's right, not unless you choose it.

Ah…excellent.

Question: Does most sex operate from competition?

Gary: Absolutely, because people think if I get this girl or this guy, I'm no longer a loser.

Sex is a very competitive area because people think they lack. They think they have to compete for the winners or the losers. At one point, I was talking with a friend who said, "Wah! I'm never going to get laid again!"

I said, "Well, there's this guy, this guy, this guy and this guy. All of them would like to have sex with you."

She said, "They're losers."

I said, "What?"

She said, "They're losers."

If the person is a winner and you have sex with him or her, then that makes you a winner too. You become a winner if a winner chooses you. You get into competitive situations to do with sex where you're looking at who's a winner, who's a loser and who doesn't count.

Does that really do anything for you, or is that a justification or a reaction to the idea that there's something wrong with you that you can't handle? Do you know what? That's competition as well.

Question: Is addiction an attempt to avoid competition?

Gary: Yes.

Wow, thank you.

Question: I just returned from seeing the X-Men movie. Forty minutes into the movie I wanted to leave so badly that I had to grip my seat and stay. I realized that I've always tried to follow the rules and get it right in order not to let loose with what I have considered my lawlessness and ruthlessness. I've stayed away from obvious competition for the same reasons. Once I had that awareness, I made the demand that I claim, own and acknowledge the lawlessness and the ruthlessness and have it available to choose. Interestingly, after I did that, I became aware of a gentleness I have never accessed before. Would you please comment?

Gary: You've been assuming a point of view about how you are not ruthless and lawless. Folks, you have to get that you are lawless. You are lawless because you are not willing to live by the rules of this reality, which is why competition is so hard for you to deal with. It's why, when you become competitive, you have to make you wrong. Either way, competition has nothing to do with choice, awareness or greatness.

Dain: And when you don't acknowledge all of what you are, you're enforcing a point of view on yourself. If you can't acknowledge some part of you, you can't have all of you, which includes the gentleness that's actually real and true for you. You ought to be able to have all aspects of you and use and be whatever is appropriate at the appropriate time.

Gary: That gentleness is a place that kills competition in yourself and others.

Dain: Yep.

Question: I had a very interesting experience of total allowance the other day. I was driving to run a group. I was fighting a sinus infection. I was irritable and bitchy, and I wanted to whack all the traffic stupids on the road. A woman whose Bars I've been running for ten months and who has gotten so much change in her life came in for the group. She asked me how I was, and I said, "Good—and I am pretty bitchy."

She said, "You go girl! Go right ahead and be as bitchy as you like." All of a sudden all my irritability and anger disappeared. How does it get any better than that?

I have had people say things like this to me before, but the energy they did it with was alignment and agreement. Commiserating just locked us both into it. This was totally different; she was not aligning and agreeing, she was not resisting or reacting; she was in total allowance. I just felt all the intensity and density disappear.

Gary: That's how acknowledgment of what is changes whatever you're stuck in—including competition. It's about acknowledging what is—not competing to find out where you're right or where you're not wrong or where you're winning or where you're not losing.

Question: As I listen to this conversation, I'm feeling heavier and heavier. Is there a misidentification and misapplication of competition as something that's necessary to survive?

Gary: Yes. The survival of the fittest is the idea that competition is the only way anything occurs. However, that is not true. In the animal world, it's not the survival of the fittest; it's survival based on the fact that some animals are inherently greater than others. They did a study on wolves years ago, which indicated that when wolves are hunting—and this is probably indicative of all predatory species—they choose the diseased in the herd, because the diseased have a particular aura.

Have you ever been around somebody you wanted to stomp to death? That's because that person had a particular aura that indicated they were not strong enough to be a valuable product in the world. When you are doing competition, you are creating you as the diseased element, which is why people start to go away from you. It's why they don't take your classes.

Trying not to compete is not the same thing as contributing. Not competing is a not-trying-to-win so that you don't become a loser.

Question: I'm looking at the ocean right now. It's as if the ocean is asking us to be as great as it is. It's like that's what we're asking of each other in not doing competition.

Gary: Yes, it's like being the ocean. It's asking everything to contribute and it's being willing to contribute to everything, so you are being that—and not doing competition.

Dain: I'd like to say something more about the lie that competition is necessary for survival. In competition, all you get is survival; you don't get thrive-al. Thriving and flourishing are not a possibility if you're doing competition, because you totally exclude the ocean that's inviting you to be as great as you are. You're saying, "I can't be part of that. I've got to do this on my own." You take yourself out of thrive-al.

The idea that competition is necessary for survival feels like it's completely locked in for me. It's as if every aspect of my being has figured that one out. It seems stuck. And it's subtle.

Gary: Is there any chance that the stuckness is the fact that you bought the lie that survival was what you were here to do?

Yes. Survival is what I have been trying to do in order to cope.

Gary: If you are living your life from "cope," you always have to create a difficulty to deal with so you can cope with what's going on.

Yeah, I totally get it! I didn't see it before. I didn't recognize it until this conversation. All of a sudden I'm multi-seeing everything. It's: "Oh, my God, I do this in every way, shape and form!" This is brilliant. Thank you.

Gary: Yeah, I see that's the place where you go into competition. If you believe in survival, then you go into competition in order to prove that you can survive. You have to do this with every person you come into contact with.

What generative capacity for the solidification of the elementals into reality by request of the quantum entanglements fulfilled as always out-creating all competition are you refusing to create and institute? Everything that is times a godzillion, will you destroy and uncreate it all? Right and wrong, good and bad, POD and POC, all 9, shorts, boys and beyonds.

Question: Can we talk about money in more detail for a minute? When I go out for dinner with people or share a taxi or do anything that involves money, I always pay the bill. I pick up on their feelings and often don't get what's mine and what is other people's. So, when they're uncomfortable about money and choose the cheapest things on the menu or count up their money because they can't afford a nice meal or when they don't really want to pay for the taxi, I'll just pay for it.

Gary: You've got a choice here. One of the things I did was to make a rule: If you invite me, you pay. If I invite you, I pay. And when people are obnoxious, I pay because it pisses them off. If they do inferior, I always make myself imperious and superior because that way I'm using their competitive limitations as a way of thumbing my nose at them. That's out-creating their limited reality.

A lot of the time I would like to pay anyway because I like to pay, and then I go into this survival thing. If I want to keep paying and be generous, my money is going to diminish, so that's the survival thing, isn't it?

Gary: Yeah, that's the survival thing—the idea that you could actually ever be out of money. You're never going to be out of money; that's not part of your reality,

Darling. I love you, you're cute as hell, but being out of money is not going to be part of your reality. That is the projection of what is delivered at you all the time. That's a projected future reality that could never be.

How many people are projecting at you that you could run out of money, you could be out of money or you won't have money if you keep spending money the way you're spending it? That's what was projected at you as a kid. Did that stop you from anything? No. You weren't going to buy that crap then and you're not going to buy that crap now because that's the competition people do to prove that they're not losers!

Everything that is times a godzillion, will you destroy and uncreate it all? Right and wrong, good and bad, POD and POC, all 9, shorts, boys and beyonds.

I'd like to change this, and it's not changing. What do I need to do?

Gary: Well it's a lie that you're petty. You're seeing the pettiness of others and you assume you must have something similar because you can perceive it.

When people have discomfort about money, and I give them money, it always blows their mind and changes their paradigm.

That's it. I can't keep going on like this, paying for other people.

Gary: According to whom?

Oh, Gary!

Dain: Okay, do this. Take the amount of money you have in the bank right now and look at how many dinners you would have to buy before you ran out of money.

(Laughing)

Dain: How many hundreds of thousands of dinners, however many it is for you, now divide that by the number of days in a year, how many years of dinners could you buy without running out of money?

Gary: Those of you who have some money have to look at this. You ain't ever going to be out of money because that's not your choice. You wouldn't do it.

One of the greatest gifts I ever got was working for the United Way. I had to go out and talk to all the charities that gave food and things to people. Then I had to talk to the people who received the stuff.

I discovered, in talking to homeless people, that they thought I was nuts for having all the money I had, because that meant I had to pay rent and I had to work!

I looked at it and thought, "I don't want to live on the street." The only difference between you and someone who has no money is that you will never let yourself have no money—because that's not your reality. "I might run out of money." No, you won't!

I find people's discomfort about paying a bill to be almost unbearable. Is it just a matter of sitting with that discomfort?

Gary: Yes, it's a matter of sitting with that discomfort and then making them have more discomfort. When people invite me out and assume I am paying, I sit there on my hands and do nothing. I sit there and sit there and let them figure it out. They are going, "Oh my God, oh my God, he's not going to pay, he's not going to pay, he's not going to pay," and when they finally get to the point where they start to reach for the bill, I say, "Oh, I've got it." You've got to learn to make people suffer. You'll pay the bill rather than allowing people to have their discomfort. I love letting them sit there in their discomfort.

I knew a lady who used to get everybody to pay for her. She would never offer to pay for anything. I would keep her on waiting. I would sit there until she was so uncomfortable she would go, "Uh, uh, uh." She knew she had to leave and she knew she had to get a ride and she knew she had to get somewhere and she couldn't use somebody else if she couldn't get me to let her use me. I would just sit there and look at her and smile as if to say, "Well, when are you going to contribute?"

I knew she wasn't going to, but I thought I might as well torture her. If she was going to torture me by making me pay, then I was going to torture her back. That's not getting even, folks. That's recognizing that the only way a person is going to become aware of what they're choosing is by using what they're choosing as a thing you can contribute to them, so they recognize what their choice is.

Make them uncomfortable enough and they might choose to stop doing that. Then again, they might not. It's not what you're trying to get them to do. It's the fact that you have to enjoy making them uncomfortable. Let's run this process one more time:

> What generative capacity for the solidification of the elementals into reality by request of the quantum entanglements fulfilled as always out-creating all competition are you refusing to create and institute? Everything that is times a godzillion, will you destroy and uncreate it

all? Right and wrong, good and bad, POD and POC, all 9, shorts, boys and beyonds.

Question: Gary, is that an example of what we were talking about yesterday, of joyfully overriding other people's limitations?

Gary: Yes, it's joyfully overriding other people's limitations. You sit there with somebody who's planning on your paying and you joyfully override their limitations. Their point of view is that they can make you pay. You make them doubt that you're going to pay. When their doubt is sufficient to make them hysterical, you pay. You override their limitations to the point where they're going "Oh my God, I might have to pay! I can't do this again!" All I want is for them to stop doing that to me, because it isn't kind.

Being joyful about it means you're out-creating. Is that it?

Gary: Yeah.

I see. I would buy all that discomfort and embody it. But being joyful is out-creating.

Gary: Being joyful is out-creating their limitations and it's out-creating their competition. Their competition under those circumstances is "Can I out-compete this person and wait long enough so he pays?" That's how they win and you lose. That's what they're trying to do. You've got to get clear about how all of this stuff works or you become the effect of the people who are sly enough to use your money against you.

Dain: What generative capacity for the solidification of the elementals into reality by request of the quantum entanglements fulfilled as always out-creating all competition are you refusing to create and institute? Everything that is times a godzillion, will you destroy and uncreate it all? Right and wrong, good and bad, POD and POC, all 9, shorts, boys and beyonds.

Gary: Nice! This conversation is making a few of you uncomfortable, which makes me happy. I am out-creating your limitations.

Dain: Joyfully so.

What generative capacity for the solidification of the elementals into reality by request of the quantum entanglements fulfilled as always out-creating all competition are you refusing to create and institute? Everything that is times a godzillion, will you destroy and uncreate it all? Right and wrong, good and bad, POD and POC, all 9, shorts, boys and beyonds.

Gary: Hopefully you've gotten a few insights into this area.

This has been a phenomenal call, you guys, just phenomenal.

Really good, thank you.

Gary: Take care everybody, love you lots!

Dain: Thanks y'all.

~~~

No Drugs of Any Kind

Gary: Hello everyone. Tonight we're going to talk about the eighth key: No drugs of any kind. A drug is anything that cuts off or diminishes your awareness in any way, shape or form. Anything that makes you less aware is a drug.

People say to me, "You don't like drugs."

I say, "I don't care if you do drugs. It's your life. Do whatever you want."

The difficulty with doing drugs is that when you do drugs you open the door to other entities taking over and using your body. Any place you lose control of your body becomes a place in which another entity can enter or use your body. That's the primary reason for not doing drugs.

Question: Is love a drug?

Gary: Well, does love erase consciousness? Or, in order to have love, do you have to create a fantasy that erases consciousness? In that case, love is a drug.

Dain: In this reality, love functions as though it is a drug, because love isn't about creating more awareness. It is usually based in a fantasy, which leads to more fantasy, with the idea that it will lead to the perfection of a fantasy eventually, but this doesn't create an awareness of what's actually possible.

Gary: Exactly.

Question: Do people use food, alcohol, extreme workouts or sex as drugs? Are they abusing their bodies and cutting off their awareness?

Gary: Anything that cuts off your awareness is a drug. You've got to be willing to be aware of everything. There are a lot of people who do not eat from a conscious place. They don't look at what their body desires; they only do what they have decided to do. The biggest drug on the planet is unconsciousness.

What about smoking cigarettes? Are cigarettes a drug?

Gary: Well, do they alter your consciousness? Do they cut off your awareness? Or do they limit the kind of awareness you are willing to have? It depends on what you're using them for. If smoking cigarettes has little to no effect on you, it's irrelevant.

Dain: There are some people who will have a cigarette and it seems to have no effect on them. They'll have one every now and again, and it's no big deal. Then there are people who are addicted to cigarettes. Every time they are about to be aware, they pick up a cigarette to stop that awareness.

So, it's not "I smoked a cigarette, therefore I am violating this key" or "I had a beer, therefore I violated this key." It's about the awareness you're cutting off, avoiding or running away from.

Gary: You can have alcohol and still be aware. But if you're using it to diminish what you're aware of, that's not good. I had the viewpoint when I started Access Consciousness that people shouldn't smoke cigarettes because cigarettes are bad for your health. What question is that? I'm sorry, some people do just fine with smoking. The important part here is to ask, "What am I using this for?"

Question: I have to ask, "How many great works of art, literature and music are created by artists who are under the influence of some drug?" I understand that in some cases the drug destroyed them—but could those works of art have been created without the drug?

Gary: That's not exactly the right question. A more interesting question is: Would they have been greater had they not been on drugs?

Dain: You're looking at this from the point of view, "Would these things have been created if the artist had not used drugs?" What about asking, "Could their art have been greater if they had not been on drugs? Would they have invited us to an even greater possibility?" The beauty of art is that it opens us up to a different possibility; it creates a question in our universe and invites us to experience a different energy.

After I graduated from college, I had a roommate who was a photography student at the Brooks Institute. He started every day by filling his bong and smoking a bowl of marijuana. He would do it in the afternoon as well. Apparently he was a great photographer, but I observed that when he was in the intensity of smoking, you could wave your hands in front of his eyes and say, "Hello. Are you there?"

He'd be like, "Dude, I'm composing my next shot."

I wonder if his level of brilliance would have been greater if he had been more present.

I used to like to smoke pot because it seemed like it was the only time I actually felt good, and yet afterwards, I always felt worse. A big part of that is that when you give up control of your body on drugs, you open the door for entities to enter. It took me a long time to get rid of those frigging things.

I also discovered that my personal sense of creativity grew dynamically as I went beyond the drugs. So I wonder what other possibilities these artists could have created if they had chosen to become more present. It would be interesting to see what else might have been possible.

Question: Last week we were talking about no competition, and someone asked if addiction was a way of avoiding competition. Gary, you said yes, it was. Can you blend that with what we're talking about right now?

Gary: Drugs are a way to avoid competition. You use drugs to cut off awareness, so if somebody is highly competitive and they cut off their awareness, what do they become aware of?

People usually do drugs and alcohol because they can't handle all the awareness they're having. That's the primary reason for drinking and using drugs of any kind. You don't know what to do with all the awareness you have, so you diminish it and cut it off with drugs.

Question: If artists are on drugs, are they the ones creating the work of art— or is some entity doing it? Take Van Gogh for example. Maybe he wasn't doing the painting. Maybe an entity took over?

Gary: That could be, but more than anything, I think artists do drugs because their vision is blurred by picking up other people's thoughts, feelings and emotions. They're psychic and they pick these things up, and this alters their perception in ways they can't figure out or handle. They use drugs to cut off the awareness of other people's thoughts, feelings and emotions.

Dain: They don't get that they're picking up the thoughts, feelings, emotions and points of view of other people—and they also don't get the awareness of their own potency. It seems that people who do drugs and get addicted to them are trying to avoid an awareness of the creative, generative energy that would allow them to create anything they wanted in their lives. And it seems like they want to avoid an awareness of their potency and power. They seem to feel they have to cut it off at all costs.

Gary: We say, "no drugs" because we're trying to get you to step into a greater level of awareness and capability.

Dain: Drugs make you gravitate backward toward a level of density. The intense vibration of space that you can be is actually much more valuable than the density you gravitate to with drugs.

Gary: Another part of it is that because most of you think that competition is wrong, you try to avoid competition while at the same time being competitive. In order to avoid competition with others, you try to make yourself into the most common denominator. In other words, you try to make yourself as unconscious and unavailable as everybody around you.

People have come to me and said, "Well, I guess I can't be in Access Consciousness."

I'd ask, "Why?"

They'd say, "Well, do you know what I do to make my money?"

"No."

They'd say, "I grow pot."

I'd say, "You're growing pot. So what?"

They'd ask, "What do you mean, 'So what?'"

I'd ask, "Are you selling it to little children?"

"No."

"Then who are you selling it to? People who deal drugs?"

"Well, yeah."

"If you made alcohol, I wouldn't have a problem about it. If you made ugly chairs, I wouldn't have a point of view about it. It's just what you do."

They'd say, "But, but, but, doesn't that mean I'm dedicating myself to unconsciousness?"

I'd say, "No, you're creating money through unconsciousness. That's where most of the money in this reality is created from—unconsciousness."

Question: Karl Marx said that religion is the opiate of the masses for a reason, because it does change your consciousness.

Gary: It doesn't change your consciousness; it eliminates it.

Yeah, well that would be a change.

Gary: It would be a change—but not for the best. Yes.

When you put an addiction across from a teetotaling, religious perspective, they're at opposite ends of the spectrum.

Gary: Yep. It keeps the masses doing exactly what they're doing on the treadmill of stupidity.

Would the same thing apply to politics?

Gary: Well, let's not go down that line. That's a drug of its own.

I'm just inquiring.

Gary: Of course it applies. How much stupidity do they have to have to become politicians? And how much stupidity do they have to believe we have to think that we want to have them there?

Can you take this right into television and a number of other media?

Gary: You can take it into everything that is called this reality. The reason we say "no drugs" is because what we want you to do is find your reality, not buy this one.

Question: I'm so grateful for a place where we can discuss this stuff in a totally different way. For so long I have heard the same conclusions and answers about drugs when I know there's a different possibility. My question relates to the drugs we are prescribed to control our bodies, for example, contraceptive pills. When I first started taking them, I was very angry that I had to use them to avoid getting pregnant. I must have been aware that there was another possibility for having choice with my body, but I didn't know what that could be.

Gary: First of all, if you go to a doctor and the doctor prescribes drugs, are you going to trust their point of view or your own? You can look at their viewpoint, say, "They have the answer," and give control of your body to them. Is that where you want to go? We're talking about control of our bodies.

For many years, I relied on the pill and only recently chose to stop taking it, as I was aware that my body was changing after doing all this Access Consciousness stuff. It was not responding the same way it had previously. I created a pregnancy not too long after that. I went through a termination and all that, which was not the total drama I tried to make it into. I received from this experience an aware-ness about how I have made being a woman and having female parts so signifi-cant, particularly because I feel I don't have control or say in how my body works and when it works.

Gary: Being a man or being a woman can be a drug, because it allows you to cut off your awareness of everything else. When you function from infinite being, infinite body, you have a totally different choice about how you function with your body.

I get that taking the pill, at least for me, was a way to avoid the awareness and the choice I could have with my body. I'm now asking, "What else is possible?" because I still feel stuck in the significance of what my body and my mind cre-ate without the drugs to control it. What really is possible with our bodies? Can we really choose to have something completely different? And what would that look like?

Gary: You might want to start running this process:

What projected future realities that can never be am I using to eliminate the awareness of my body with total ease? Everything that is, will you destroy and uncreate it times a godzillion? Right and wrong, good and bad, POD and POC, all 9, shorts, boys and beyonds.

Question: Gary and Dain, this has been an amazing series. I'm delighted and wowed. I have a question about my daughter. We have an interesting, amazing, powerful, beautiful, twisted, bizarre, demented relationship. There are drugs involved, and the legal system is already in the picture. These are my tickets and they are working when I'm not jumping out of them—allowance, no significance, staying present, awareness versus what I wish for her, and not being vested in the outcome. I opened the Foundation manual last week and found another one: no resistance. My world is still opening from the impact of those words: resistance to drugs versus no drugs, resistance to jail, resistance to anything.

All these things are working, yet I still feel like a pull toy or a yo-yo. I keep getting in trouble with wanting her to choose something different. What is it that keeps sucking me back in?

Gary: What keeps sucking you back in are the projected future realities about being a mother that can never be. Run all of those about being a mother, about being a mother to her and about not being a mother and about not being a mother to her.

Also run the projected future realities that she's going to die and the projected future realities that she's going to jail.

Question: I'm apparently addicted to unconsciousness. How do we handle the addiction part?

Gary: Well, the addiction part is the fact that addiction is what you use to try and hide from your awareness. So you might ask:

How much of my awareness am I trying to eliminate with the drugs I am choosing? Everything that is, will you destroy and uncreate it times a godzillion? Right and wrong, good and bad, POD and POC, all 9, shorts, boys and beyonds.

If you're talking about someone else's addiction, know that you can't solve someone else's addiction. You can only encourage it. You could say this: "I get that you would rather die than be present, so if there's anything I can do to help you, please let me know." That's called a wedgie.

Question: When I was younger, I drank a lot, and I eventually decided to quit. I thought, "Great, I'm going to be aware and conscious now." Then I would go to a party and if someone was smoking pot, I would get high or if somebody was drinking, I'd be drunk. Is that a capacity? How could I make that different or be more in choice with that?

Gary: You've got to acknowledge what your body does. If you're the kind of person who takes drugs out of other people's bodies, you're going to be aware of the drugs they use. You may try to make it real or to make it yours because you're aware of it.

Ask, "Is this person taking drugs? Is this person doing drugs?"

You described going to the party and having all those things happen. You're in competition to be like others. This is why people try to get together in groups. They never want to be totally alone. Groupthink is competition, brought together as a team effort, for the destruction of the species. That's what drugs and alcohol are mostly about.

In this reality, people make unconsciousness a team sport. Everybody is competing to see who's the drunkest, most stupid and least aware. People compete to be, do, have, create or generate unconsciousness.

Gotcha. The expression I always use with teams is "Don't forget: There's no 'I' in team."

Gary: Exactly. That's what happens when you become part of a team.

Yeah, you give up your individual…

Gary: Yes, people want to be part of the team. That's why they look for community and the things they think community will give them. They're looking for who they belong with and all that kind of stuff, because they're competing to be part of a team. Most people are willing to join the team of unconsciousness.

Question: I was raised with people who have the point of view that drugs are conscious and taking drugs is about having more consciousness and being more consciousness. There's also the Native American point of view; for example, the traditional peyote ceremony is part of their religion and it was about being conscious.

Gary: Hold just a minute. The idea was that you took drugs and altered your consciousness and then you became aware of other realities. It was about the awareness of other realities; it was not about consciousness.

Yes, that's the accurate wording, thank you.

Gary: Taking drugs was never about consciousness, even in the 1960s. It was about altered states of consciousness that were supposed to give you awareness of other realities. I grew up in the 1960s; I did the drugs; I was good at it; I was better than any of you will ever be. The point of view was that you couldn't get there any other way. That's the lie.

Dain: That's the biggest lie in all of this stuff, and it's the one that sticks you—the idea that you can't get that effect (or something greater) if you don't use drugs. I don't know about you, but I've had much greater experiences with Access Consciousness than I ever had on drugs, even the psychedelic kind.

We recently did an Energetic Synthesis of Communion call that was more like a psychedelic trip of possibilities than anything I have ever experienced. And the only hangover you get from that is greater awareness. The idea that there's no other way to deal with your awareness or become aware of other realities and other possibilities except through using drugs is a huge lie that has been perpetrated on people.

The other thing is, when you do drugs, you activate your sensory cortex, which turns up your talents and abilities. Everything you perceive is intensified and locked into your sensory cortex. So, every limitation you think you're overcoming while you're on drugs, you're just hiding away into a deep corner of your mind that you can't access unless you're on the drug.

Gary: You can't even access those things while you are on the drug. Basically you take these things and you store them in the sensory cortex. They then get activated based on some trigger that you have no control over.

I never heard it put that way, and I finally got it. Thank you.

Gary: We live in a drug culture right now. There's always a drug that's supposed to make you feel better, look better or have sex more easily. Dain and I were working with a woman who had gone to raves when she was younger. She did all kinds of drugs. The drug she used had been locked into her body so completely that she couldn't even feel her body. We did some work on the sensory cortex aspect of her drug use and later, when I touched her arm, she almost jumped out of the car because it was so sensitive. Her body had been de-sensitized by the drugs she had used.

Have you used drugs to de-sensitize your body, de-sensitize your awareness, and de-sensitize your awareness of the insanity of this reality? Everything that is, will you destroy and uncreate it times a godzillion? Right and wrong, good and bad, POD and POC, all 9, shorts, boys and beyonds.

A lot of people who do drugs do it because it makes them feel like they're outlaws, because it's against the law. They're going against the norm by doing drugs. If it weren't against the law, they wouldn't have the need to do it. Taking drugs wouldn't have the romance, verve and vitality of being an outlaw, taking a chance and living on the edge. People love to play Russian roulette with their lives.

Somebody sent me a cartoon that says, "Our way of life is being threatened by the dark force. We must defend our way of life." What is this dark force that threatens our way of life? It's our way of life!

It's the way of life we choose that determines what kind of awareness we can have. What kind of awareness would you like to have? What kind of awareness are you choosing not to have that you could have?

Did you ever decide that you were the wild child of all your friends? Many people have done that. Have you been the weirdest, the wildest and the wackiest while simultaneously competing to be normal? It doesn't work for you, yet you keep thinking that it's somehow going to work out. It's the drug of choice in this reality—to try and be normal, while trying to be an outlaw, while trying not to be normal, while not being normal. It's a Möbius strip of insanity.

Question: I want to ask about a different sort of drug situation. I've worked with a lot of people who are depressed, and once I began to use Access Consciousness tools with them, I realized that a lot of their depression was about not fitting in. They cut off so much of themselves that they couldn't be who they were. They couldn't access their potency, and then they went on anti-depressants, which flattened them out and made them zombies. That's supposed to be "better." It's crazy what we do. More and more of what's called mental illness is just a sign that people know there's something wrong with this reality, but they don't know what to do with it. Could you talk about anti-depressants and anti-anxiety medication?

Gary: Those drugs are a way of dealing with the fact that you can't handle what you're aware of. I suggest you read *Brave New World* by Aldous Huxley. The people used a substance called soma, which was basically an anti-depressant. It made everybody happy with things exactly as they were. That's the same thing that's being accomplished here with drugs, whether they're legal drugs, street drugs or any other kind of drugs. It's the idea that you can get to the point where you don't care about what's happening around you. And you don't care what's happening to you. That's the purpose of ninety-nine percent of all drugs. They'll say the drug is for all kinds of things, but that's not true. It's a way to make you content with the insanity that's going on around you, as though you will now fit in and you will not have a problem with what's happening.

We did some advanced body work recently and after I had an anti-aging process run on me, I had a sense of contentment that was reminiscent of the days when I would do drugs in order to cut off my awareness so I could have a sense of contentment. Years ago, I used to smoke pot every morning so I could have a sense of contentment with my life even though I wasn't content at all. After doing this process, I had the contentment without a drug. I was simply content with my life.

Dain: I've had a very similar experience with the advanced body processes. It's a contentment that goes beyond me. It's as if the contentment is in the space around me, so when I'm around people, they come out of the pain and suffering they think they need to experience. A sense of peace oozes through them.

Dain, what you said about people who have no idea how to express their potency and their capacity was brilliant. They do anti-depressants, and it takes them even further away from their potency. It's as if they don't have an awareness of their potency or the capacity to express the difference they are. The depression is about not being able to be that and do that. It comes with not being able to express that capacity and potency in life and living. I can see that's a huge reason why people go into depression in the first place. The success rate I'm having using Access Consciousness tools with these people is amazing.

Gary: I have a process here to help you a little bit if you want it.

What generation and creation of secret agendas, beingnesses, fantasies and projected future realities that can never be as the perfection of the drug-induced corpus callosum of sensory cortex filing systems are you using to lock into existence the positional HEPADs* you are instituting to choose drugs and unconsciousness as preferable to total awareness? Everything that is times a godzillion, will you destroy and uncreate it? Right and wrong, good and bad, POD and POC, all 9, shorts, boys and beyonds.

Question: What's the corpus callosum?

Dain: It's the wonderful thing that joins both halves of your brain.

Thank you.

Dain: What generation and creation of secret agendas, beingnesses, fantasies and projected future realities that can never be as the perfection of the drug-induced corpus callosum of sensory cortex filing systems are you using to lock into existence the positional HEPADs you are instituting to choose drugs and unconsciousness as preferable to total awareness? Everything that is times a godzillion, will you destroy and uncreate it? Right and wrong, good and bad, POD and POC, all 9, shorts, boys and beyonds.

Question: It seems that people are using drugs to cut off their feelings of guilt or shame or responsibility.

Dain: The interesting thing here is that ninety-eight percent of their thoughts, feelings and emotions don't belong to them. Ninety-nine percent

---

* See glossary for definition.

of people are doing ninety-eight percent of their drugs to get rid of the 98,000 percent of feelings that aren't actually theirs.

In Access Consciousness, we give people a way to be aware and acknowledge what actually is, which makes them feel lighter. Often this is what they thought they were going to get from the drugs. Instead they always feel heavier after they do drugs. We're giving them a form for their awareness and their capacities that will continue to create lightness, which I think is what they were looking for in the first place.

Yes, that's true for any addiction.

Gary: If everything you perceive when you're doing drugs and alcohol goes into the sensory cortex, you don't have access to it with any kind of ease. It can only be triggered by an outside source that was part of the original conditioning. Say you took the drug then you heard a piece of music. Every time you hear that music, it stimulates that same response you got with drugs, but you have no control over it.

If someone I'm working with is feeling guilty, I talk about guilt as a distracter implant that society and the culture use to try to control us. Many people think guilt is real. They think it's theirs, and when we talk about it, it seems to create more awareness in their universe. They see that they're drinking because of distracter implants, and we use Access Consciousness tools to destroy those implants.

Gary: That's exactly why they're drinking—the guilt and the shame are created by the fact that they know they're not supposed to be doing it. They know they want to do it and they know that they don't know why they're doing it and when they become aware, they have a choice. It's "Okay, I can have total awareness or I can cut my awareness off. Which one would I like here?" Different possibilities open up. Let's run the process again.

What generation and creation of secret agendas, beingnesses, fantasies and projected future realities that can never be as the perfection of the drug-induced corpus callosum of sensory cortex filing systems are you using to lock into existence the positional HEPADs you are instituting to choose drugs and unconsciousness as preferable to total awareness? Everything that is times a godzillion, will you destroy and uncreate it? Right and wrong, good and bad, POD and POC, all 9, shorts, boys and beyonds.

Question: Does this clearing unlock all the stuff we've locked into the sensory cortex?

Gary: I hope so. I have no idea. As we have been talking, I have been feeling this energy—and I turned it into a process. Hopefully it will start to unlock that stuff and give you more awareness and more choice.

Question: When I was a teenager, I was anorexic for many years. I know that I was aware of the insanity that my parents were perpetuating, mostly between each other and that I felt impotent to do anything about it. There was no place I could contribute to it and I knew my big issue was control.

Gary: Whoa, whoa, whoa, darling. Number one, please listen. When you say, "my issue was" or "my issue is" you're locking in a lie.

It's not your issue. An issue means something that is given to you, so it can't be yours. An issue has been given to you. It is not something that is ever yours. The whole idea of "my issue" is a travesty the psychological community has visited on people. It's the idea that the thing that was given to you as a point of view is yours. It isn't yours. Ever. This is really important, please get this.

Yes, I see that. If I make it mine, I can never be free of it.

Gary: Exactly, you can never change it and you can never get clear—because you're functioning from a lie.

I used to alter my consciousness or what I was aware of with starvation, sleep deprivation and over-exercising. That would totally take me out of being present to what was happening.

Gary: Those were things you locked into your body with the adrenaline pump you used—and there are a lot of people who use an adrenaline pump as a drug.

Will the process that you're running now address that?

Gary: I believe it will. If you've had any drug issues or drug use or if you were subjected to drugs and alcohol as a kid, you might want to put this process on a loop and run it nonstop until you suddenly find change in your world. Let's do it again, Dr. Dain.

Dain: What generation and creation of secret agendas, beingnesses, fantasies and projected future realities that can never be as the perfection of the drug-induced corpus callosum of sensory cortex filing systems are you using to lock into existence the positional HEPADs you are instituting to choose drugs and unconsciousness as preferable to total awareness? Everything that is times a godzillion, will you destroy and uncreate it? Right and wrong, good and bad, POD and POC, all 9, shorts, boys and beyonds.

Question: When I used to smoke pot on the odd occasion, it was too intense for me, so I would avoid it. I have the same point of view about total awareness, that it would be way too intense.

Gary: Well, total awareness will be intense, but it will also be intensely spacious. Drugs are about the intensity of density. Total awareness will give you intensity of space. The intensity of space is not contractive, impelling or impactful. It's expansive. It's about possibility and joyfulness. So yes, you will have an intensity of awareness.

We've misidentified and misapplied taking drugs with the idea that we were getting more aware. We thought drugs were going to create awareness or consciousness. That's the line we were given about the purpose of drugs. We assumed that consciousness would create the same intensity of the altered state of awareness that we got from drugs, and that's not the case. Let's do the process again, Dain.

> **Dain:** What generation and creation of fantasies, beingnesses, secret agendas and projected future realities that can never be as the perfection of the drug-induced corpus callosum of sensory cortex filing systems are you using to lock into existence the positional HEPADs you are instituting to choose drugs and unconsciousness as preferable to total awareness? Everything that is times a godzillion, will you destroy and uncreate it? Right and wrong, good and bad, POD and POC, all 9, shorts, boys and beyonds.

Question: What's coming up for me is that the choice for drugs and anti-consciousness is a choice for a closed system and separation. It's a total separation, whereas awareness is more like the Kingdom of We.* Can you talk about that a little bit?

Gary: The big reason we say no drugs is because if you're doing drugs, the primary reason you're doing it is to separate you from you. You separate you from your awareness and you from everybody else. At the same time you're trying to be like everybody else. That creates the Kingdom of Me.

Once, many years ago, when I was doing drugs, a friend of mine left some money with me. I decided that I needed his money, so I took it. I thought it was fine for me to take it because it was in my house. I had the use of it; therefore it was mine. I would never have done such a thing under normal circumstances. It would have been outside my reality of what was possible.

I then had to go out and sell some of my things in order to create the money to pay the guy back. It took me two weeks to get the money—and he needed the money at the time he needed it, which is why he had given it to me in the first place. I lost a friend, I lost his trust and I lost trust in myself by choosing that. We do those kinds of things when we're doing drugs.

---

* See glossary for definition.

Dain: If we were able to be as the Kingdom of We—if we could be in this reality with our awareness of everybody else's stuff and not feel like we were losing ourselves, drugs wouldn't be necessary or relevant. They would be truly irrelevant to our lives. In this reality, we're not given the tools to create that, so it seems as though we need to fight the fight any way we can. If we were just given the tools to live and to be as some sense of connection rather than becoming swallowed up and inundated with the insanity that this reality is, we'd have a totally different set of choices available.

Gary: Yeah, unfortunately, I think all of us are competing to see whether we can be as stupid as everybody around us.

Question: Is some of this also that we refuse to be or acknowledge where we have connections with each other and with the Earth and the energies we are looking for? What's coming up for me is how many times I had me and I gave it up for other people's points of view or the lie of what drugs would give me.

Gary: Yes, you give you up instead of having an awareness of what is possible. You give you up in favor of the drugs. That's the reason no drugs is one of the keys.

I'm not talking about refusing to take medication you need because your body has an imbalance. You have to ask your body, "Do you need this?"

I worked with a guy who was on blood pressure medication; his blood pressure was too high. His doctor kept telling him he needed to take more of his blood pressure medication—except it never made him better. It only lowered his blood pressure a little bit. Finally I asked him, "What are you creating that is producing high blood pressure?"

It turned out that he was creating an upset, which raised his blood pressure and allowed him to take blood pressure medication, which kept him from being able to get an erection—because his wife didn't want to have sex. This is bizarre, but it is the way we create these situations.

Question: Could you talk about how surgical drugs affect us?

Gary: After surgery, run MTVSS* on the immune system points. You should also run the molecular de-manifestation* and de-molecular manifestation* of the drugs you took. They put too many drugs in our system all the time, thinking that's the way to make sure we're unconscious. They think we're not actually aware while on drugs, which is insane. A lot of things occur during operations; you should also do zero sum of trauma* and other body processes to eliminate the effects of what were done to your body while you were under drugs.

---

* See glossary for definition.

A great deal of what is done to us under drugs invalidates and destroys our body. We want our body to cooperate with us. Does it work for us to invalidate it? No, if we do that, our body is going to eventually give up its connection to us.

Do we make decisions while we're unconscious in surgery? And then afterward, do we not have access to them?

Gary: Yes, that's why we're doing this process. When we're under anesthesia, all the information about our experience goes into the sensory cortex. I had a friend once who was hypnotized to find out why he had such a strange point of view about his penis. He found out that while he was under anesthesia during a surgery, someone in the room was making fun of his penis. He ended up with an off-kilter point of view of what that person said, and it affected him in very negative ways.

Let's do the process one more time, Dain.

Dain: What generation and creation of fantasies, beingnesses, secret agendas and projected future realities that can never be as the perfection of the drug-induced corpus callosum of sensory cortex filing systems are you using to lock into existence the positional HEPADs you are instituting to choose drugs and unconsciousness as preferable to total awareness? Everything that is times a godzillion, will you destroy and uncreate it? Right and wrong, good and bad, POD and POC, all 9, shorts, boys and beyonds.

Gary: Friends of mine who are nurses have told me about the jokes they made about patients while they were in surgery.

If somebody makes fun of your body while you're under anesthesia, these things go into your sensory cortex, and then you have a reaction to them without even realizing what you are reacting to or where a point of view comes from. That's the travesty of talking during surgery. I actually insisted there be no talking during my surgery, and my doctor agreed. I wanted a friend of mine in there to ensure there wasn't any talking, but my friend wouldn't agree to do that. At one point during the surgery, I actually came out of the anesthesia and heard them talking about strange things. Would I trust a doctor after that? Not in a million years. That's why it's important to do this process as well as the processes I've mentioned after you have had surgery.

Question: Last year my father had two operations, one on his prostate and another on one knee. Both times he was put under anesthesia. The first time it was supposed to be in-and-out in one day, but when I got there, he was delirious. I had to stay overnight with him—and it wasn't my father in that body.

The next evening I was able to bring him home and he came back. The second time, he had a knee operation. He wasn't able to have the same general anesthesia because of the reaction he had earlier, so they gave him an epidural, but he reacted the same way. He wasn't even remotely like my father. He had to spend six days in the hospital when he should have been out in three. They wouldn't release him because of his state of mind. Is there anything that can be done for him now?

Gary: Your dad came back from the hospital with another being in his body. But your dad is still there. Remove the entity that inserted itself into his body at the time of surgery. In a situation like this, there is a seventy percent chance you can get it to leave.

When someone goes under the knife and dies while under anesthesia, that person hangs around the operating room, waiting for their body to show up. As soon as they feel a body under anesthesia, they'll step into it because it feels like theirs did.

Do I just do the entity clearing that you generally do with the Access Consciousness? Can I do that long distance? Is that possible? I'm here in the States and he's in the UK.

Gary: Of course you could.

Okay. Thank you.

Gary: Let's do the process one last time, Dain.

Dain: What generation and creation of fantasies, beingnesses, secret agendas and projected future realities that can never be as the perfection of the drug-induced corpus callosum of sensory cortex filing systems are you using to lock into existence the positional HEPADs you are instituting to choose drugs and unconsciousness as preferable to total awareness? Everything that is times a godzillion, will you destroy and uncreate it? Right and wrong, good and bad, POD and POC, all 9, shorts, boys and beyonds.

Gary: Are you beginning to see why drugs are not an asset in your life?

Question: I drank a lot for a long time. When you're in a blackout or unconscious, does it have the same effect that drugs have in surgery?

Gary: Yes, whatever you experience bypasses your cognitive capacity and goes directly into your sensory cortex. You come out the other side of the experience in a reactive state. You react to smells or music or sounds and you have emotions about events that have nothing to do with any information you can access. You didn't think about these things because you were impaired by the drugs.

Get the Access Consciousness reference materials and look up the information on the sensory cortex. Go through it and see where it applies to you and use those processes.

Okay. Thank you.

Gary: You're welcome.

This was a brilliant call, you guys. Thank you.

Yeah, thanks, Dain and Gary.

Dain: Thank you.

Gary: Thank you, everybody, for being on this call. I hope it helps you understand the key, no drugs of any kind. We're not asking you to eliminate medicines your body needs. We're asking you to eliminate anything that cuts off your awareness.

We want to give you an awareness of what your body truly desires. We're interested in your having a willingness to be more in communion with your body, more in communion with the Earth, more in communion with you and more in communion with the Kingdom of We and the possibilities that creates.

~~~

Do Not Listen to, Tell Or Buy the Story

Gary: Hello everyone. Tonight we're going to talk about the ninth key: Do not listen to, tell or buy the story. Unfortunately, Dain can't be with us tonight.

So, what's a story? What constitutes a story? What's the purpose of a story? The purpose of a story is to validate your point of view. It's a way to explain and justify your choices and to make it real that the choice you made is right. Most people have the point of view that if they can get something right then everything in their life will work. But is that really correct? Is that what's really going to work?

Question: Does "story" always imply the past or the future—and not the present moment? Can there be a story from the "now" moment?

Gary: Not really. If you're really being present in life, there is no story. One of the things we do with processing in Access Consciousness is, instead of buying the story and listening to the story, we ask, "Okay, so what's really going on here? What's underneath this?"

The only reason people have a story is to justify their choice. They need to justify why they're choosing what they're choosing. They need to validate that they are right in choosing to have this upset or this problem, whatever it is. They need somebody to evaluate and find them right. So, their story is about the validation, justification and rightness of their point of view. None of those things has anything to do with what's really going on. Stories are usually created based on conclusions that don't have anything to do with what's really happening.

Question: How can I help my thirty-five-year-old daughter, who would rather be dead than continue to deal with intense emotions and psychological pain? She believes all the lies that this reality holds with gratitude.

Gary: She doesn't believe the lies with gratitude—but she does believe the lies. All you've got to do is ask a question, "What would you really like to create, darling? If death is truly more important to you than living, I understand." That's all you can say to anyone.

Question: Do we need to eliminate the word why from our vocabulary—because the only response to a why question is a story?

Gary: It's not only that. Why is like a fork in a road. If you take the right bend all the time, you go in a circle and eventually end up where you started. That's what keeps the story going. Instead of you getting an awareness of what is really going on, you get stuck in the story. Have you ever noticed how somebody who has a story will tell it over and over again as though it's going to get them somewhere—except you never get anywhere with a story.

Have you ever heard somebody say, "I did such-and-such and that's because of this?" When you go into because, you're going into justification.

Question: Is story an answer?

Gary: Yes. A story is the answer to the rightness of your point of view. It's the answer that validates every choice you've made, it's the answer to the explanation, it's the answer to the relationship you would like to have with somebody and it's the answer to something that doesn't occur.

Why do we have to justify the choices we make instead of recognizing we just choose? My point of view is that when you choose in every ten seconds, you can eliminate the story, be present in every moment of every day and do whatever you want to do.

Ninety-nine percent of the people who tell a story can't see it for what it is. So, it's pretty simple: If you want to get clear, don't listen to, tell or buy the story.

Question: Is a point of view a story? Are you saying everything is just a story?

Gary: No. A point of view is something you use to lock into existence something you've decided is so. Points of view are basically locked-in conclusions you come to in order to have a sense that somehow you exist. Most people think they are the sum total of their points of view.

The purpose of a story is to validate your point of view. It explains and justifies your choices and shows that the choice you made is right.

Gary: People believe that underneath every story and every point of view is the real "reason and justification" why the person did something, but that reason and justification has nothing to do with what the person actually chose. A story is the justification for your choice; it's not the reality of what you chose or why you chose it.

Question: What is the difference between a story and an example? Does an example become a story when you add words like because, but or feelings? Would you please talk about buying the story?

Gary: An example is what you do to show people something or to give them an idea of how something applies. A story is something that proves your point of view. How something applies is different from the story.

The words you use aren't that important; it's more about whether your intention is to explain something or to justify your point of view.

When you use the story as an example, then it is not about the rightness or the wrongness of your point of view. It's about showing someone how something applies. That is a story as an example. Don't tell the story unless you are using it as an example. Don't buy the story by listening to other people's points of view about how they think it has to be or how you're supposed to be with it.

Buying the story is when someone tells you what point of view you're supposed to buy into—and you do that. When people tell you what you're supposed to experience, what you have experienced, how something is supposed to be or what you're supposed to do—and you do that—you're buying the story.

Question: What do you say to people who love a story? There are people who build their lives on story: writers, new agers, storytellers, preachers, teachers, historians and Access Consciousness practitioners. There are people who do workshops telling their story.

Gary: There are a lot of people who tell stories. It's fine to tell a story if that's what you want to do. I'm trying to give you tools that will get you out of difficulties in doing your life. Buying the story eliminates your capacity to choose; buying the story eliminates choice. When people do the story, they've made a choice. They've decided what the choice is and they won't change their story because they don't want to change their choice. People tell stories to justify the points of view they take.

People can tell stories all they want, but you don't have to listen to them if you don't want to.

Have you ever watched somebody who was trying to justify their point of view? They use a story to justify and prove their point of view.

I do it when I'm facilitating classes. I use stories to give people an awareness of what I'm trying to talk about. Most people are more willing to listen to the story than they are willing to look at what is real.

Question: Is a story the way we learn and remember things like language?
Gary: No.
Is a story the way we all get brainwashed into contextual reality?
Gary: Yes.
Is choosing to say some words and not others not story?

Gary: No, when you are creating communication, it requires that you be aware of the words you use because the words you use determine the energies that get created between you and another.

So, how do you stop buying the story?

Gary: You just stop.

In Access Consciousness, you talk about the power of words and using correct wording. Is incorrect wording just another story?

Gary: No. Story is always a justification. Story is the reason and justification for the choice you make. That's why you create a story.

Question: When you say, "Do not listen to the story" what do you mean by the word listen? Through my years of being a social worker and teacher, I was taught to listen to people. But sometimes listening feels like I'm allowing someone to do a power-over move on me. It seems like they are manipulative; they are dominating the conversation with blather rather than communicating.

Gary: Yes, that's one of those places where you don't want to listen to the story. When that happens, you should say, "Hold on a minute, will you? I need some clarity here. I do not get the purpose of what you're telling me." They have to re-assign the way in which they are justifying what they're doing, and in so doing, the story usually ends or it changes. Both of which are good for you, because it gets you out of having to listen to crap.

Question: I have always valued listening without questioning. "Oh, she's such a good listener" has seemed like a positive thing to say. Now I'm questioning that. Truth, do people ever really listen anyway? Most people use listening as a way of deciding what they can say or do that will lead to the conversation they want to have.

Gary: Do you all get that? My mother-in-law was perfect at this. She would talk with you about anything and wait until you said the right word that allowed her to jump in, take over the conversation and lead it where she wanted it to go. She considers herself an incredibly interesting person. But people who are incredibly interested by their own point of view are not necessarily listening at all; in fact, they're usually listening for key words they can respond to that will allow them to take over the conversation and make everything work the way they want.

Question: It seems like people are more interested in telling their points of view than listening. Why have we been taught in this reality to listen—as if it's a good and noble thing?

Gary: Well, it is good and noble to listen because that way people can take advantage of you, and we all know that's the purpose of life, isn't it? To let people take advantage of you.

Question: What do people mean when they say listen? Listening could be training in perceiving energy.

Gary: If you listen to the story, you'll notice that it often does not match the energy of what's going on. Why not? Because the person who is telling the story is validating, justifying, explaining, rationalizing and regurgitating it as though that's going to create something different.

Many people I know, including people who do Access Consciousness, tell the story. How do you not listen to the story? Do you walk away or zone out? Do you cut them off, interrupt them, ask a question, listen to the energy of what they are saying rather than the words and throw in a wedgie?

Gary: You definitely listen to the energy of what they are saying, and then, yeah, wedge and walk.

Question: Is a wedgie a way of giving them a different possibility without telling them?

Gary: No, it's a way of asking a question, which requires them to look from a different place or their butt blisters, whichever comes first.

Question: What contribution can I be to myself and my friends when it seems like they are obsessively caught in their story?

Gary: My favorite thing is to say, "Oh my God, I forgot! I've got an appointment. I've got to go, see you later."

Question: How come six of The Ten Keys are stated in the negative form? Just curious.

Gary: Because that's the way people will hear them. Most people do not hear the words *will you* or *do this*. They only hear *don't do this*. It was just easier at the time to state them in the negative form. And it works. That's the real reason. It works.

Question: When I'm in the role of an Access Consciousness facilitator and someone goes on and on, and I've already got the gist or the energy of what they're saying, what are some things I can say that will gracefully shut them up?

Gary: You can say, "Shut up," "Stop, stop, stop," or "Listen. Did you hear what you said?"

They'll say, "What? What did I say?"

Then you have to repeat what they said.

They'll say, "Well yeah, but that's not what I meant."

You'll say, "Yeah, but that is what you said, and that is what you meant because it matches the energy of what you're saying far more than what you think you're saying. But let's go into analyzing this, shall we? Let's try to take this apart so you can get some freedom here." That's how you talk to them gracefully. You've all heard me say, "Shut up" to people, haven't you? Or "Whoa, whoa, whoa?" Sometimes you need to do that.

Question: A story can be such a subtle thing, like "rain." What do you know about rain? There's a ton of story in just one word.

Gary: That's not a story; that's an awareness. Awareness and story are not the same thing. People use story to eliminate awareness. They use story to justify what is not awareness as though it is true.

Question: I see people connecting through shared stories: stories of divorce, stories about having teenagers, stories about buying their first car. What's that all about?

Gary: It's about insanity, which is the way most relationships are created. People create judgment to create connection. What they're looking for in shared story is "Do we have the same judgment? Are we on the same page? Are we judging everything alike?" If so, that means they are together.

Is it really true that we are together, or is that a lie we buy and perpetrate on ourselves to make sure we have someone "there for us?"

Question: Are all stories basically beingnesses?

Gary: No, most stories are projected future realities.

But they're about the past. How are they projected future realities?

Gary: Because they're trying to get you to align and agree with their point of view as though that's going to change and create something different in the future.

Oh, okay. How can you tell a story from beingness?

Gary: You can tell a story from being if you are doing it to create greater clarity. Telling a story for awareness means you're telling it for awareness; you're not telling story for conclusion. Ninety-nine percent of the people tell stories from beingness; they do it to create a conclusion in your world or theirs and in order to make things look a certain way.

Thank you, that's great.

Question: And more clarity means more awareness?

Gary: Yes.

Question: When someone gives you information that sounds real about someone else, what awareness is needed so you can know that it is information—and not a story?

Gary: People tell you all the time about others; for example, so-and-so is doing bad things. Is that an awareness, or is that a judgment? Usually when people are telling a story about others, it's a judgment they are trying to soft-pedal into your world. They make it seem as though it's not important that they're saying it, but it requires you to come to some kind of conclusion. When people give you information about another person, you can usually tell by the way it feels energetically whether it's judgment or whether they're communicating an awareness.

Question: I had a powerful but contrary experience with a dental session this week. I had a violent, early problem with a dentist when I was five. I hit him hard; he then slapped me, swore at me and physically threw me out of his office. It has left me tortured about dental appointments. I have been having mercury removed from fillings as they are forty years old, and I have been forcing myself to go to appointments before bigger issues arrive. Since we just had the no drugs of any kind call, I have been struggling with not judging myself for craving those numbing consciousness-altering drugs.

Gary: First of all, if you are having pain and suffering, taking drugs is acceptable. If you are taking them for a short amount of time in order to accomplish a particular result, there's no problem. If you are using them long term in order to prove that you don't have to be aware or present, it's not good.

When the nitrous oxide hit, I forced myself to observe and inventory the room through the irrational terror I was experiencing. I literally walked through every item I perceived, from sound to smell to color to size comparison of the dentist's hands. Since I couldn't remember the details of all that happened to me as a child, I just grabbed the biggest things: his hands, the smell and the sounds, my size in the chair, my own emotional terror and most importantly, was any of that kid stuff happening now? The nitrous seemed to reduce the emotionalism and helped me focus on details. It was as if it amplified things. That confused me based on our last call, but I continued to focus on inventorying the now and making a demand for change.

Gary: Once again, you just mentioned you demanded a change and you demanded awareness. So you made that demand and this is what's happening for you when you do that.

I had done that exercise during other appointments, but my mind skittered around like a frog on an interstate highway with no results. This time I came to an immediate awareness that I had been running from that experience for much of my life. I've had trouble telling people that I am in pain or sick and expecting to receive kindness or assistance. My mother was very unsympathetic with my behavior in the dentist's office when I was five, and she sent me back to that same dentist for years. Still it was a huge piece of personal competition: "I can do it and I won't ask for help. Damn you for not knowing what I needed and not helping me in any way." To recognize it and move on is life changing. It relieves me of the burden of forcibly standing in my place and getting slapped or having my bad expectations rewarded, not so much physically as emotionally. Intuitively I know what I need and I can provide it. People tell me they feel a contained explosive energy in me.

Gary: That wouldn't be surprising since you've been on suppress forever. I suggest you do some processing on the suppression of anger:

What generation and creation of the suppression of anger as the primary source for the elimination of other people's reality are you using to lock into existence the positional HEPADs* you are instituting as the wrongness of you and the rightness of other people's points of view? Everything that is times a godzillion, will you destroy and uncreate it all? Right and wrong, good and bad, POD and POC, all 9, shorts, boys and beyonds.

I recognize I stepped fully into the now experience. Almost at exactly the same moment, the present dentist said, "You're in pain, yes? I will give you something for that right now. You should never be in pain. Always tell me when that happens and we will take care of it immediately." We became simpatico in the same instant. I'm still very emotional about this. What's happening there? It seems like if I actually came to full awareness, I wouldn't be emotional.

Gary: It's not that full awareness eliminates emotions; full awareness eliminates negative emotions. What you have been experiencing is positive release.

Three hours in the dental chair felt like fifteen minutes.

Gary: Yeah. When you get to the place where you have gratitude and you make a demand, clarity comes. You asked for clarity in the demand that you made and that's exactly what occurred. I congratulate you on being so intense and so great in that.

The expectation of harm or aggression has definitely passed, at least with the dentist. I moved into greater ease with making myself comfortable and asking for help. I feel calmer as well. How do the drugs work in that situation?

Gary: Because you made a demand, all you could do was use them for your benefit. Now people might say, "When I smoke dope, I make a demand that I be conscious with it," but that's not what you're doing. You made a demand to overcome the limitation you were in. When you are smoking pot recreationally, you are not making a demand for anything; you are just smoking recreationally.

Did the drugs actually help me separate from the trauma and drama of the story enough to bring the situation into clearer focus?

Gary: Yes, and that's the reason you want to eliminate the story. You want to create clear focus so you can see what's really there, not what you

---

* See glossary for definition.

thought was there. Your thoughts and emotions are your justification. You were five years old and you had to justify that your mother was doing the right thing or not doing the right thing and you had to make you wrong for forty years. You made the story a justification for many of your fears. The idea of not telling the story or buying the story is to get to the point where you can go behind the story and release what's got the story locked into your reality.

I now realize this information is from the unconscious. Much of it was held inside, outside my awareness. Telling myself that the fear wasn't rational or that the distant event wasn't happening or real any more didn't bring me awareness. Please, what process can be used to find these blind spots of childhood, specifically those that are related to trauma and the story? I have irrational fears with authority figures, and I am rebellious as all get out. I suspect that the experience with the dentist when I was a kid isn't the only reason.

Gary: You might want to run:

What fantasy, beingness, secret agendas, projected future realities and projected present realities for always fighting authority have I made so real that even in the face of total awareness and consciousness, I cannot change, choose or cure it? Everything that is times a godzillion, will you destroy and uncreate it all? Right and wrong, good and bad, POD and POC, all 9, shorts, boys and beyonds.

Question: Recently there was a bombing in Oslo, which has brought up a lot of points of view in the Facebook Access Consciousness group I'm in. There are also places in the world where war is going on and starvation and sexual violence are being used in warfare. What questions can we ask to not get caught up in the trauma and drama of it all? What is the reason people dwell on these kinds of stories?

Gary: Bad news is always the best news from human reality's point of view. You have a choice about how you respond to it. You can look at what's going on and ask, "Why are these people choosing this?" Some people choose their death. Why? Because if they choose their death, they get to choose how it goes, who misses them and all that kind of stuff. You wouldn't think people would have that in their "awareness," but they do, and they don't necessarily desire to change it much.

Question: I was very well trained in justifying my point of view in my family because there was such non-allowance of differing points of view. You said you can tell a story for the purpose of clarity. Could you talk more about that, please? I can see how it's a slippery slope, for example, with my sister. I see that I could use the idea of facilitating clarity to justify my point of view.

Gary: The reason you tell a story is to justify your point of view. That doesn't lead to clarity, nor does it lead to possibility. You want everything you do to create clarity so you have a greater possibility in every moment of every day, in every way you are and in every way you can be. If you don't have that, what are you actually creating?

Limitation.

Gary: Yeah. So, if you don't wish to create limitation, you have to create from the sense of possibilities that are available.

In the dynamic I described, where I felt complete non-allowance, what choices did I have?

Gary: Hold on just a minute. The moment you feel no allowance, stop talking. There are two reasons you do that. When you stop talking, the other person has to go into question. If they go into question, who's in control?

Awareness.

Gary: Yeah. And you want to have awareness.

Yes. I see that I could have chosen to say, "It's an interesting point of view" that they were in non-allowance or whatever their point of view was—and not care so much and not be so vested in having their agreement or approval.

Gary: The whole purpose of telling a story, buying a story or listening to a story is to get people involved in something that is not changeable or solvable. Why would people want to do that? Because if they can get you involved in something that's not solvable or not changeable or something requires you to think about it for long periods of time, then they have eliminated you being present in your own life. It's a form of disempowerment. That's the reason I say, "Don't tell the story, don't buy the story and don't listen to the story." A story only has one purpose—to disempower you. Is that where you want to live?

Question: I had a client recently who said, "I'm looking for clarity. I need clarity. Clarity will help me choose," but she stayed in the story, which prevented clarity, which then prevented choice. I'm wondering if what she was saying about clarity was some type of illusion to keep stuck-ness in place.

Gary: That's one of the greatest difficulties—dealing with people who don't want to be aware while they *say* they're interested in being aware. If someone is telling you a story, you could say, "Could you hold a minute? I need some clarity here. I'm not getting what you're talking about." This requires them to look from a different place, talk from a different place or choose from a different place rather than continue down the same storyline.

If the person starts over again and tells the same story again, that's when I say, "Wait a minute. You just said you wanted awareness."

They'll say, "Yes, well, just let me tell you about this. It's really important," and they'll tell the story again.

I will say, "Okay, my rates just went up."

They'll say, "What do you mean?"

I'll say, "If I have to listen to the story, my rates go up. You started down
a storyline that doesn't match the energy you came in here with, which you
said was the problem you had to solve. So, we can deal with the real energy
of what's going on—or we can deal with your story. My rates double when
I have to listen to the story."

Story is the way people justify their choices. No choice is a choice.
If somebody says there's a choice of x, y or z and nothing else, there is a
possibility that there's something else there they haven't acknowledged or
looked at.

*Question: Often when I'm working with addicts or alcoholics, I listen to a
story. I ask them, "Tell me about your drinking" or "Tell me about your food addiction" and they go into stories—but I get a lot of information from that.*

Gary: You're eliciting a response from them in order to get the information you need to know where to go, and that works. But if people go on
and on about their story—if somebody walked in and said, "My mother
treated me badly and that's the reason I drink. I can't believe she treated me
so badly. She was so mean to me and she was so bad to me and she was
blah, blah, blah," are you dealing with the drinking problem, or some other
problem?

Exactly. Okay.

Gary: Have you noticed that when a person goes on and on about a
story, they never get over it?

Yes. I don't let them stay in their story, but I do get information from it.

Gary: That's fine, but there are a lot of people who tell the story, and the
story continues for a long period of time. They keep going back to it. Why
do they go back to the story? Because they bought the lie that the story is
what has to be changed.

There are people who say that if you're not happy with the story that
you should change the story. No, if you're not happy with the story, there's a
very good chance that the story is not the problem. The problem is whatever
came before the story. You've got to get to whatever came before the story or
you're not going to get a result.

*Question: Sometimes I talk to people who seem like they are lost in an uncon-
scious loop of story. What could I do to create more awareness for them?*

Gary: To change anything, you have to go to what came before the story—not what happened during the story. People loop back and tell the same story over and over again because they're trying to deal with what they think the story is, rather than dealing with what created the story. That's the thing that needs to change.

Question: When I'm present with someone like a client, who continually, endlessly tells the story, is there anything I can do to point them toward the possibility of a different choice? Or do I just sit there and listen?

Gary: Why would you want to do that?

Exactly, it's painful.

Gary: You've got three choices. You could sit there and listen, you could turn on your heel and walk away, or you could say, "You know what? I love the fact that you tell that story all the time."

Thank you.

Question: Would you please talk more about using people's story to your advantage, in the Kingdom of We?*

Gary: When someone has a story, I always notice the energy of what is true. This is usually the first sentence out of their mouth, and it's the strongest energetically. People say things like, "I did this because…" or "I did this just…" or "I did this but…" The first element of what they said is the problem. The *because* or the just or the but leads in to the story that rationalizes, justifies and explains what they did. It makes the story real for them. Is it real? Or is the first thing that was said the reality that nobody's willing to have?

Question: When I'm busy in my story and disempowering myself, I can get caught and go down the rabbit hole so far so fast…

Gary: I know, isn't it fun?

No, it's not.

Gary: It is! You've got to get that it's fun for you or you wouldn't choose it. And when you get to the end of your story, if you start to say, "Wow, that was really fun!" you'll stop doing it so much.

Do you mean to acknowledge that it's fun even though it's torturous?

Gary: It only became torturous after you heard yourself talk too much and said, "Wow, I am boring myself to death!"

Is that the way to get out of it?

Gary: Yeah. Say, "I was boring myself to death. You know what? Story sucks. What am I doing?"

---

* See glossary for definition.

Question: Are all of the things called mental illness, like anxiety, depression, and paranoia, based on stories?

Gary: Yes.

Wow!

Gary: Buying a story is a lie that requires the person to continually lead himself or herself into a lack of awareness and a lack of choice.

I love it. What can we do to change all of this?

Gary: This is the reason we ask you not to listen to, buy or tell stories. If you get clear on what a story is and why people get stuck in their story, you will be able to recognize it—and you will know there's a lie there. When you see that someone is trying to live from a lie, the thing in their life that is screwed up suddenly becomes obvious. Most people think the reason they are screwed up is because of the story they tell. They tell you the story of why they're screwed up, thinking that eventually they're going to get better. Does that ever really work?

No, not at all.

Gary: Never. So what other choices do you have?

Question: How can you work with someone who has spent their life with a psychotherapist and become completely hooked on stories?

Gary: That's what psychotherapy is about. You tell your story over and over again until it "discharges" enough of the charge that you have on it—and then you move on to another, slightly different story. When somebody I'm working with is addicted to the story, I say, "You've got a choice here."

They ask, "What do you mean, I have a choice? I don't have a choice."

I say, "Yes you do. We always have choice. Do you believe it's a free will universe?"

If they say yes, then you've got 'em. If they say no, you shut up and walk away.

Question: I can speak to that, too. As a psychotherapist, when people do the story, I say, "Okay, so if you weren't telling me that story, what would you be aware of?"

Gary: Brilliant!

Question: Can you talk about what comes before the story and how to change that, with some examples?

Gary: A lady came to me who wanted to change her relationship with her mother. I asked, "What is it you want to change about your relationship with your mother?"

She said, "Well, my mother is a bitch."

I said, "It doesn't sound like you want to change your relationship with your mother. It sounds like you want to change your mother or you just want to tell her off."

She said, "Yes, but you don't understand her."

I asked, "What do you mean I don't understand her?"

She said, "Well, every time I say anything to her, she goes, 'blah, blah, blah.'"

I said, "Okay, let's go back to this again. What is it you really want from your mother?"

She had it all justified that her mother needed to change to make the relationship work for her. When I finally asked, "What do you want from your mother" enough times, she suddenly realized that what she really wanted was for her mother to care about her in a particular way. She had decided she wouldn't receive anything that didn't match her mother choosing that specific way of showing her that she cared. Once we got to that, everything started to change for this woman.

Could we look at something I do? I create failure. I go into a load of crap about things that aren't changing. I say, "This isn't changing and that's not changing."

Gary: Yeah, because you try to believe that the story is real.

I've tried looking at the point where it was created, but it wasn't just one point, there were many, many points.

Gary: What came before that creation of the story?

For me just looking at it going...

Gary: You've got to look for what came before the creation of the story.

There's no one single thing. There are lots of incidents that just constantly...

Gary: Incidents are what people use to accumulate information to deliver the story or to make the story real. It's the way they justify what's going on. What came before that? Who you were before the incident occurred? Basically go before that incident. You ask, "What happened before that incident? And what happened before that incident? And what happened before that incident?" You can actually work backward in time to the first time you made the decision or the choice that you could or couldn't do something. That's what opens it up.

Right now that feels inconceivable to me. It goes back to when I tried to gift me and was rejected. It goes back even before that, to the womb. Where do I let go of this?

Gary: Are you talking about your own personal story here?

Yeah.

Gary: Is your story real to you?

Ha! Yeah, otherwise I wouldn't be talking about it.

Gary: You lied to me.

I know it's a story, yet it feels embedded in my molecular structure.

Gary: I understand, but you've made it real. I asked you, "Is your story real?" and you couldn't answer the question to start with.

I was trying to find a way to say no, but it is real to me. I was looking at how I hang on to it.

Gary: It's actually not real. You're making it real. Why are you making your story real?

I'd like to know that, Gary, I'd like to change it.

Gary: Are you vested in the outcome?

I'm not sure what you mean by that.

Gary: If you want to make your story real, then you have to hold on to whatever occurs no matter what. You want to make your story real if you want to make it truth. You have to justify it and add to it in order to keep it in existence. So how much of what you have defined as your story of you and your life is based on a lie? A lot, a little or megatons?

Megatons.

Gary: Everything that is times a godzillion, will you destroy and uncreate it all? Right and wrong, good and bad, POD and POC, all 9, shorts, boys and beyonds.

Question: It seems like you can't have a story unless you're buying into identity, like: I'm a woman, I'm a mother, I'm a this, I'm a that. So, if you destroy all your identities you can't have stories. Is that accurate?

Gary: Yes. I don't have a story because people are always saying, "Your stories are boring." I say, "That's because I don't have any new ones. I don't create any new ones. That would be valuable based on what? As soon as I get rid of something if I can remember the story, I use it forever." Most of you use your story forever—but you use it to keep it in existence.

People use stories to keep their identities in existence.

Gary: Yes, and they keep their stories in order to keep what they have decided is true that actually isn't true about or for them. They try to keep that in existence too.

Wow.

Question: If there's a story, isn't it just a story as long as it has an emotional attachment? If there isn't an emotional attachment, then is it still a story? When is it a story? And when is it not a story?

Gary: A story is anything that justifies your choices or your actions. If you're trying to justify anything with your story or your actions, you're telling a story or you're living the story as though the story is you.

But then don't we have to try to defend a false sense of truth in that story?

Gary: No, you do that when you get emotionally attached to the story. That's a whole other universe. Emotional attachment is much different than just being aware "Okay, this is a story."

Okay, I've got it. Thank you.

Question: In my practice, I work with infants who have come through birth trauma. Part of my goal is to give them a sense of expansiveness beyond their trauma. Obviously, I can't do that with words. Do you have any insights on how to do that, so the story doesn't become the life?

Gary: Have you read the book, *Talk to the Animals?*

No.

Gary: In that book, I describe the zone of awareness every animal has outside of its body. When they are in a traumatic or a fear-inducing experience, oftentimes their zone collapses. Kids who come through with birth trauma tend to have their zone totally collapsed so they have no sense of their personal space.

Are you saying their space is inverted?

Gary: Yes. You have to stand anywhere from eight to twelve feet away from them and grab their zone and pull it out and then extend it another twenty feet behind you.

Okay.

Gary: It's very simple. There's a description of how to do it in *Talk to the Animals.* That would be the easiest way you could learn how to give them a sense of expansiveness with ease. When an animal is injured, usually its zone will collapse and it will tend to not recover well.

Deer were the one creature that I could not get to expand their zone again. Once they were injured and their zone collapsed, they never seemed to come back. I have had dynamic success with horses and cows. I've also had some amazing success with wild animals when they were in rescue centers.

Thank you. I'll give it a try. It will probably help a lot of kids.

Gary: If it works, great—and if it doesn't, go back to what you're doing. Always do what works. Don't do it the way you *think* it has to be.

You can also do this when somebody gets compulsive about a particular story and they go over it again and again. Or you can run their Bars with trifold sequencing systems.*

Question: Going back to the story and wild animals. The other day, I was at the rescue center where I volunteer. I was cleaning a raccoon cage, but I was not being aware, and as I put my hand into the back of the cage to clean it, one of the raccoons bit me. I removed my hand immediately and I noticed that the raccoons didn't have a story about it.

As soon as I saw that, it was all fine. I could approach it in a different way. It was a huge bite. It broke the skin and I had a bruise for about five minutes and then everything went away. It was "Wow! That's interesting!"

Gary: Animals never have a story about anything. Their point of view is, "The sun is up, can I sing? The sun is up, where do I go?" They don't have the point of view that anything has to look a certain way or be a certain way or work a certain way. They're just here. They look at what's available and ask, "Now, where do we go? What do we do?"

Yeah, and the raccoons didn't make a decision about me. It was just an arm in a place that didn't work.

Gary: Yeah, I was at a wild animal center in New Zealand where they let us go in a cage with a bunch of leopards. Suzy was petting them and one was sitting behind me. I was wearing a crocodile belt, which was very stiff. The belt was sticking out about three inches in the back because of the way I was sitting. All of a sudden, the leopard reached forward and grabbed it. I said, "Stop that!"

The trainer was shocked, because if a wild leopard had done that to a regular person, the person would have screamed or yelled or gotten weirded out and thought the animal was trying to bite them. I didn't. I knew he was just checking out my belt, so I said, "No, stop that." The animal had no point of view about it. There was no story for the animal and there was no story for me. And the trainer didn't have a story, either, because he didn't have to deal with a difficulty or a problem.

You've got to get that no story gives you total presence. Story eliminates your presence because story is always about something that happened in the past; it's never about actually being in the present.

Question: Could you talk about the idea that story is locked into our molecular structure?

Gary: What you lock into your molecular structure is lies.

---

* See glossary for definition.

When we do that, is it even ours? Or is that just a pattern that's come from the field as it were?

Gary: The science of this is that when you intersect a thought, feeling or emotion with one of the molecular structures of your body, you actually elipticize the cellular structure and that's the beginning of "disease." You lock it in through the thoughts, feelings and emotions, the sex or no sex point of view that you take.

This has to do more with judgment than anything else. When you try to justify your story based on your judgment or when you try to justify your judgment based on your story, you can lock that into the cellular structure of your body. That's a reason we try to get people to do body classes. The body processes are extremely dynamic in unlocking this stuff, so you will have greater freedom with your body than you have had in years.

I get that and I'm locking that stuff in, but is it even mine to start with?

Gary: It doesn't matter.

But we're taking it on as ours.

Gary: Don't tell the story, listen to the story or buy the story. For example, let's say you're Jewish and your family feeds you what it means to be Jewish. The rest of the world impels their point of view about what it means to be Jewish. So you lock that into the cellular structure of your body and you lock that into your life as though it's real. It's not real. Are you a Jew or are you an infinite being? You've got to get the difference. It doesn't matter whether you're South African or English or American or Aussie or Swedish or anything else. You've got to get that these are culturally impelled points of view. You also get them about being a man or a woman.

So, we're actually unlocking lifetimes and generations of time and patterning?

Gary: Yeah, exactly. That's the reason we say, "Don't tell the story, buy the story or listen to the story." I had a friend who was Jewish and I didn't know he was Jewish because I don't have a point of view about what Jewish is. I didn't have the point of view that it meant anything. He was having a terrible time and I asked, "What's wrong?"

He said, "You don't know what it's like to be Jewish."

I asked, "What do you mean?"

He said, "People talk about how you look and stuff."

I said, "I don't understand. You look like a person to me."

He said, "No, no, no. It's as if people keep trying to see if my nose is big.

I said, "I don't see a big nose. What are you looking at?" He was creating a whole universe based on that.

If we choose, as you say, to come into the family we come into, do we then have a proclivity to come in with that patterning or that story, so we just repeat the story that we're trying to get out of?

Gary: I don't believe so. I think we come in with the idea that we're going to change the story. And when we fail to change it, we start buying the story and making the story more real for us.

Question: When I first meet people, they often start asking me questions like "Who are you?" and "Where are you from?" Are those questions part of a story? Are those people looking to interface with something in particular?

Gary: People create connections through judgment. And they create separation through judgment. When people ask me, "Where are you from?" I say, "Everywhere." When they ask, "What do you do?" I say, "Anything."

They say, "No, no, no, I need to know what you do. What do you do?"

I just ask them about what they do, and they will say, "I do this, this and this." They don't really want to know what I do. They just want to choose whether they can judge me and separate from me or be close to me.

I went out with a woman one time. She said, "I think we'll get along beautifully. You like good pens and El Caminos, and so do I."

Uh…I think there's a little more to life than good pens and El Caminos. That's my awareness. That's what is true for me.

She "needed" to have a connection to somebody who had similar ideals. She thought that if you liked the same things, then you would get along well in a relationship. That's the way the majority of the world functions. That's the reason they ask you to tell your story. They want to find out whether they can reject you.

Question: My French students keep asking me questions about your story. They want to know everything about you, what kind of business you were in before you created the Bars, and so on. I'm stuck with that because I don't want to go down that path.

Gary: Well, you could tell them, "From his point of view, his past doesn't exist. Everything he did before he came to Access Consciousness was exactly right in that it prepared him for what he's doing now. What he did doesn't really matter. All of it applies to what he's doing. What if everything you have done"—and this is the question you want to ask them—"is preparing you for what you're going to do? It's not as though your story is the value of you."

Question: You talked about animals not doing story. What's the difference between a decision and a story? If they go through water in a certain place and they get bitten by a snake, for example, they won't go through water in that area again. They have conclusions, computations and decisions. What's the difference?

Gary: They don't have a story about it because they're not looking at it from "Okay, now that I've been bitten by a snake, I have to be a crazy animal all the time" or "I have to do x, y or z or I have to blah, blah, blah."

We create justifications for everything, none of which has anything to do with choice. Story is a way of eliminating true choice.

So, if they choose not to go through that water again so they won't get bitten by a snake, isn't that a story? They're saying, "I'm not going through water again because there could be a snake in it."

Gary: That's a conclusion, but it's not a story.

So, "going through water means getting bitten by a snake" is not a story. It's a conclusion.

Gary: It's a conclusion. You can have a conclusion about anything. It's a story when you use it to justify what you choose.

Right, so they lock that into their bodies as well. My horse has been abused. He was pushed and kicked, and all that is locked into his body. And a lot of horses won't let you put a saddle on them. They'll kick like crazy because a saddle means this...

Gary: Those are conclusions they come to, but they don't have a story about it.

Other than asking them to destroy and uncreate that, would bodywork be a good way to...

Gary: Bodywork is great, and it's also a matter of getting them calm. I knew a lady who had a stallion that would buck. I could put somebody on his back in a stall and then lead him out and he wouldn't buck. But if you put a saddle on him when he was in the open, he would buck. Saddle meant "fight," people meant "it's okay." That's conclusion; that's not a story.

Bodywork would be putting your hands on them and asking them what their body requires? That would be enough to release the abuse?

Gary: Exactly.

Question: Does the clearing statement take them to the moment before the story or the decision?

Gary: Yes. That's the reason someone can tell a story and you can ask, "Would you like to POD and POC that?" If they say yes, there's no problem; if they say *no*, there's a problem.

A lot of people will say, "Yeah, I'll POD and POC it and then I'll put it right back in place—because my story about what I've got as a problem is more real than the problem."

Question: Could you help me get how I've misunderstood and misapplied the importance of details? I see that when I ask you to facilitate or assist me in anything, I'm stuck in thinking that telling you all the details about it will assist you in assisting me.

Gary: Probably the best way I can give you this is to ask, "When you're in your house and you shut your eyes, do you know where all the furniture is?"

Yes.

Gary: Can you walk around your apartment without bumping into everything?

Pretty much, yeah.

Gary: "Pretty much" is not the same thing as *yes.*

Okay, I guess, yes then, I could get it to yes.

Gary: If you can get it to yes, then aren't you being aware of everything other than the story of your eyes?

(Laughing) Yes.

Gary: That's because you're being aware of the energy of all things and not just what you see. The thing about the story is not just looking at what you hear, but being the awareness of the energies that come before the story or that get altered because of the story.

And to go beyond that is what would give me a choice for something new.

Gary: Well, it will give you greater clarity than anything else will. Your family always wanted you to justify why you chose everything. If you have to justify why you choose everything, do you really have choice?

No.

Gary: No, they didn't want you to have choice; they wanted you to choose what they thought was important for you to choose.

Right.

Gary: Most families do this. You've got to see that it doesn't matter what they wanted you to choose. It only matters what you choose and what works for you.

Okay. And is there ever any value in telling the story to celebrate something or for inspiration? I have stories that I tell because they reveal the magic that I created in my life.

Gary: That's fine.

I just wanted to make sure that it wasn't just a waste of time or that there wasn't an identity in that.

Gary: You've got to know what you're trying to do and what you desire to create. If you desire to create clarity or inspiration, that's one thing. That's not a story. There is no justification involved when you wish to inspire people. It's a story when you're using it to justify something.

Question: If someone's telling me a story, sometimes I'll ask, "If you took all the facts of that, could you tell a different story?" When they do that, they can see it's just a story.

Gary: That's one way of getting them to change their perspective so they come out of justification. Everybody has to use a technique that works for them.

In Access Consciousness, we use the clearing statement to energetically clear what came before the justification that created the story. We just go to the energetics of it and POD and POC it.

Some people do the psychological thing. Some groups say you just need to rewrite the story to get a different ending. But what if you just had no story at all—and no ending? What if there was nothing to have a story about? Other people just want to hold on to their justifications. It might be interesting to ask them, "What's your justification for keeping this story?" Steve Bowman just asks people, "Would you like to change that?" Sometimes that's all it takes for people to drop the story.

Question: It seems like when we go to story, we're expressing a preference for solidity over exploring the fullness of space.

Gary: Yes, when you're doing story, it's always about diminishing the space that's available.

And that's what keeps the story solid.

Gary: Yeah, that's what keeps it solid. You've diminished the space in an attempt to keep something real that isn't. Stories are almost always a lie about what's really going on.

Is it also identifying ourselves with density? We're identifying ourselves as that density, and the space gets overlooked?

Gary: At the beginning of this conversation, I said the purpose of the story was to justify, rationalize, explain—and what else? To prove the rightness of your choice. Those are the reasons one has a story. You make the story solid and real, and then you have to justify every choice you made thereafter. Is that really where you want to live? That's the reason I say, "Give up the story." This is the worst key of all.

Question: The worst? Why?

Gary: It's the worst one because everybody tells stories. And all of you are trying to see how it's appropriate or not appropriate to justify your story.

I want to say thank you. The question you gave us, "Do you believe it's a free will universe?" opened up a whole universe of possibility for me. It enabled me to ask myself a couple of questions: What story am I using to justify the limitations in my life? What story is my life justifying?

Gary: There you go. Stories are justifications. I hope you all got some clarity from this conversation.

~~~

No Exclusion

Gary: Hello everyone. This is our final conversation about The Ten Keys. Tonight we're going to talk about the tenth key: No exclusion.

I'd like to start by reading an email that came in, which I personally appreciated tremendously:

Gratitude and thanks. Thank you for doing this amazing teleclass. I cannot even begin to tell you all the amazing stuff that has happened during these weeks. I have stepped into so much more potency and wow, who knew it was only a choice and not even hard? No words can say how much this contributed to my family, my work, my home and my life. Having been in deep depressions for a decade or so, I have a smile on my face knowing I can choose and create so much I never dreamed possible. I can only say a godzillion thank yous for being who you are and allowing us to know that we be. I also want to send gratitude to the participants of this class—what amazing contribution you be—and to me, for choosing to follow the energy and see what else is possible.

Dain: Yay!

Gary: I'm very grateful for this email. I hope all of you have gotten some dramatic change from these calls—and if you haven't, I hope you will go back and listen to the calls again a few thousand times. Each key, if you apply it, will take you to a level of freedom that could set your life on fire and create something greater than you ever knew was possible.

Okay, does anyone have a question?

Question: Could you clarify the difference between awareness and any violation of The Ten Keys?

Gary: These are the keys to total presence, total awareness and total possibility in every choice you would like to make. It's not about whether you violate them. It's about looking at them and seeing how to use them to make your life better.

How do we know we are having an experience of awareness and are not just trapped in the logic of non-interesting point of view, story, competition or significance?

Gary: That's the reason we gave you The Ten Keys, because each one of them will take you out of the place of conclusion and assist you to move into the place of awareness.

I seem to confuse functioning with awareness and getting it right. What's the experience of functioning from awareness versus functioning from a point of view?

Gary: Awareness has no point of view.

Dain: When you're functioning from awareness, there's a lightness. There's no need to prove that what you're saying is right. There's no need to say a frigging word to anyone about anything.

Gary: Unless someone asks you a question.

Dain: Right. When you have a need to tell someone something or a need to be vindicated in your point of view, that's not awareness.

Awareness has no need attached to anything. It doesn't need to be verbalized. There's a lightness to it. It's a freedom that, to some people, initially feels like "Oh, I don't care anymore." It's actually a state of greater caring, but you have far less point of view, and the strange thing is that having a point of view is what most people in this reality define as caring.

What is the experience of functioning from awareness versus functioning from judgment and calling someone an ELF?

Gary: First of all, calling someone an ELF is not about judgment. It's about observing that somebody is being an ELF, an evil little f---. That's not a judgment. It's an observation.

You have the point of view that if you say something negative, it's a judgment and if you say something positive, it's not a judgment. No. Positive can be as big a judgment as negative.

Dain: And sometimes a lot bigger. The question is "Is there anything negative, about acknowledging that somebody is an ELF?" Is that negative— or are you just observing what is?

Gary: You're just observing what is. When you have just what is, it's light.

How does one keep from making functioning from awareness significant?

Gary: If you're functioning from awareness, it won't get significant. It will just be what is.

Dain: If it's significant, you're not functioning from awareness any more.

How do I know I'm functioning from awareness versus functioning in a story I like?

Gary: Well first of all, in awareness, you usually don't have anything in particular to say. You're just there and you're enjoying it. You're looking at what's going on and you're saying, "That's nice, that's not nice. That's good, that's not good. That's fine, that's a choice, oh well." It's much more …I would like to say blasé, but it's not blasé. It's basically a sense of peace. Nothing seems that important and nothing is that significant.

Dain: The other thing that happens when you function from awareness is that if you get a new piece of awareness or information, you're willing to change your point of view instantly.

If you're in the story, you try to keep the part you like going. You do this even when the other players in the story aren't willing to have it—and even when things are not going in the direction you think they're going. You keep trying to take it where you want it to go. That's the difference between awareness and being in a story you like.

Is it correct to assume you and Dain function from awareness 100 percent of the time and everyone else has a lesser percentage?

Gary: That's funny. No, not quite.

Dain: (Joking) And no, the answer is totally yes. Absolutely.

Gary: No, it's not. You're so lying, Dain.

We don't function from 100 percent awareness, but we function from far more awareness than other people do because if anything feels slightly funky in our worlds, we try to do something to find out what it is and change it.

Dain: A lot of people ask Gary or me a question only if things are wrong or if they run into a wall they can't get around; otherwise, they never, ever ask us questions. Once I got the tools of Access Consciousness, I said, "These tools will change things." I started to ask questions about everything and anything that was remotely "off" in my world. What is this? What do I do with it? Can I change it? How do I change it? What's that going to take?

There are far greater possibilities for awareness available than anyone in this reality will tell you. Awareness is the key to the freedom that you've been looking for. But because awareness is the key to being different, nobody wants you to know this. What would it be like if you stopped excluding from your life the truly amazing infinite possibilities that can occur when you ask questions about things you would normally not ask questions about?

Question: Is an ELF always an ELF or do they get to participate in life in ten-second increments?

Gary: The purpose of getting you to recognize an ELF is not about making a judgment; it's the recognition that this person tends to do evil shit. Once you acknowledge that, they tend to change of their own volition.

Dain: They have choice in ten-second increments, just like you do—and just like everybody else does. It's just that they tend to continue to choose to be an ELF for whatever reason.

Gary: But if you acknowledge it, they will tend to change.

Dain: Especially when you acknowledge it without a sense of judgment. I knew a lady who was an ELF. I was really busy at one of the places I was traveling to and I made time to work with her son because I saw this kid had possibilities available. I cancelled three other sessions so I could work with him.

She called me twenty minutes before she was supposed to show up and said, "Sam has decided he doesn't want to go to the session."

I said, "You know what? You are such an ELF."

She called me a day later and said, "Thank you so much for acknowledging me that way," and she actually turned into a nice person.

You don't have to exclude their ELF-dom by judging it. You can create a different possibility when you acknowledge someone as an ELF and you do it from no judgment.

Gary: You want to participate with them in ten second increments to see when they're doing ELF and when they're not doing ELF—not to have a conclusion that they are an ELF and always will be.

Gary, sometimes you talk about your ex-wives—and Dain talks about his step-mom. Will your exes and Dain's step-mom always be the way they were—or can they grow?

Gary: They can change if they choose to. It's always their choice; unfortunately, we don't get to make that choice for them.

Does our holding a point of view about someone make it more difficult for them to change?

Gary: Yes, and that's the place where you're excluding change as a possibility for them.

Dain: Please realize Gary doesn't actually have a point of view about his ex-wives, and I don't actually have a point of view about my step-mom. We're not putting that out as a point of view; we're using that as humor to try to get people to see things...

Gary: From a different direction. I'm always surprised when my exes go back to where they were functioning from. I somehow expect that with me working on all of my kids and with them being connected to my kids, that they will change. It is more startling to me that they don't change than that they do the same thing again.

Question: If somebody's being inconsiderate, mean or whatever, can you get to a point where nothing bothers you? Or is that an illusion I'm creating?

Gary: Well, trying to have nothing bother you means it's already bothering you—and that's excluding the place where you can be in humor about them. When somebody's an ELF, I find them humorous. I think they're funny.

Even if it messes up your day or messes up class or has an effect that messes things up for you?

Gary: I'm not willing to get stuck in somebody else's point of view. If you're allowing your day to be messed up by someone, to some degree you're buying something about them. The idea is to get you to the point where nothing affects you and you're just there, being you.

So, you just let it go, like Dain did with that lady?

Dain: Yeah, I would just acknowledge, "Wow, this lady is an ELF. Who would do that to somebody?" She did things like that all the time based on her precious little son. Was I frustrated that I cancelled three people and she didn't show up? Yeah. And when I called her an ELF, I just acknowledged what was. It wasn't from a place of judgment.

Gary: Nor was it from a place of anger. Anger is beside the point. No exclusion means you don't have to give up your anger about it.

Dain could have said, "That was a f---ed thing to do. You're such an ELF." But he didn't have to do that because when you get to the point where you're willing to include your anger in the computation of things, you start to change everything and everyone around you by that alone.

Dain: You don't try to exclude that anger, which takes a lot of energy and a lot of judgment.

Gary: And you don't try to exclude the awareness you have of what they're not willing to be and have.

When you guys do angry, it's very different from the way we do angry.

Gary: We don't exclude our anger from our lives. I don't exclude anger; anger is one of the many things I can be, do, have, create or generate. So if I get angry, know I'm angry.

Dain: That's true. It's very tough to miss.

Gary: I don't try to suppress my anger or my upset about anything.

Dain: But because of that, it's there—and then it's not there anymore.

Gary: Yeah, instantaneously I can flash it and it's gone. It's like being a flasher. I can wear my trench coat and cover up my nakedness and my vulnerability with anger or I can experience my anger and move on. I would rather experience it and move on.

I was hoping you'd say that nothing ever bothered you.

Gary: No exclusion gives you a place where almost nothing bothers you—because you're willing to experience everything. You're willing to include every emotion, every point of view, every reality and every awareness. The thing about no exclusion is to stop trying to cut off your awareness. That's what you do when you try to make yourself good or right or you try to come to conclusion or any of that stuff. Those things are about excluding your awareness and your capacity to choose.

Thank you.

Question: This key gives me trouble with one person in particular. I find myself in so much resistance and reaction to her. I avoid her at all costs.

Gary: This is definitely exclusion.

She leaves messages on my phone, and I simply cannot bring myself to call her back. I simply cannot press the call button. I had not seen this person for several years and when she showed up again, she had been through some major trauma. In the past, I was the one who tried to help everyone out of their messes, a habit I have given up since I discovered I was being a superior asshole and that many people like the messes they are in and don't require me to fix them.

Gary: You are correct about that.

But rather than come to a place of allowance with this woman, I find myself refusing to get manipulated by her victimization.

Gary: Therein lies the rub. You have to be in allowance of the fact that she likes being a victim, which is why she keeps coming back as a victim, because, from her point of view, being a victim gives her some credibility in life.

I'm going to give you a process here. We've talked before about how the basic elements of creation are being, receiving, choice, question, possibility and contribution. Somewhere we got weirded out and we began to think that contribution was the most important product and the most important aspect of these four things.

Question: Can you explain more about how we think the contribution part is the most important element? I'm not getting that.

Gary: Contribution is receiving and gifting at the same time. We somehow think the greatest source of creation is what we can contribute to others or what others can contribute to us, whereas question, choice and possibility, if they are added to contribution, expand everything to a degree that's unbelievable.

Dain: We give up question, choice and possibilities for contribution. We believe someone or something or some choice or some way of being or not being is going to provide for us. This is a huge disservice because we cut off the majority of the generative, creative elements that we have available when we do that.

You can't choose anything unless you have the point of view that it is a contribution to you. For example, being a superior asshole. You would never choose to be that unless you thought somewhere it was going to be a contribution to your life, your living and your reality.

Gary and I found that with fantasies, beingnesses and secret agendas, what you think is a contribution is often 180 degrees from the actual contribution.

Gary: The process is:

What contribution is _____ to my life, my living and my reality? Everything that is times a godzillion, will you destroy and uncreate it all? Right and wrong, good and bad, POD and POC, all 9, shorts, boys and beyonds.

Dain: Let's say there is some Spanish music playing in the background. If you wanted to exclude it, you would ask:

What contribution is this Spanish music to my life, my living and my reality? Everything that is times a godzillion, will you destroy and uncreate it all? Right and wrong, good and bad, POD and POC, all 9, shorts, boys and beyonds.

Gary: And you would also ask:

What contribution is no Spanish music to my life, my living and my reality? Everything that is times a godzillion, will you destroy and uncreate it all? Right and wrong, good and bad, POD and POC, all 9, shorts, boys and beyonds.

Dain: For most things, you want to run both sides of the question. One of those sides will usually have a lot more energy than the other.

You can try running:

What contribution are petulant, angry, withdrawn, covert and controlling women and men to my life, my living and my reality? Everything that is times a godzillion, will you destroy and uncreate it all? Right and wrong, good and bad, POD and POC, all 9, shorts, boys and beyonds.

Gary: You all need to run that one nonstop for about 365 days so you can get over every relationship problem you ever had.

Dain: What contribution are petulant, angry, withdrawn, covert and controlling women and men to my life, my living and my reality? Everything that is times a godzillion, will you destroy and uncreate it all? Right and wrong, good and bad, POC and POD, all 9, shorts, boys and beyonds.

Gary: Today I was running, "What contribution is breeding horses to my life, my living and my reality?" It nearly knocked me out of the plane. Then I ran the other side, "What contribution is not breeding horses to my life, my living and my reality?" That was equally hideous. I had walked into breeding horses backward without realizing what I was doing. Running this process was a major element in beginning to see from a different place.

I'm trying to get you to see that you've got to look at both sides of the coin. I'm not an asshole. I am an asshole. The reality is that we have those two points of view in existence, and we're always trying to prove one and disprove the other. But we're both. I'm an asshole. And I know that I'm an asshole. I don't try to deny it or change it. I'm an asshole. Is there a problem?

Let's say you notice you're being a superior asshole. You can run:

What contribution is being a superior asshole to my life, my living and my reality? And everything that doesn't allow that to show up, times a godzillion, will you destroy and uncreate it all? Right and wrong, good and bad, POD and POC, all 9, shorts, boys and beyonds.

What contribution is not being a superior asshole to my life, my living and my reality? And everything that doesn't allow that to show up, times a godzillion, will you destroy and uncreate it all? Right and wrong, good and bad, POD and POC, all 9, shorts, boys and beyonds.

Or if you're being mean to people, run:

What contribution is being mean to my life, my living and my reality? And everything that doesn't allow that to show up, times a godzillion, will you destroy and uncreate it all? Right and wrong, good and bad, POD and POC, all 9, shorts, boys and beyonds.

What contribution is not being mean to my life, my living and my reality? And everything that doesn't allow that to show up, times a godzillion, will you destroy and uncreate it all? Right and wrong, good and bad, POD and POC, all 9, shorts, boys and beyonds.

These are ways you can start to come out of places where you're stuck in the way you act and react to people.

Question: I was talking about the woman who plays the victim and manipulates me. Getting manipulated requires me to be aware—and to not put up walls, correct? Yet I have what seems an undeniable urge to put up walls and exclude her anyway.

Gary: If you're putting up walls in one area of your life, you have done it other places in your life as well. If you put up walls, you're cutting off your awareness. You attempt to put up the wall when your awareness is not carrying through for you. You might want to run:

What contribution is putting up walls to my life, my living and my reality? And everything that doesn't allow that to show up, times a godzillion, will you destroy and uncreate it all? Right and wrong, good and bad, POD and POC, all 9, shorts, boys and beyonds.

What contribution is not putting up walls to my life, my living and my reality? And everything that doesn't allow that to show up, times a godzillion, will you destroy and uncreate it all? Right and wrong, good and bad, POD and POC, all 9, shorts, boys and beyonds.

Question: There's a person who consistently shows up in my life, and I simply do not want to be around her, as time and again she proves that she's an ELF. I don't want to play with her again. How do I not do exclusion?

Gary: What are you excluding when you're not playing with her again? Admiration? Gratitude? What? I'll give you two—one or two or both?

Are those my only choices?

Gary: Yeah.

Dain: He's trying to make it easy.

I'm confused.

Gary: No you're not!

(Laughing)

Gary: You're just trying to weasel out of answering. Are you excluding gratitude? Yes or no?

Yes.

Gary: Are you excluding admiration? Yes or no?

I say no.

Gary: You're not excluding admiration?

For her evilness and ELF-ness?

Gary: I didn't ask you that. Are you excluding admiration?

Yes.

Gary: So, now you want to know how to get rid of her?

Yes.

Gary: Gratitude and admiration.

Oh, man!

Gary: (Laughing) You're excluding the two weapons that will get her to move away from you!

Dain: It used to fry my brain too. I totally understand how it does not compute for you right now, but if you look at this, you may realize that you can have gratitude and admiration for this person. It's important to understand this. This is the one area people ask the most questions about. They ask about people they don't want to be around anymore.

Time and time again, I've seen Gary have gratitude and admiration for ELFs. Initially I thought, "How can you be nice to this person?" The answer is that gratitude and admiration are the two things people cannot stand. It will make them run away from you faster than anything you can imagine.

Gary: They'll run away at the speed of sound, let me tell you. You just say, "I'm so grateful for you. You have taught me so much."

They'll ask, "What? What are you talking about?"

You say, "Well, I'm just so grateful for you. I admire the way you live your life."

They'll ask, "What do you mean by that?"

You say, "Well, who is most important to you in your life? I admire the fact that you can do that."

They have to run away from you, because otherwise they would have to go into judgment of themselves. Your judgment of them and your exclusion of your admiration and your gratitude keep them coming back. They want to beat on that barrier to gratitude and admiration because they know if they ever make it through, they will have to leave—but as long as they don't make it through, you're still their victim.

You can truly be in admiration and gratitude for them? You are truly grateful for them?

Gary: Yes, I'm grateful to people who try to rip me off. It's "Wow, thank you so much. I'm grateful for the information I got. I'm grateful for the fact that I can see where you're functioning from. I'm grateful for the fact that I don't have to make myself a victim to your supposed victimhood. I admire the fact that you can make your life so horrible and still manage to walk and talk." It's true admiration—not B.S. I'm not doing B.S. I don't do B.S.

Dain: If you can look at what Gary's saying and get even an inkling of the energy of it right now about the person you're talking about, and then if you run this process, some interesting things might happen.

What contribution is this person to my life, living and reality? And everything that doesn't allow that to show up, times a godzillion, will you destroy and uncreate it all? Right and wrong, good and bad, POD and POC, all 9, shorts, boys and beyonds.

What contribution is excluding this person to my life, living and reality? And everything that doesn't allow that to show up, times a godzillion, will you destroy and uncreate it all? Right and wrong, good and bad, POD and POC, all 9, shorts, boys and beyonds.

Gary: When you resist someone, when you exclude them, you contract yourself. You stop you from receiving.

Dain: That's what occurs when you try to exclude someone from your life, living and reality. You contract yourself and eliminate your receiving.

Thank you. That's really helpful.

Gary: You're welcome.

Question: What is the difference between contribution and value?

Gary: *Contribution* is gifting and receiving simultaneously. *Value* is what we think makes someone or something important.

What if you're making being a contribution important?

Gary: Being a contribution is not about you having awareness, so when you make being a contribution important, you're excluding what gives you the freedom to choose something different.

When someone says, "I resist that person" or "I avoid that person at all costs," where is the question? Do you hear a question anywhere?

No.

Gary: What choice do you have under those circumstances?

None. I see that valuing being a contribution takes me out of choice as well. I think that's how I've lived my entire life.

Gary: Yeah, most of us have. Everybody makes contribution more valuable than question, choice and possibility. Rather than going to question, choice or possibility, which could give you more awareness, you go to the conclusion: "I have to contribute to them" or "I can't contribute to them." Those are the two choices we tend to make for ourselves. Neither of them is about the question, which would be, "Okay, so what would make this person decide to leave me alone? What possibilities are there?"

Dain: When you're trying to exclude someone, you're trying to find what part of you you've got to cut off in order to exclude them. It feels heavy.

Gary: You've got to exclude you in order to exclude them.

Dain: That part is actually the killer. No exclusion probably wouldn't even be one of The Ten Keys if exclusion didn't cause you to exclude you. In order to exclude anything or anyone else, you have to exclude you. That's the way it works. Recognize that it's a gift to you to stop excluding. It's not about them. You're not doing it for them. You're doing it as a gift to you. It gives you the possibility for a different point of view. As long as you're doing exclusion, you're going into what they contribute or what they don't contribute or what you have to contribute or what you don't want to contribute. You're not going to any question, any possibility or any choice. And ultimately, you should have total choice, total question and total possibility.

If you're only looking at the contribution that you can or can't get from these people or the contribution you must give or can't give to these people, you're excluding the other elements that are about creation.

Question: I seem to be going to a place in my sleep that appears as true consciousness or my reality. It feels really beautiful and full of light. It's like a semi-dream state and requires no action in this reality, yet at the same time, it seems to be exclusively of this reality.

Gary: You cannot exclude this reality. You have to include this reality—but in including this reality, you've also got to do choice, question and possibility. Once again, you're trying to see whether this reality contributes to your reality. This reality may not contribute to your reality, but if you exclude it, you are excluding your awareness—because this reality is included in your awareness.

I make the choice not to participate in this reality from this place.

Gary: Not participating is an exclusion of you in the participation of your life, because you live in this reality as well as having your own.

You're excluding yourself when you're not willing to control utterly this reality with your question, your choice and your possibilities.

I am perceiving two realities—my reality and this contextual reality of planet Earth. These realities seem to be exclusive of each other.

Gary: That's the mistake. You've got to ask the question and get the choice and the possibilities that could create it by including and not excluding.

What clearing statements could I use to have contextual reality as part of my reality with total ease?

Gary: What contribution is contextual reality to my life, my living and my reality? And everything that doesn't allow that to show up, times a godzillion, will you destroy and uncreate it all? Right and wrong, good and bad, POD and POC, all 9, shorts, boys and beyonds.

What contribution is not having contextual reality as part of my life, my living and reality? And everything that doesn't allow that to show up, times a godzillion, will you destroy and uncreate it all? Right and wrong, good and bad, POD and POC, all 9, shorts, boys and beyonds.

Could you please talk about inclusion of this contextual reality with perceiving, knowing, being and receiving?

Gary: Yes, you cannot have total perceiving, knowing, being and receiving unless you are including this reality.

Question: I have a question about inclusion and exclusion. I find that my Access Consciousness events are attracting some people who society would call misfits. These people are clearly looking for inclusion but when they come to the events, the reason they have become misfits is quite apparent. At times, this has a result of making the events less joyful for the rest of the people who are attending.

Gary: Hey, inclusion is "There are crazy people and there are not crazy people." Most people you think are not crazy are actually far crazier than the ones you know are crazy.

It's not about making your Access Consciousness events joyful, because joy is not the purpose of the events you have. Joy is a sideline that occurs if you do a great job. The events should be about creating awareness. If you create awareness, at the end, everybody will be joyful because they have gotten more awareness. Don't make your events about creating joyful experiences because not-so-joyful is often the greatest question, possibility and choice that someone can have.

Question: The first experience of exclusion in our psyche was our parents.

Gary: Now, that's an interesting point of view. What part of that is a question? It's not a question; it's a conclusion—and if you are concluding, you're excluding. You don't think your parents are part of your reality.

It was filled with judgment and punishment.

Gary: What was filled with judgment and punishment? Your experience with your parents? Okay, that's an interesting point of view. What part of that did you create or generate?

The one person you exclude any time you do exclusion—is you. Everything you've said is about exclusion—exclusion of your awareness as to what else is possible here. What choices do you have? What question can you ask that would make this all disappear?

Question: Why do we choose to come into this limited reality? There's got to be another possibility.

Gary: The reason you choose to come into this limited reality is because you've come to so many conclusions that you will have to come back and do it again until you get it right.

Dain: And here's the other thing to get: It is a choice. The thing about doing conclusion and inclusion or exclusion is that it's a choice. Why do you come to this limited reality? Because you haven't gotten to the place yet where this reality is an interesting point of view. Even what goes on with your parents is an interesting point of view. Until you get to "interesting point of view," the polarity of this reality will keep sucking you right back in to it as though you have no choice.

The first thing to get is that it's all choice. With this call and all of Access Consciousness, we're hoping to expose you to the awareness that you have different choices available than you ever knew were available. We hope you have the openness and the invitation to start choosing them.

Question: I have a client who has somebody who is trying to harm him, poison him. Can I use this clearing with him? Would it work?

Gary: Yes, it would help a lot. If nothing else, he'll become aware of when and where it's happening.

How would I phrase it?

Gary: What contribution is (the name of the person who is trying to harm him) to my life, my reality and my living? Everything that is times a godzillion, will you destroy and uncreate it all? Right and wrong, good and bad, POD and POC, all 9, shorts, boys and beyonds.

Gary: If you think there's more than one person, then put "these people" into the blank. You can also do the process that Dain gave earlier about the mean, petulant and angry people, and add "poisonous people" to that list.

Dain: So it would be:

What contribution are petulant, angry, withdrawn, covert, controlling, poisoning women and men to my life, my living and reality? And everything that doesn't allow that to show up, times a godzillion, will you destroy and uncreate it all? Right and wrong, good and bad, POD and POC, all 9, shorts, boys and beyonds.

Gary: You can use this process with anything. We choose things that don't work because we think they are making some contribution to our creation of our life.

Question: What can I do if someone else is excluding me?

Gary: Ask: What question, choice and possibility do I have here? And run the process:

> What contribution can this person excluding me be to my life, my living and my reality? And everything that doesn't allow that to show up, times a godzillion, will you destroy and uncreate it all? Right and wrong, good and bad, POD and POC, all 9, shorts, boys and beyonds.

That sounds great. It feels so light. I kept looking at all the ways I've been excluding this person, but it is actually the opposite. She has been excluding me.

Dain: There was a girl who contacted me after the class we did in Mallorca. She was with a guy who kept coming down on her with all kinds of judgments. She said, "This whole time I thought I had been excluding him. I thought it was all about me, but I've realized it is exactly the opposite. He has been excluding me. He's in total judgment of me and I couldn't see it."

Many times that's the way it works when you think you're excluding somebody else. Much of the time they're actually excluding you; they're in judgment of you.

That's awesome. Thank you very much.

Question: When I read the invitation for this telecall, the question popped up in my head: How often do I include myself? I have a family and I have taken on different roles in this life. I see that a lot of the time, I ignore what I would like. I don't even think to ask what would work for me in different situations. I think of others all the time. Actually, when I was a child I was constantly told by my parents that they didn't like selfish and spoiled children and they didn't want us to be like that. I remember how often I felt guilty if I got something the way I wanted it to be. At an early age, I was entrained to look after others and I became a family caretaker. If there was an argument, I had to sort it out. Could you please talk about excluding ourselves?

Gary: If you are not including you, if you are excluding you in any computation about what you choose, you are actually discounting you. You are not making you part of your own life and living. You could run something like:

What contribution is not being a part of my life and living to my life, my living and my reality? And everything that doesn't allow that to show up, times a godzillion, will you destroy and uncreate it all? Right and wrong, good and bad, POD and POC, all 9, shorts, boys and beyonds.

Question: I recently became aware that when I have a strong and immediate response to exclusion of anyone or anything, it is because it comes too close to a soft spot or a hard-to-look-at place within myself. Might it not be beneficial to include in my own processing an acceptance of something that is within me that I wish to exclude?

Gary: Yes, but if you feel yourself doing that, what you're not willing to do is to be vulnerable. You have to be vulnerable enough to perceive, know, be and receive everything.

Question: What does saying "no" without exclusion look like?

Gary: Whenever I am going to get together with my family, I always ask Dain if he would like to go out and have lunch or dinner or whatever with my family. I'm always willing for him to say no because he doesn't need to go there.

Does he invite me to go with his family? No. Why doesn't he invite me? He's aware that inviting me to visit with his family would not be helpful to him or to anyone else, including me. It would not make his life or his family's life easier. That's where you say no. It's not exclusion—because you realize there are other people involved who may not be able to receive what another person is going to give or contribute.

Dain: It's the awareness that including someone in a particular situation may not work out well for anyone. Have you ever had a friend that you liked but nobody else did? That person felt weird when they were with your other friends. Or have you ever dated somebody that no one around you liked? That person felt weird around your other friends. In a situation like this, when you are aware of the difficulty it would create in everybody's world, it can be a kindness to not invite that person to an event. Is that exclusion or is that awareness?

Gary: That's awareness. Exclusion is when you say, "I don't like this person, so I'm not letting them come."

Are there people I exclude from things I'm involved in? Yeah. Why? Because I know that they're not going to fit. Last year at Christmas time, I had someone here who worked for Access Consciousness. She had gone out with my youngest son. My son's second baby's mommy came to the house, met this woman, went ballistic and left in a hissy fit. She was doing exclusion.

I could not exclude this woman since she works with us. I could not exclude her from our Christmas party since she was away from home and didn't have any family here. I wasn't going to exclude her. But I wouldn't exclude the woman who my son had his baby with because I didn't consider that kind either. She, however, called the line. So in the future I will tell her, "Okay, I will invite you, but you cannot throw a hissy fit if somebody is here." I'm going to call the rules. Is that exclusion? Yes, but it's choosing. I'm willing to choose from the possibilities, the choices and the question.

Dain: Gary and I have both noticed that some people in Access Consciousness think, "I don't ever have to do anything that feels uncomfortable" or "I don't have to go anywhere there might be any heaviness" or "I don't have to be involved in anything that's not total lightness and joy." Not necessarily. You have commitments in your life that you've made. You need to honor those—for you. It's a way of not excluding you. For example, say you're looking at not going on the family vacation. You might look at the energy that will get created if you don't go, and you'll know, "If I don't go, it's going to be absolute hell. My family's not going to like me, they're going to kick me out of the will," or whatever it is. Go on the damn vacation. Suck it up for a week if you have to and realize there are things you need to do so you're not excluding you from your life. You have made commitments to other people, for example, by virtue of coming in to a particular family.

When you decide on your own that you're going to exclude people and situations from your life, people may end up feeling like you're their enemy or that you are not included in the family. That's because you've made unilateral decisions to exclude them from your life.

Gary: You're excluding the awareness of what you're going to create by the choice you make. You've got to be willing to look at what your choice is going to create. Exclusion of all possibilities, all questions and all choices is the place in which you exclude the awareness of what's going to make your life easier and greater in every moment.

Several years ago Simone wanted to come and have Christmas with us in Santa Barbara because we're way more fun than her family, but there was no great reason or excuse for her to come here except that she wanted to. She asked me, "Do I really have to spend the time with my family?"

I said, "Well, I'm getting *yes*."

She said, "Damn it, I was getting that too, but I didn't want to hear it. I wanted to think that I could get away without having to be with them at Christmas time."

I said, "Well, you know what? You need to be there." So she stayed home—and she had the best Christmas she'd had in years. Why? Because she came from a place of not excluding what she would like (which was to come to Santa Barbara) as well as not excluding her family nor the awareness of what her choice would create in the world. The end result was that everything worked out better for her and everybody concerned. That's where you've got to function from.

Dain: One of the big pieces of this is the awareness of what your choice is going to create in your world and in other people's worlds. We were talking about the difference in energy between excluding somebody and being totally present as you. It's a very different energy.

When you say, "I'm choosing to be with my family based on the awareness of what it will create and what's actually going to happen," it's a totally different energy than when you say, "I hate this. I don't want to be here, but I've got to be here."

It's a totally different thing when you recognize you're at choice. That's part of what we're hoping to open up—you being at choice in a far greater range of circumstances than you would be if you were excluding you.

People tend to exclude themselves from things that they previously thought they had to do. They decide, "Well, now that I'm in Access Consciousness and I've got choice, I don't have to go there or do that anymore." You're doing something that is unkind to you to try to prove that you're doing something kind to you.

Gary: If you don't exclude your awareness of what your choice is going to create in the world, then you begin to include the possibilities that can occur as a result of the choice you have in the world.

No exclusion means you don't give up any of the questions, any of the choices, any of the possibilities—and you don't have to give up being contributed to or contributing to others.

Most of you think that choosing for yourself is excluding others. You think that in order to choose for you, you have to exclude others. No, you can choose for you based on including others as well. Does that mean you have to go against what you want to do? No. Does that mean you have to follow the obligation? No. It means you have to choose from total awareness.

Every one of these Ten Keys can be applied individually. I got an email from somebody who said that she loved The Ten Keys. She said, "I realized that if you just took one of them, and used it in every situation you came across, your whole life would change."

That's the whole idea. You can use any of the keys at any time. We are doing The Ten Keys calls because we hope they will get people to see the choices they have available. That's why we abused you and hopefully amused you a little bit too.

Let's try these processes:

What contribution is Access Consciousness to your life, your living and your reality? Everything that is times a godzillion, will you destroy and uncreate it all? Right and wrong, good and bad, POD and POC, all 9, shorts, boys and beyonds.

What contribution is not having Access Consciousness to your life, your living and your reality? Everything that is times a godzillion, will you destroy and uncreate it all? Right and wrong, good and bad, POD and POC, all 9, shorts, boys and beyonds.

What contribution is not totally embracing and using The Ten Keys to your life, your living and your reality? Everything that is times a godzillion, will you destroy and uncreate it all? Right and wrong, good and bad, POD and POC, all 9, shorts, boys and beyonds.

What contribution is totally embracing and using The Ten Keys to your life, your living and your reality? Everything that is times a godzillion, will you destroy and uncreate it all? Right and wrong, good and bad, POD and POC, all 9, shorts, boys and beyonds.

Question: The continuing line of the last ten calls seems to be what determines whether the energy flows or not.

Gary: Yep. For me, it's always about a sense of the lightness of everything. Nothing is solid, hard, stuck or difficult. When you get to something that creates a sense of space, there's a lightness to it, and that's the place you want to go. Every one of these keys is designed to give you the space, so you can be the space to have the space so you can choose more space and choose a different possibility.

I get a sense I'm looking at all the dead-end alleys—and all of a sudden there are no dead-end alleys.

Dain: That's perfect.

Yeah, there's just a superhighway. Zoom.

Dain: Gary and I function from that place pretty much all the time. That's where I *didn't* function from eleven years ago. By using these Ten Keys, I have created a different reality.

When you have the superhighway going on and something else comes up, it's "Oh! I've got plenty of room to handle this on the superhighway.

Cool. What choices do I have available? What possibilities are available? What questions can I ask here to change this?"

Contribution allows more of that superhighway to be in every situation you're dealing with. It's a different way of being in the world than most of us have been taught, so we've got to teach ourselves.

So, from that perspective, even if the choice is uncomfortable, like when you were talking about family, it's not impossible to have a choice that looks bad, but feels right.

Dain: Yeah.

Gary: You may feel like it's bad, but what comes out is usually greater than what you thought it could be because you're on the superhighway. The best way I can describe it is: There are no more brick walls that fall in front of you to smash yourself on.

Question: I have a question. I'm going to try to offer you the energy of it without going into the whole story. It's about an experience I had in receiving assistance this weekend. It was very uncomfortable and I felt like I was allowing an invasion or a hijacking of my life. I didn't know if I was doing allowance and no exclusion or what else could I have chosen.

Gary: You're going to have to give me a little bit more detail.

I was staying in a hotel, and my hard drive crashed. I don't know anything about stuff like that. Another hotel guest, a complete random stranger, offered assistance. We were supposed to meet in the lobby, but instead he showed up at my door and insisted on coming into my room. I didn't want him in my room. Next thing I knew, he was lying on my bed and I noticed a terrible body odor. Then I realized he didn't really know what he was doing because I have a Mac and he's got Windows. This went on and on, and I couldn't get him out of my room.

Gary: Hold, hold, hold. First of all, you blew the deal. What you should have said (with the door closed) is, "I'm sorry, I was raised as a nice Southern girl and Southern girls don't allow gentlemen in their room. So we need to go downstairs because I am not comfortable with this." It's called not being a doormat. Allowance is not being a doormat. Allowance is "This is not going to work. Thank you so much for coming by, but this is not going to work."

Dain: And it's not exclusion.

Gary: No, it's awareness. This is not going to work. You knew when he showed up at your door it wasn't going to work. Why did you go against your own awareness?

What came up was my family. I was used to putting up with all sorts of crap just to get a little dropper full of goodness.

Gary: Yeah, well that's a nice story. Are you going to make that real for you?

No!

Gary: Good. You've got to choose what you know is right for you. Each of these Ten Keys is about getting you to the awareness of what works for you, what's right for you and what's going to make your life easier. It's about where you're going to have the superhighway of ease. When somebody shows up at your door and that's not what you've asked for, you say, "I'm sorry, I'm not available right now, I'll meet you in the lobby in half an hour."

Okay.

Gary: It's taking control, darling. The whole idea of The Ten Keys is to give you a place where you're willing to have control instead of allowing yourself to be used or abused.

Yes, and then that goes back to remembering to include myself.

Gary: Exactly, you've got to include you in this whole thing. You're excluding your needs, wants, requires and desires in favor of everybody else's. That doesn't work. You can't do that to yourself. Okay?

Yes, thank you.

Question: As you're talking about no exclusion, I see that I have a sense of superiority in the relationship with my body that makes me punish and abuse it in different ways. I have excluded my body from participating in its wants and desires. Do you have a process to integrate the body and the entity into wholeness?

Gary: First of all, let's talk about the relationship between the being and the body. Close your eyes and reach out and touch the outside edges of you, the being. Not the outside edges of your body—the outside edges of you, the infinite being. Go out to the farthest reaches of where you, as a being, are. Now go farther. Are you there too? Could a being that big fit inside a human-sized body? No. Your body is inside you, the being.

It's about integrating the body into the infinite being that you are, because the body has to have an infinite sense of space as well.

As my friend, Dr. Dain, says, "It's your point of view that creates your reality. It's not reality that creates your point of view." If you see your body as inside of you, the being, instead of something outside of you—or something you have excluded from your space—you may have a different way of being with it.

You have to include what your body desires and requires. If you don't get that your body needs rest, for example, then you become more and more exhausted and your body begins to hurt and you start to create illness—because your body has to try and override where you're ignoring it.

Question: I want to take that superhighway back to the physical form and ask you to give me the nitty-gritty on how the superhighway opens into the physical form.

Gary: You're going to require the Advanced Body Class.

I understand that and I will get there. I promise I will, but right now I'm here.

Gary: So what you've got to do is run:

What contribution is my body to my life, my living and my reality? And everything that doesn't allow that to show up, times a godzillion, will you destroy and uncreate it all? Right and wrong, good and bad, POD and POC, all 9, shorts, boys and beyonds.

What contribution is not having a body to my life, my living and my reality? And everything that doesn't allow that to show up, times a godzillion, will you destroy and uncreate it all? Right and wrong, good and bad, POD and POC, all 9, shorts, boys and beyonds.

Can you take those questions through every aspect of your physical form as well?

Gary: Yeah. If you have a pain in your body you can ask, "What contribution is this pain to my life, my living and my reality?"

Recently I was walking and I had all kinds of pains in my body. I asked, "Wow, what contribution are these pains to my life, my living and my reality?" Fifty percent of them went away the first time I did it!

I still have some issues with giving back other people's stuff. It's as if I can't delineate it clearly enough or my body doesn't choose to delineate it clearly enough so that I can give it back, even though I know it's not mine.

Gary: So have you acknowledged the fact that you're a healer?

Oh yeah.

Gary: Okay, so you might want to run:

What contribution is being a healer to my life, my living and my reality? And everything that doesn't allow that to show up, times a godzillion, will you destroy and uncreate it all? Right and wrong, good and bad, POD and POC, all 9, shorts, boys and beyonds.

What contribution is not being a healer to my life, my living and my reality? And everything that doesn't allow that to show up, times a godzillion, will you destroy and uncreate it all? Right and wrong, good and bad, POD and POC, all 9, shorts, boys and beyonds.

Question: At the beginning of this call, Dain said that when you're functioning from awareness, you need not say a word. When we do bodywork, are we mostly functioning from awareness?

Dain: Yes ma'am, this is true.

And if we're functioning from awareness, we can act more quickly?

Dain: Exactly! You actually become a vibration that allows something totally different to occur, which is pretty darn cool.

Question: Do you find that most people do exclusion on the outside, as in "I won't be with that person" or "I won't do that thing" rather than doing exclusion from themselves, as in "I won't be bitchy or mean?" Do we do exclusion more on the outside or the inside—or both?

Gary: It's both. It fluctuates back and forth depending on the day and the people you are around.

Dain: And any time you try to exclude someone else, you have to exclude you as well.

Gary: Yeah, and that's the bad part.

There's probably no excluding something from the outside without having it be an internal exclusion?

Gary: Well, if you're trying to exclude someone or something from your life, you're also excluding you in that process.

Here's an example—a story. I used to hate dog shit, and everywhere I went, I stepped in it. When I finally started to POD and POC everything that made me think I couldn't include dog shit in my reality, the dog shit started to tell me it was there, and I never stepped in it ever again!

That's funny.

Gary: I said, "No exclusion includes dog shit. All I do when I exclude dog shit is step in it." That's pretty much the way it works in every aspect of your life. Whatever you try to exclude, you have to step into again and again and again.

When children are young, they are usually in a state of non-exclusion. It seems like they include themselves and everything.

Gary: That can be true, but it is not necessarily true. It depends on the kid. It's an individual thing.

But little children don't exclude themselves.

Gary: Well they usually don't, but some do. It depends on the age they learn to do it. They can learn it when they're three months old—or earlier sometimes. You can't take the point of view that children are naturally wonderful because some of them aren't.

I was in a restaurant with my daughter, Grace, and her baby the other day. Every time the waiter came up to the table, the kid would look at him, expecting to be talked to, because when we were in New Zealand, everyone talked to the baby when they walked by. They know he is not just a baby; he is a being. They would talk to the baby, and the baby would smile and do his thing.

When the waiter in California came up to the baby, the baby would wait and watch, expecting to be spoken to. It was amazing to watch this little guy, waiting for the waiter to address him and engage him. When the waiter didn't speak to him, he looked at the waiter as if to ask, "What's happening?" He's three and half months old.

He already hates it when you don't include him in the conversation.

When you're having a conversation with someone, all you have to do is turn to the baby and ask, "Well, what do you think about that?" or say, "I can't wait until you can talk so we can hear what you have to say about this." The baby will sit there and make little cooing sounds, trying to be part of the conversation.

Every being wants to be part of the conversation; every being wants to be involved. When you exclude kids from being involved, you have excluded them from your life, and that means they have to make themselves count by being in someone else's life.

Question: When we sleep, do we exclude ourselves or do we include ourselves?

Gary: It depends on what you think is important for that night. Some people get out of their bodies and go away for the night.

You mean they exclude themselves?

Gary: They go away and do other things during the night instead of just being aware.

You call it dreams, but that's not necessarily the case. Have you ever had the experience of waking up startled? Or have you woken up and had the sense that something was wrong? That's a place where you excluded you from your body during the night. You're getting stuck with the impact of everybody else's points of view when you come back into your body.

You leave your body alone and you go out to do whatever you do. Some people go out and work all night, but when they come back into their body, they wake up startled or maybe depressed and unhappy. How much of that is actually theirs? None of it. Sometimes they come back and they're so tired. They say, "I felt like I was working all night" or "I felt this terrible stuff going on all night long."

You have to ask your body, "Body, are you tired?" Ninety-nine percent of the time, the body is not tired because it got eight hours of rest. You were the one who was out fighting battles and doing things.

You and your body are slightly separate in that way, and you are excluding you from your body when you aren't totally aware of your body.

Is that the same as when you have nightmares and other people's points of view are torturing you?

Gary: Those are different things. Sometimes it's memories of past lives that you were either happy or unhappy with. There are no pat answers to dreams. And there are no pat answers to most anything in life. It's about being in question, seeing the choice and the possibilities and being able to know when something is truly a contribution to you. When something is a true contribution, it expands your life; it doesn't contract any part of it.

The same thing applies with people. People who expand your life are major gifts. They are the people who contribute and gift to you. They are part of what creates expanding the superhighway to greater awareness. Those are the people you want to keep around. Those are people you want to support as long as possible.

Dain: They're the ones who keep expanding the space. They make your life easier. They contribute to the choices, possibilities and questions that you never even thought of.

Gary: I would like to conclude our conversation now. I want to thank all of you for being on these calls, and I hope that they have created a greater sense of space and some dramatic changes for you. Each key, if you apply it, will take you to a level of freedom that could set your life on fire and create something greater than you ever knew was possible.

We adore you!

Dain: Thank you, we adore you all!

~~~

The Clearing Process

In Access Consciousness, there is a clearing process we use to destroy and uncreate blockages and limitations.

Here's a brief explanation of how it works: The basis of the universe is energy. Every particle of the universe has energy and consciousness. There is no good energy or bad energy; there is just energy. It is only your judgment that makes anything good or bad. Energy is present, mutable and changeable upon request. It is the substance by which transformation occurs. Everything you say, everything you think and everything you do generates what occurs in your life. Whatever you choose puts the energy of the universe, the energy of consciousness, into action—and that shows up as your life. This is what your life looks like in this very moment.

Point of Creation, Point of Destruction

Every limitation we have was created by us somewhere throughout all time, space, dimensions and realities. It involved making a judgment or a decision or taking on a point of view. How and why the limitation was created does not matter, nor does any other part of its story. We only need to know *that* it was created. We call this the point of creation (POC). The point of creation energetically includes the thoughts, feelings, and emotions immediately preceding the decision, judgment or point of view we took on.

There is also a point of destruction. The point of destruction (POD) is the point where we destroyed our being by taking on a decision or a position that was based on a limited point of view. We literally put ourselves into a destruct universe. The point of destruction, like the point of creation, includes energetically the thoughts, feelings, and emotions immediately preceding the destructive decision.

When you ask a question about a blockage or limitation, you call up the energy that has you locked into it. Using the clearing statement, you can then destroy and uncreate the blockage or limitation (as well as the thoughts, feelings and emotions connected to it). The clearing statement allows you to energetically undo these things so you have a different choice.

The Clearing Statement

These are the words that make up the clearing statement:

> Everything that is, times a godzillion, destroy and uncreate it all. Right and wrong, good and bad, POD and POC, all 9, shorts, boys and beyonds.

You don't have to understand the clearing statement for it to work, but if you wish to know more about it, there is additional information in the glossary.

With the clearing statement, we are not giving you answers or trying to get you to change your mind. We know that doesn't work. You are the only one who can unlock the points of view that have you trapped. What we are offering here is a tool you can use to change the energy of the points of view that have you locked into unchanging situations.

To use the clearing statement, you simply ask a question designed to bring up the energy of what has you trapped, including all the crap built on it or hiding behind it, then say or read the clearing statement to clear the limitation and change it. The more you run the clearing statement, the deeper it goes and the more layers and levels it can unlock for you. You may wish to repeat processes numerous times until the subject being addressed is no longer an issue for you.

How Does the Clearing Process Work?

Asking a question brings up an energy, which you will be aware of. It's not necessary to look for an answer to this question. In fact, the answer may not come to you in words. It may come to you as an energy. You may not even cognitively know what the answer to the question is. It doesn't matter how the awareness comes to you. Just ask the question and then clear the energy with the clearing statement:

> Everything that is times a godzillion, will you destroy and uncreate it all? (Say yes here, but only if you truly mean it.) Right and wrong, good and bad, POD and POC, all 9, shorts, boys and beyonds.

The clearing statement may seem nonsensically wordy. It is designed to short-circuit your mind so that you can see what choices you have available. If you could work everything out with your logical mind, you would already have everything you desired. Whatever is keeping you from having what you desire is not logical. It's the insane points of view you wish to destroy. The clearing statement is designed to fry every point of view that you have so that you can start to function from your awareness and your knowing. You are an infinite being, and you, as an infinite being, can perceive everything, know everything, be everything and receive everything. Only your points of view create the limitations that stop that.

Don't make it significant. You're just clearing energy and any points of view, limitations or judgments you've created. You can use the full clearing statement as we've given it here, or you can just say: POD and POC and all the stuff I read in the book.

Remember: It's about the energy. Go with the energy of it. You can't do this wrong. You may find that you have a different way of functioning as a result of using the clearing statement. Try it. It may change everything in your life.

Glossary

Allowance

When you are in allowance, everything is just an interesting point of view. There is no judgment of something being right or wrong or good or bad. You have no resistance or reaction to anyone or anything, and there is no need to align and agree with any judgment or point of view. In the space of allowance, you are aware of everything and you have total choice and possibility.

Bars

Access Consciousness Bars are a hands-on body process. An Access Consciousness facilitator uses a light touch on the head to contact points that correspond to different aspects of one's life and invite any stuck energy in that area to start moving again. Running the Bars begins to destroy the computer bank that has been dictating everything in your life.

Beingness

We try to prove that we are being *something* rather than being what we are; we take on a beingness to prove we are being. For example, if you take on the beingness of a smart businessperson, you will feel you can only be you when you are being a smart businessperson. What if you didn't have to prove you were anything? What if you were just being you?

Clearing Statement (POD/POC)

In Access Consciousness, there is a clearing process we use to destroy and uncreate blockages and limitations, which are really just stuck energy. Once we become aware of an energy that we wish to clear, we use the clearing statement. It may seem like the clearing statement is about the words (which are expressed in short-speak) but really, it is the energy of the clearing statement that changes things, not the words. The words of the clearing statement are: Right and wrong, good and bad, POD and POC, all 9, shorts, boys and beyonds.

Right and wrong, good and bad is shorthand for: What's right, good, perfect and correct about this? What's wrong, mean, vicious, terrible, bad, and awful about this? The short version of these questions is: What's right and wrong, good and bad?

POD and POC

POC stands for the **P**oint **o**f **C**reation of the thoughts, feelings and emotions immediately preceding your decision to lock the energy in place. POD stands for the **P**oint **o**f **D**estruction of the thoughts, feelings and emotions immediately preceding any decisions to lock that item in place and all the ways you have been destroying yourself in order to keep it in existence. When you "POD and POC" something, it is like pulling the bottom card out of a house of cards. The whole thing falls down.

All 9 stands for the nine different ways you have created this item as a limitation in your life. They are the layers of thoughts, feelings, emotions and points of view that create the limitation as solid and real.

Shorts is the short version of a much longer series of questions that include: What's meaningful about this? What's meaningless about this? What's the punishment for this? What's the reward for this?

Boys stands for energetic structures called nucleated spheres. There are thirty-two different kinds of these spheres, which are collectively called "the boys." A nucleated sphere looks like the bubbles created when you blow in one of those kids' bubble pipes that has multiple chambers. It creates a huge mass of bubbles, and when you pop one bubble, the other bubbles fill in the space. Have you ever tried to peel the layers of an onion when you were trying to get to the core of an issue, but you could never get there? That's because it wasn't an onion; it was a nucleated sphere.

Beyonds are feelings or sensations you get that stop your heart, stop your breath or stop your willingness to look at possibilities. Beyonds are what occur when you are in shock. The beyonds include everything that is beyond belief, reality, imagination, conception, perception, rationalization, forgiveness as well as all the other beyonds. They are usually feelings and sensations, rarely emotions, and never thoughts.

Distracter Implants

Distracter Implants are designed to lock you into this reality and take you out of being you. They have nothing to do with what is really going on, yet we try to address them as if they are real. We use distracters to distract us from what's really true so we don't have to look at what is underneath them. The twenty-four distracter implants are: Blame, Shame, Regret, Guilt, Anger, Rage, Fury, Hate, Love, Sex, Jealousy, Peace, Life, Living, Death, Reality, Business, Doubt, Relationship, Fear, and Addictive, Compulsive, Obsessive, and Perverted Points of View.

Elementals

Elementals describe the pure essence or basic form of things; they are the molecular structures that exist in all realities. The basic elements for the construct of reality are energy, space and consciousness (ESC), and we can ask these elements to come into solidification as what we want based on the quantum entanglements. (See the definition of quantum entanglements for more information.)

Energetic Synthesis of Being

Energetic Synthesis of Being is a way of simultaneously working with the energy of individuals, groups of people and their bodies. ESB shows you how to access, be and receive energies you always sensed were available but you didn't seem to have access to.

Humanoid

Humanoid is the name used to describe people who are willing to have more, be more and do more. They are usually creators of great art, literature and ideas. They like experiencing the elegance and aesthetics of life, enjoying the adventure of life or doing things that make the world a better place. Humanoids often feel like they don't fit in anywhere. They tend to be in judgment of themselves and wonder, "What's wrong with me that I don't fit in?"

Implants

Implants are thoughts, feelings and emotions as well as other things that are put into our physical form with electricity, drugs, vibrations, lights and sounds, as a way of controlling, helping or not helping us. Implants are a means to dominate, manipulate and control us and our bodies. You can't be implanted unless you align and agree or resist and react to something. For example, if you align with a religious leader, you can be implanted with all sorts of fears and superstitions. When you have no point of view about religion, no amount of preaching will make an impact on you; it will just be an interesting point of view.

Kingdom of We

When you function from the kingdom of we—the kingdom of consciousness and oneness—you are asking for everything to be easier for you. But "you" includes everybody around you. The kingdom of we is a place where you choose from everything and how it works for you and everybody around you, not from the kingdom of me. We keep trying to "choose for me", which means you are going to choose against everybody else to choose for you.

Molecular De-manifestation

Science tells us that if we look at a molecule, we change its shape and its structure by virtue of looking at it. So, whenever we put our attention on something or decide it needs to be a certain way, we create an effect on it. Molecular de-manifestation is a hands-on Access Consciousness body process that uncreates the molecular structure of something so it ceases to exist. It's a way of getting something to disappear.

De-molecular Manifestation refers to creating something where it did not exist before. You ask the molecules of something to change their structure and become what you would like them to be. *Manifestation* means the *way* something shows up, not *that* it shows up. You are not manifesting new molecules; you are asking the molecules to change so the possibilities of what can manifest are different.

MTVSS

MTVSS (Molecular Terminal Valence Sloughing System) is a dynamic hands-on Access Consciousness body process. MTVSS undoes the diminishment, aging and disintegration caused by the valence shifting systems of the chemical and molecular structures of the body.

Positional HEPADS

For every fixed point of view you take, you have to cut off awareness. Positional HEPADS (Handicapping, Entropy, Paralysis, Atrophy, Destruction) are a position you took about any subject, and then you start to handicap yourself about what can occur. You create entropy, which is creating chaos out of what was order before. You create paralysis where you are unable to function. You create an atrophy in which you start to break down the structure so that it cannot be generative. Then you create destruction. These are the five elements of what occurs every time you take a position about anything.

Positional HEPADS are what you create with every fixed point of view you take. This reality says you're only right and not wrong when you have the right fixed point of view and that's it. So you spend your whole life trying to get the right fixed point of view and the right position. That way you can fit in, you can benefit, you can win and you cannot lose. Then everything will be just fine. Except that's part of the construct for everything you know that doesn't work in your life and doesn't work here for you.

Handicapping – As humanoids you'll handicap yourself for the race because you know you're faster than all the humans, faster than everybody around you, more aware, and more fun. Somebody normal would handicap themselves by tying one leg and one arm behind them. Not you, you tie two arms and two legs behind you, gag your mouth and still run the race. That's the handicapping you do with taking positions and points of view. That's how much you have to handicap you to be in the human race.

Entropy – When you take what is ordered in your life (being you) and you make that chaotic, trying to become what other people want you to become, thinking that finally someone is going to accept you, see you, love you, and care for you totally. They're not. Entropy is also when things fall apart and devolve over time. This is why your body devolves over time; it's why your relationships fall apart over time (if you don't put huge amounts of energy into them.)

Paralysis – When you think you don't have any other choices available. You eliminate everything other than the one position you've taken.

Atrophy – When you let go of the things you are good at because nobody else thinks it's a good thing. You let the natural capacity you have shrink and disappear. Atrophy is also muscles shrinking and becoming useless. Have you seen people in the world who take a lot of fixed points of view? Their mental capacities shrink and become useless. Their capacity for joy shrinks and becomes useless and non-existent. Their capacity for creation and generation shrinks and becomes non-existent.

Destruction – When you look at yourself as a wrongness. We all know what destruction is. Where you're using your energy against you, so you can destroy instead.

Basically you're confining and defining and avoiding choice and question through all of this. So you take these positions and points of view and you end up creating a constriction, destruction and a handicapping of you in everything you actually are as a being.

If there is something in your life that you are not happy with and it is not changing, then you want to ask: How many positional HEPADS do I have holding this in existence?

Out of Control

Being out of control is not being uncontrolled. Being *uncontrolled* is resisting and reacting to control, especially control done from judgment, where you use force and superiority to stop yourself and others. When you are *out of control* you are out of the control of control. Being out of control is being totally aware. You don't try to control the way things are generated; nothing and no one stops you, and you don't need to stop or limit anyone else.

Quantum Entanglements

Quantum entanglement is the scientific term that describes a molecule in the present time, location, dimension or reality that has a resonance with a molecule in another time, location, dimension or reality. Quantum entanglements are the strange ways that energies interconnect with each other to create things as solid and real in this reality. They are the seemingly random, chaotic way the universe delivers what you ask for and are, in essence, your connection with the creative, generative elements of the universe. If you didn't have quantum entanglements, you would not have psychic awareness, intuition or the capacity to hear somebody else's thoughts.

Secret Agendas

An agenda is a format you are supposed to follow. Secret agendas are decisions we make or conclusions we reach about the format of our life that we are no longer aware of because we decided to keep them a secret. You may have made these decisions at an earlier point in your life, but often they were made in previous lifetimes. Anything you decided that you cannot now recall is a secret agenda. It creates reaction instead of action, reaction instead of choice, answer instead of question, and conclusions instead of possibilities.

Sex and No Sex

The lower harmonic of receiving is sex or no sex. That does not mean copulation or no copulation. **Sex** is walking tall, strutting your stuff, looking good, and feeling good about yourself. **No Sex** is an exclusionary universe where you feel, "I don't exist," "I don't want anybody to look at me" or "I don't want anybody around me ever." People use their points of view about sex or no sex as a way to limit their receiving.

Trifold Sequencing Systems

Trifold Sequencing Systems is an Access Consciousness process that allevi-ates current or past trauma that a person keeps going over again and again, but is never able to get out of. Trifold Sequencing Systems undoes this per-petual loop so they can go beyond it.

Wedgie

A wedgie is when you take hold of somebody's underwear and pull it up so high it creates discomfort. An energetic wedgie is a question you ask that creates discomfort in someone's universe. To drop a wedgie is to wait for an opening, drop a question like a bomb and walk away. It takes six to eight weeks for it to fester and blister, and when it does, the person will ask a question that's really a question. Change is then possible—but not until then.

Zero Sum of Trauma

Zero Sum of Trauma is a hands-on Access Consciousness body process that undoes the cumulative effect of trauma on the body. When people have experienced repeated trauma, they get used to the pain they are living with. The body adapts to this new level of pain and diminished function as though it is normal. The Zero Sum of Trauma process undoes whatever locks the trauma into place.

About the Authors

Gary M. Douglas

The illustrious best-selling author and international speaker, Gary Douglas, pioneered a set of transformational life changing tools and processes known as Access Consciousness® over 20 years ago. These cutting edge tools have transformed the lives of thousands of people all over the world. In fact, his work has spread to 173 countries, with 2,000 trained facilitators worldwide. Simple but so effective, the tools facilitate people of all ages and backgrounds to help remove limitations holding them back from a full life.

Gary was born in Midwest USA and raised in San Diego, California. Although he came from a "normal" middle class family, he was fascinated from an early age with the human psyche and this interest grew into a desire to assist people to "know what they know" and expand into more awareness, joy and abundance.

These pragmatic tools he has developed are not only being used by celebrities, corporates and teachers but also by health professionals (psychologists, chiropractors, naturopaths) to improve the health & wellbeing of their clients.

Prior to creating Access Consciousness® Gary Douglas was a successful realtor in Santa Barbara, California and also completed a psychology degree. Although he attained material wealth and was regarded as "successful," his life began to lack meaning and so he began his search to find a new way forward—one that would create change in the world and in people's lives.

Gary is the author of 8 books including the best selling novel *The Place*. He describes the inspiration behind the writing. "I wanted to explore the possibilities for how life could be. To allow people to know there actually is no necessity to live with the ageing, insanity, stupidity, intrigue, violence, craziness, trauma and drama we live with, as though we have no choice.

The Place is about people knowing that all things are possible. Choice is the source of creation. What if our choices can be changed in an instant? What if we could make choice more real than the decisions and stuck points we buy as real?"

Gary has an incredible level of awareness and care for all living things. "I would like people be more aware and more conscious and to realize we need to be stewards of the earth not users and abusers of the earth. If we start to see the possibilities of what we have available to us, instead of trying to create our piece of the pie, we could create a different world."

A vibrant 70-year-old grandfather (who is almost "ageless") with a very different view on life, Gary believes we are here to express our uniqueness and experience the ease and joy of living. He continues to inspire others, teaching across the world and making a massive contribution to the planet. He openly proclaims that for him, "life is just beginning."

Gary also has a wide range of personal and other business interests. These include: a passion for antiques (Gary established "The Antique Guild" in Brisbane, Australia in 2012), riding spirited stallions and breeding Costarricense De Paso horses, and an eco retreat in Costa Rica set to open in 2014.

To find out more, please visit:

www.GaryMDouglas.com

www.AccessConsciousness.com

www.Costarricense-Paso.com

Dr. Dain Heer

Dr. Dain Heer is an international speaker, author and facilitator of advanced Access Consciousness® workshops worldwide. His unique and transforming points of view on bodies, money, future, sex and relationships transcend everything currently being taught.

Dr. Heer invites and inspires people to greater conscious awareness from total allowance, caring, humor and a deep inner knowing.

Dr. Heer started work as a Network Chiropractor back in 2000 in California, USA. He came across Access Consciousness® at a point in his life when he was deeply unhappy and even planning suicide.

When none of the other modalities and techniques Dr. Heer had been studying were giving him lasting results or change, Access Consciousness® changed everything for him and his life began to expand and grow with more ease and speed than even he could have imagined possible.

Dr. Heer now travels the world facilitating classes and has developed a unique energy process for change for individuals and groups, called The Energetic Synthesis of Being. He has a completely different approach to healing by teaching people to tap into and recognize their own abilities and knowing. The energetic transformation possible is fast—and truly dynamic.

To find out more, please visit:

www.DrDainHeer.com

www.BeingYouChangingTheWorld.com

www.BeingYouClass.com

Access Books

Conscious Parents, Conscious Kids
By Gary M. Douglas & Dr. Dain Heer

This book is a collection of narratives from children immersed in living with conscious awareness. Wouldn't it be great if you could create the space that would allow your kids to unleash their potential and burst through the limitations that hold them back? To create the ease, joy and glory in everything they do in consciously take charge of their own lives?

Money Isn't The Problem, You Are
By Gary M. Douglas & Dr. Dain Heer

Offering out-of-the-box concepts with money. It's not about money. It never is. It's about what you're willing to receive.

Talk to the Animals
By Gary M. Douglas & Dr. Dain Heer

Did you know that every animal, every plant, every structure on this planet has consciousness and desires to gift to you? Animals have a tremendous amount of information and amazing gifts they can give to us if we are willing to receive them.

Being You, Changing the World
By Dr. Dain Heer

Have you always known that something COMPLETELY DIFFERENT is possible? What if you had a handbook for infinite possibilities and dynamic change to guide you? With tools and processes that actually worked and invited you to a completely different way of being? For you? And the world?

Divorceless Relationships
By Gary M. Douglas

A Divorceless Relationship is one where you don't have to divorce any part of you in order to be in a relationship with someone else. It is a place where everyone and everything you are in a relationship with can become greater as a result of the relationship.

Magic. You Are It. Be It.
By Gary M. Douglas & Dr. Dain Heer

Magic is about the fun of having the things you desire. The real magic is the ability to have the joy that life can be. In this book you are presented tools & points of view that you can use to create consciousness and magic—and change your life in ways you may not even be able to imagine.

Right Riches for You
By Gary M Douglas and Dr. Dain Heer

What if generating money and having money were fun and joyful? What if, in having fun and joy with money, you receive more of it? What would that be like? Money follows joy; joy does not follow money. As seen on Lifetime Television's *Balancing Act Show*.

The Place, A Novel
A Barnes and Noble Best Seller by Gary M Douglas

As Jake Rayne travels through Idaho in his classic 57 Thunderbird, a devastating accident is the catalyst for a journey he isn't expecting. Alone in the deep forest, with his body shattered and broken, Jake calls out for help. The help that finds him changes not only his life but his whole reality. Jake is opened up to the awareness of possibilities; possibilities that we have always known should be but that have not yet shown up.

Embodiment:
The Manual You Should Have Been Given When You Were Born
By Dr. Dain Heer

The information you should have been given at birth, about bodies, about being you and what is truly possible if you choose it…What if your body were an ongoing source of joy and greatness? This book introduces you to the awareness that really is a different choice for you—and your sweet body.

Sex Is Not a Four Letter Word but Relationship Often Times Is
By Gary M Douglas and Dr. Dain Heer

Funny, frank, and delightfully irreverent, this book offers readers an entirely fresh view of how to create great intimacy and exceptional sex. What if you could stop guessing—and find out what REALLY works?

Conscious Leadership
By Chutisa and Steve Bowman

The Conscious Leadership book is a gift to every individual, leader and organization dedicated to creating a life that is greater than what they now have, and to making a difference in the world. It is an invitation for those people who choose to be more conscious in their leadership, with an emphasis that no particular way is right or wrong.

About Access Consciousness®

Access Consciousness® is an energy transformation program which links seasoned wisdom, ancient knowledge and channeled energies with highly contemporary motivational tools. Its purpose is to set you free by giving you access to your truest, highest self.

The purpose of Access is to create a world of consciousness and oneness. Consciousness includes everything and judges nothing. It is our target to facilitate you to the point where you receive awareness of everything with no judgment of anything. If you have no judgment of anything, then you get to look at everything for what it is, not for what you want it to be, not for what it ought to be, but just for what it is.

Consciousness is the ability to be present in your life in every moment, without judgment of you or anyone else. It is the ability to receive everything, reject nothing, and create everything you desire in life-great than what you currently have, and more than what you can imagine.

- What if you were willing to nurture and care for you?
- What if you would open the doors to being everything you have decided it is not possible to be?
- What would it take for you to realize how crucial you are to the possibilities of the world?

The information, tools and techniques presented in this book are just a small taste of what Access Consciousness has to offer. There is a whole Universe of processes and classes.

If there are places where you can't get things in your life to work the way you know they ought to, then you might be interested in attending an Access Consciousness® class, workshop or locating a facilitator. They can work with you to give you greater clarity about issues you haven't yet overcome.

Access Consciousness® processes are done with a trained facilitator, and are based on the energy of you and the person you're working with.

Come and explore more at: www.accessconsciousness.com or www. drdainheer.com

Access Seminars, Workshops, & Classes

If you liked what you read in this book and are interested in attending Access seminars, workshops are classes, then for a very different point of view read on and sample a taste of what is available. There are the core classes in Access Consciousness®.

Being You, Changing the World, Intensive 3.5 Day Class
Facilitated exclusively by Dr. Dain Heer
Prerequisites: *None*

What would it be like if you created a bigger life and a reality worth playing in? Are you always asking for more, and looking for that 'something' we all know is possible? What if that 'something' is YOU? What if you, being you, is all it takes to change everything; your life, everyone around you, and the world?

This 3.5 day event is designed to take you from having a life run on autopilot—into becoming FULLY ALIVE and totally present as the infinite being you truly are. It will open you up to an expanded awareness of a life without judgment and empower you to know that you know.

With the Access Consciousness tools, perspectives and verbal processing that these days offer, you can start changing any area of your life that isn't working for you—like relationships, money and body—and start creating the future you truly desire.

You'll also experience Dr. Dain Heer's unique transformational process called The Energetic Synthesis of Being and receive an experience of *being you* that is impossible to describe, that you won't find anywhere else and that will stay with you for the rest of your life, if you allow it!

This class has no prerequisites and every event is uniquely created by the people who choose to come. Together, we'll go on a journey of creation...to a space that has never existed before.

What if you, truly being you, is the gift and the change this world requires?

Access Bars® (One day)

Facilitated by Certified Access Bars® Facilitators worldwide

Prerequisites: *None*

Do you remember the last moment in your life when you were totally relaxed and nurtured and cared for? Or has it been a little too long since you received healing and kindness without any judgment for your body or your being?

The first class in Access is Access Bars®. Did you know there are 32 points on your head which, when gently touched, effortlessly and easily release anything that doesn't allow you to receive? These points contain all the thoughts, ideas, beliefs, emotions, and considerations you have stored in any lifetime. This is an opportunity for you to let go of everything!

Each Bars session can release 5–10 thousand years of limitations in the area of your life that corresponds with the specific Bar being touched. This is an incredibly nurturing and relaxing process, undoing limitation in all aspects of your life that you are willing to change!

How much of your life do you spend doing rather than receiving? Have you noticed that your life is not yet what you would like it to be? You could have everything you desire (and then some!) if you are willing to receive lots more and maybe do a little less! Receiving or learning Access Bars® will allow this and so much more to show up for you!

Access Bars® have assisted thousands of people change many aspects of their body and their life including sleep, health and weight, money, sex and relationships, anxiety, stress and so much more! At worst you will feel like you have just had the best massage of your life. At best your whole life can change into something greater with total ease.

Taking Access Bars® class is a pre-requisite for all Access Consciousness® core classes as it allows your body to process and receive the changes you are choosing with ease.

Access Foundation

Facilitated by Certified Access Facilitators worldwide

Prerequisites: *Access Bars®*

After the Access Bars®, this two-day class is about giving you the space to look at your life as a different possibility.

Unlock your limitations about embodiment, finances, success, relationships, family, YOU and your capacities, and much more!

Step into greater possibilities for having everything you truly desire in life as you learn tools and questions to change anything that's not working for you. You also learn a hands-on body process called Cellular Memory that works wonders on scars and pains in the body! If you could change anything in your life, what would it be?

Access Level 1

Facilitated by Certified Access Facilitators worldwide

Prerequisites: *Access Foundation*

After Access Foundation, Level 1 is a two-day class that shows you how to be more conscious in every area of your life and gives you practical tools that allow you to continue expanding in this your day-to-day! Create a phenomenal life filled with magic, joy, and ease and clear your limitations about what is truly available for you. Discover the five Elements of Intimacy, create energy flows, start laughing and celebrating living and practice a hands-on body process that has created miraculous results all over the world!

Note: It is recommended that you attend Foundation and Level 1 consecutively, as they work together. Foundation and Level 1 manuals change at least every six months. If you do the classes separately and choose to do Level 1 after the class manuals have been revised, then you will have to repeat Foundation.

Access Levels 2 & 3

Facilitated exclusively by Gary Douglas (Founder of Access Consciousness®) and Dr. Dain Heer

Prerequisites: *Access Bars®, Foundation and Level 1*

These two classes are offered by Access Consciousness® founder Gary Douglas, or Dr. Dain Heer. During these four days you will gain access to a space where you begin to recognize your capacities as an infinite being.

As you begin to recognize how different you are, you start becoming aware of the choices that you make, the choices you would like to make, and what you would like to generate as your life with ease...financially, in relationships, in your work and beyond...

Generating your life is different from creating it. For creation to occur, there always has to be destruction. Generating your life is a moment-by-moment increase in what is possible in your life. When you stop creating from your past you can start generating a future that is unlimited. What if sensing the possibilities could replace judgment of everywhere you are right or wrong?

What else would you like to add to your life? And what catalyst for change could you be in the world if you unleashed the real you? Would you be willing to function from the energy, space and consciousness you truly be? And would you be willing to be more of you than you have ever been before? With ease, joy and glory? And maybe just a little bit of happiness too?

The Energetic Synthesis of Being (ESB)

Facilitated by Dr. Dain Heer

Prerequisites: *Access Bars®, Foundation and Level I*

This intensive takes you deeper into the wondrous adventure of Dr. Dain Heer's Energetic Synthesis of Being (ESB). The ESB is a unique way of transforming limitations into possibilities and healing, for you, the world and the planet.

During this 3-day intensive, Dain works simultaneously with the beings and bodies in the class to create a space that allows the change everyone is asking for to show up. In working with one person, everyone is invited to that change. You and your body will be introduced to a level of being and energetic awareness that goes beyond everything you've experienced before.

The molecules in your body start to change—and you become aware of the catalyst you are for a different possibility in the world. The result is an acoustical wave of oneness that encompasses the present and the future. What if you didn't have to separate anymore from anyone or anything... including you?

What if you could have it all...and all of you, starting now? What would you be able to create as your life and in the world?

The new prerequisites for the ESB Intensive are described below. This allows the group to build on the awareness from these classes and take the step into the unknown, allowing magic to be created, continuously.

This is your invitation to become the acoustic wave of change you've always perceived possible and now can...BE.

*New prerequisites for participating in a Level 2/3 or an "advanced class" with Gary or Dain:

• If this is the first time you're taking a Level 2&3 or an ESB, you have to have done "Foundation & Level 1" (with any facilitator) within the last 12 months.

• If you're repeating Level 2&3 or ESB or another advanced class with Gary and/or Dain, you have to have either done "The latest F/L1" OR a "Tele Call Series" OR "a full class with Gary and/or Dain" within the last 12 months. (A full class means a class between 3–7 days long)

• An advanced class is any class with Level 1 or higher as the prerequisites facilitated by Gary or Dain.

• A tele call series is any series of calls with Gary or Dain with at least 3 calls.

Access Consciousness® 3-Day Body Class
Facilitated by Access Body Class Facilitators worldwide
Prerequisites: *Access Bars®, Foundation and Level 1*

What if your body was a compass or guide to the secrets, mysteries and magic of life?

The Access Consciousness® 3-Day Body Class was created by Gary Douglas and Dr. Dain Heer. Facilitated by Access Consciousness® 3-Day Body Class Certified Facilitators, during these three days you will receive and gift numerous hands-on body processes that unlock the tension, resistance, and dis-ease of the body by shifting energy dynamically. There are over 40 hands-on processes, as well as lots of verbal processes, in the Body Class manual that will allow you to deal with most issues that exist in bodies today.

People who have attended the 3-Day Body Class have reported dramatic shifts and changes with body size/shape, an overall relief from chronic and acute pain, and their relationships and money issues seem to get easier too.

The 3-Day Body Class is designed to open up a dialogue and create a communion with your body that allows you to enjoy your body instead of fighting against it and abusing it. When you start to change the way you relate to your body, you start to change how you relate to everything in your life.

Do you have a talent and ability to work with bodies that you haven't yet unlocked? What do you know? Or are you a body worker—massage therapist, chiropractor, medical doctor, nurse—looking for a way to enhance the healing you can do for your clients? Come play with us and begin to explore how to communicate and relate to bodies, including yours, in so many new ways.

Advanced Access Body Class with Gary Douglas

Prerequisites: *Levels 2 & 3, 2 x Access Consciousness® 3-Day Body Classes*

This class offers a unique set of new body processes that have been created to give your body the possibility of going beyond the limitations of this reality.

What if you could undo the limitations that you have locked into your body that currently create an alteration of the way your body functions, so that it becomes far more efficient and also less needful of what people have defined as the best of this reality?

What if food, supplements and exercise have almost nothing to do with how your body truly functions? What if you could have ease, joy and communion with your body far beyond what is considered possible right now? Would you be willing to explore the possibilities?

Connect with Access Online

www.AccessConciousness.com
www.GaryMDouglas.com
www.DrDainHeer.com
www.BeingYouChangingtheWorld.com

www.YouTube.com/drdainheer
www.Facebook.com/drdainheer
www.Twitter.com/drdainheer

www.Facebook.com/accessconsciousness
www.RightRecoveryForYou.com
www.AccessTrueKnowledge.com